MW00462249

"For many years, there has existed [a need] cal gospel of grace to LDS indivi[duals] and, with hopeful and tender hea[rt] of the Bible and a loving approach to sharing Truth, Eric Johnson has met this need. It should be a standard for many years to come in introducing biblical Truth to LDS."

Dr. Lynn Wilder
Author, *Unveiling Grace: The Story of How We Found
Our Way out of the Mormon Church*

"*Introducing Christianity to Mormons* is a unique book. Eric has studied and taught Christian beliefs for years, and so he captures the heart of core doctrines with clarity. And yet he has spent his life studying the LDS Church and engaging Mormons, so he presents Christian beliefs in a respectful and understandable fashion. This is the first book I will now recommend for those with an LDS background who want to understand Christian teachings."

Sean McDowell, PhD
Biola University professor, coauthor of *Evidence That
Demands a Verdict* and *More Than a Carpenter*

"With every passing year, the distinctions between Christianity and the LDS Church are increasingly confused. Most contemporary LDS consider Mormonism a denomination of Christianity, even though their founders would never have described it that way. Now more than ever, we need a guide to help us navigate the differences and engage our LDS friends with compassion and truth. That's why this book is so timely. No one does a better job than Eric when it comes to understanding the differences, focusing on the essentials, and reaching Mormons with love and urgency. If you know Mormons, let this book prepare and guide you every step of the way."

J. Warner Wallace
Dateline-featured Cold-Case Detective,
author of *Cold Case Christianity*

"Have you tried to share your faith with an LDS (Mormon) friend only to walk away confused by the discussion? Eric's book offers the Christian great insights on Mormon beliefs, along with guides for more meaningful discussions."

Sandra Tanner
Cofounder of Utah Lighthouse Ministry, coauthor
of *Mormonism: Shadow or Reality*

"When sharing the Christian faith with members of the LDS Church, using precise language is always paramount. Christians have often expressed frustration when their LDS counterpart gives the impression that they have few disagreements with what Christians have historically believed, even though one of the foundational teachings of their church is that Christ's church fell into a state of complete apostasy after the death of Jesus' apostles. Eric Johnson cuts through this theological fog and offers information that will make for effective conversations."

Bill McKeever
Director of Mormonism Research Ministry (Utah),
coauthor of *Answering Mormons' Questions*

"I have long felt the need for a book that takes LDS beliefs and language into account when explaining the message of Christianity. Eric Johnson has created that book. He has combined theological clarity and a lucid writing style with his extensive experience talking to Mormons to produce a resource I will give away often."

Ross Anderson
Author, *Understanding Your Mormon Neighbor*, executive
director, Utah Advance Ministries

"I wish I'd had this book when starting out in ministry in Utah. I'll be giving many copies of it away. It will be a great help to those who don't understand the differences between the religions that find their origin in the teaching of Joseph Smith and traditional Christianity, to those who are leaving some form of Mormonism for Christianity, and for Christians who live and serve in Mormon communities."

Loren Pankratz, PhD
Lead pastor, The Bridge Community, Centerville, Utah

"Eric Johnson gives us a multifaceted jewel in this book. Viewed from one side, it is an articulate primer for the historic Christian faith. Viewed from another side, it gives Christians the resources to anticipate and field common LDS questions and objections. And from yet another angle, a Latter-day Saint could encounter the material as a winsome and conversational polemic for the core of Christianity. Truth and grace march in lockstep through its pages. As a pastor and theologian in LDS country, I heartily recommend it!"

Dr. Bryan Hurlbutt
Lead pastor, Lifeline Community, West Jordan, Utah

INTRODUCING

CHRISTIANITY

TO MORMONS

ERIC JOHNSON

HARVEST HOUSE PUBLISHERS
EUGENE, OREGON

Cover design by Brock Book Design Co., Charles Brock

Cover Photo © anatolir, BigAlBaloo / Depositphotos

Interior design by KUHN Design Group

For bulk, special sales, or ministry purchases, please call 1-800-547-8979.
Email: Customerservice@hhpbooks.com

Introducing Christianity to Mormons
Copyright © 2022 by Eric Johnson
Published by Harvest House Publishers
Eugene, Oregon 97408
www.harvesthousepublishers.com

ISBN 978-0-7369-8549-9 (pbk.)
ISBN 978-0-7369-8550-5 (eBook)

Library of Congress Control Number: 2022931413

Printed in the United States of America

22 23 24 25 26 27 28 29 30 / BP / 10 9 8 7 6 5 4 3 2 1

For more than three decades, my wife has supported me in ministry endeavors and has never complained. Thank you, Terri Lynn, for your many sacrifices as well as your encouragement to finish this project. I love you.

ACKNOWLEDGMENTS

Many people helped me tremendously in this project. First, I want to acknowledge Sharon Lindbloom, a friend and associate at Mormonism Research Ministry. Her valuable advice and constructive criticism to my first two drafts is greatly appreciated. Thank you, Sharon, for the hours you dedicated to this project!

Mark Ridgway, Tom Hobson, and Karen Taylor took the time to read both drafts of the manuscript and provided suggestions that were both beneficial and helpful. Kaz Dombrowski, Carissa Flores, Sherry Frazier, Michael Hodge, Jerry Jenkins, Michael Kempton, Robert McKay, Neal Powell, Devin Rill, Shane Roe, Sandra Tanner, Kim Thorne-Harper, and Eric Wendt read the first draft and offered their encouragement.

Bill McKeever, the founder of Mormonism Research Ministry, allowed me to push nonessential ministry assignments aside during the fall of 2020 and the winter/spring of 2021 to work on the manuscript. The camaraderie Bill and I share and what I have learned from him over the past three decades is evident in what has been written in this book.

J. Warner Wallace, I appreciate your kick-in-the-tail encouragement from the very beginning to reformat my original idea and write something that both a Christian and a Mormon could benefit from.

Steve Miller at Harvest House Publishers, thanks for your commitment to publishing quality yet niche Christian literature (including this) that many other Christian publishers would never touch. I also appreciate Rodney Morris for his careful editing of the original draft.

And Hannah, my youngest daughter, thanks for helping me come up with the idea.

I pray that this book will encourage Christians to share their faith with the Latter-day Saints, a people to whom I have dedicated much of my life to reaching. Soli Deo Gloria.

CONTENTS

MICAH WILDER

In my library are several books authored or coauthored by Eric Johnson. His newest effort, *Introducing Christianity to Mormons*, is a welcomed addition to his already impressive collection of informative works. Eric effectively lays out a clear and undeniable case for the orthodox Christian faith while juxtaposing it with the convoluted gospel of Mormonism. This book is an essential addition to anyone's library.

In the apostle Peter's first letter to the church, he encourages the saints of God, "In your hearts honor Christ the Lord as holy, always being prepared to make a defense to anyone who asks you for a reason for the hope that is in you; yet do it with gentleness and respect" (1 Peter 3:15). The significance of this exhortation cannot be understated: As Christians, we are to defend the gospel, but to do so gently and respectfully. In the more than a decade that I have had the honor of knowing Eric Johnson, he has epitomized this scriptural appeal in his apologetic approach to unbelievers.

Since the inception of our continued friendship, I have been greatly encouraged by Eric's passion for the gospel of Christ and burden for reaching the Mormon people with truth. I am humbled by those whom God has called to be missionaries to the LDS people—because I myself am a former Latter-day Saint. To the glory of God, my life was radically transformed by the power of God's Word that was delivered to me through faithful Christian missionaries who stepped out of their comfort zone and shared the good news of Jesus with me. At that time of my life, I had no reason to consider any truth outside of my religious construct, but by the grace of God, seeds were planted in my heart that ultimately came to fruition.

All too often, Christians have the perception that Mormons—among others—are unreachable. It's easy to assume they are too entrenched into their religious beliefs, and this creates in some people a hesitancy to share the gospel with them. "What's the point?" I have heard many ask. "They will never change." Yes, they can. I am evidence of that. But as Scripture says, "How then will they call on him in whom they have not believed? And how are they to believe in him of whom they have never heard? And how are they to hear without someone preaching?" (Romans 10:14).

I thank God for Eric's faithfulness to the Mormon people, and for the love and compassion he displays in every facet of his ministry. It is my prayer that this book will 1) encourage Christians to lovingly share their faith with Latter-day Saints, and 2) challenge Latter-day Saints to investigate their own faith and discover the sufficiency of Jesus alone for salvation.

—Micah Wilder

INTRODUCTION

"Do your best to present yourself to God as one approved, a worker who has no need to be ashamed, rightly handling the word of truth."

2 TIMOTHY 2:15[1]

I've never heard this before," whispered the elderly gentleman who was wearing bib overalls and sporting a worn-out John Deere baseball cap on his mostly bald head. "It's all a bit confusing."[2]

It was a hot summer day in July 1987 in Manti, Utah. I was part of a short-term missions group sharing our faith in this very religious state. In fact, more than nine out of ten residents in Sanpete County, Utah, were members of The Church of Jesus Christ of Latter-day Saints.

For two years I had attended postgraduate seminary classes in San Diego, California. Desiring a different type of ministry experience, I decided to spend a summer in Utah. It was, I must say, a baptism by fire. If you take out a map and put your finger on the center of the state, it should land on this town of fewer than (at that time) 2300 people. From my experience, most of the residents in this community at that time had never been spoken to by a Bible-believing Christian.

After answering my fellow missionary's knock on their door, this octogenarian and his wife politely invited us inside. Sitting on their 1960s upholstered living room couch, I asked them how long they had lived in Utah. The husband replied, "All my life." Telling us he was born just 14 years after the Manti LDS *temple**was dedicated in 1888, he had

---

* The first time a unique and important term is used, it is italicized to indicate the word is defined in the glossary.

followed in his father's footsteps and became a farmer who never had a reason to travel beyond Salt Lake City located two hours away by car. The couple could get three TV stations—but only, he said, if their roof antenna was positioned exactly right, though he admitted the feed still came in a bit fuzzy. Of course, the Internet would not become available for a few years more.

Knowing that there were no Christian churches in this entire county, I asked, "Have you ever heard of the TV evangelist Billy Graham?"

"Nope," he responded with a shrug. As his wife handed each of us frosty glasses of lemonade, I sensed a golden opportunity.

"Could I share with you what the Bible teaches?" I asked.

"Sure," he replied, "we have plenty of time."

Having had a stuttering problem in elementary school, I spoke in rapid-fire succession—bam, bam, bam. It was a technique I had developed during my early years as I tried to overcome a childhood disability. Meanwhile, I was oblivious to the couple's confused body language. My intentions were right, but my form during the 20-minute conversation was akin to a locomotive careening out of control.

After we left, I realized that the information I hoped to convey had flown over their heads and crash landed in the heap pile of missed connections. This could have been the very first time anyone tried to share the Christian message with this lovely couple. Unfortunately, it would probably be the last time as well.

A few minutes after we left, my companion and I stood under the shade of a tree as we bowed our heads and prayed for this couple. That night, before I went to sleep, I vowed that I would improve my serve so I could better explain the gospel in future encounters. Over the past three and a half decades, I have learned through thousands of conversations that it *is* possible to communicate Christianity in a way that most Latter-day Saints can understand. This is the reason I have written this book.

ARE MORMONS CHRISTIAN?

Evangelical *Christians*[3] and members of The Church of Jesus Christ of Latter-day Saints (abbreviated LDS, with the followers referred to as

Latter-day Saints or *Mormons* and the religion known as *Mormonism*)[4] face barriers when trying to communicate with each other on doctrinal issues. This is because adherents of these faiths share many of the same theological terms—including *atonement*, *grace*, and *gospel*—but these words can be defined differently depending on one's background and presuppositions. This can cause great confusion as well-meaning people tend to talk past each other and, ultimately, cause hurt feelings.

The question asked in this subheading has been the source of many emotional debates between Latter-day Saints and evangelical Christians.[5] In the past few decades, it has become common for many Mormons to insist that "we're Christian too." The intended impression is that there are few, if any, theological differences. Those who insist that there are discrepancies could be labeled as contentious or rude. More than once I have been asked, "Who are you to tell me that I'm not a Christian? Are you suggesting that I'm not a nice person?" This is certainly *not* the message I want to convey!

I normally encourage believers to refrain from introducing this controversy in conversations with Latter-day Saints. After all, this tactic is the perfect recipe for alienating Mormons, whether friends or acquaintances. At the same time, it is not hard to show critical differences between our faiths. Dallin H. Oaks, the first counselor in Mormonism's First Presidency, explained, "The Church of Jesus Christ of Latter-day Saints has many beliefs in common with other Christian churches. But we have differences, and those differences explain why we send missionaries to other Christians."[6]

A feeling of religious superiority common amongst some Mormons is demonstrated by LDS Apostle Bruce R. McConkie who wrote: "Modern Christians, as part of their various creeds and doctrines, have inherited many myths, legends, and traditions from their ancestors—all of which views they falsely assume are part of true religion…Indeed, it would be difficult to assemble a greater number of myths into one philosophical system than are now found in the philosophies of modern Christendom."[7]

Insisting that Christians believe a "number of myths" while commissioning church "missionaries" to be sent "to other Christians" are sure signs that these leaders do not consider anyone outside their church's organization to be as *Christian* as they consider themselves to be. The idea is based on how LDS Church founder *Joseph Smith* supposedly "restored" true doctrines considered to have been lost soon after the death of Jesus's apostles in what is known as the *Great Apostasy*.[8]

An official church lesson aimed at children under 12 years of age encourages the instructor to "explain...that the true Church was not on the earth at that time. Jesus wanted his teachings and his Church restored to the earth."[9] Because of this, only LDS baptismal rites are considered efficacious; only this church's *priesthood* is deemed authoritative; and only by work done in church temples can families have any hope to live together throughout eternity. The list could go on. It can be concluded, then, that if Mormonism is true, *all* other religions—biblical Christianity included—are false and their adherents who had knowledge of Mormonism will not be eligible to receive the very best this religion has to offer.[10]

If Christianity needed a "restoration" because God's authority had been lost, then this religion—if Joseph Smith was indeed authorized to be a prophet—is desperately needed. On the other hand, if Christianity did not lose God's authority and true beliefs can be found by correctly interpreting the Bible, then Mormonism is in error and *its* doctrines ought to be rejected.

Historically, Christians have defended their beliefs while condemning *heresies*. Here is a quick comparison of the major doctrines of Mormonism and evangelical Christianity:

DOCTRINE	MORMONISM	EVANGELICAL CHRISTIANITY
Nature of God	Heavenly Father has a body of flesh and bones (Doctrine and Covenants 130:22) who lived in a previous existence as a human.	God the Father is spirit (John 4:24) and has eternally existed as God (Ps. 90:2; Isa. 43:10; 44:6,8).
Jesus	The firstborn child of Heavenly Father who is the Savior of humanity. Jesus is a god but not equal to the Father.	Jesus is *fully* God who came to the earth as a man and died on the cross. He then bodily resurrected from the dead.

DOCTRINE	MORMONISM	EVANGELICAL CHRISTIANITY
Trinity	Rejection of the Trinity. God is one in purpose but not one in essence. Each person in the Godhead is a separate god (tritheism).	One God in three persons who is both one in essence as well as purpose. Each Person is fully God but retains His own personality.
Salvation	Depending on the context, "general salvation" is the ability for a person to gain one of the three "kingdoms of glory" through the atonement and grace offered by Jesus, something all humans will receive. "Individual salvation" is equated with eternal life/exaltation; those who qualify for this realm will exist as gods and goddesses throughout eternity.[11]	Three distinctions: 1) Past tense, comes by grace through faith and not by works (Justification); 2) Present tense, good works in a believer's life (sanctification); 3) Future tense, existing in heaven with glorified bodies forever (glorification).
Humanity	All people are commanded to repent by successfully keeping the commandments of God.	Original sin came through the disobedience of Adam, tainting all people and preventing a relationship with God.
Scripture	The Old and New Testaments (King James Version) of the Bible as well as the Book of Mormon, the Doctrine and Covenants, and the Pearl of Great Price. Also, those authoritative teachings given by current church leaders.	The 66 books of the Old and New Testaments constitute the Word of God. There is a closed canon, with no additional books or writings accepted as authoritative.
Heaven/Hell	Heaven (celestial kingdom) is eternal existence with one's earthly family; hell is equated with a place called "outer darkness" and is not a possibility for most humans.	Heaven is eternal existence with God. Hell is eternal separation from God, a possible destination for those who reject Him.

DOCTRINE	MORMONISM	EVANGELICAL CHRISTIANITY
Church	The Church of Jesus Christ of Latter-day Saints. Through the Great Apostasy that took place soon after the death of Jesus's apostles, God's authority was lost from the earth before it was restored by Joseph Smith in 1830.	Depending on the context, the church generally refers to all true believers who have placed their faith in Jesus as Savior. No religious organization or denomination holds a monopoly on Christianity.

It must be understood that people can be sincere in their beliefs and yet be sincerely wrong. Christian philosopher J.P. Moreland explains, "Reality is basically indifferent to how sincerely we believe something. I can believe with all my might that my car will fly me to Hawaii or that homosexuality is caused solely by the brain, but that fervency doesn't change a thing. As far as reality is concerned, what matters is not whether I like a belief or how sincere I am in believing it but whether or not the belief is true."[12]

He adds, "If someone used blind faith and bought the first house he or she saw with a For Sale sign in front of it, but made no effort to get information about the house and neighborhood, we would consider that person foolish. Why? Because when we use our reason and base decisions on the best assessment of the evidence we can make, we increase our chances that our decisions are based on true beliefs...Now if this is the case for day-to-day issues, why should we suddenly abandon the importance of reason and evidence when it comes to religion? We should not."[13]

Maintaining truth in spiritual matters is crucial. Paul didn't mince words when he described the gospel of those legalists who insisted that dietary law and circumcision were necessary for saving faith. Galatians 1:8-9 states, "But even if we or an angel from heaven should preach to you a gospel contrary to the one we preached to you, let him be accursed. As we have said before, so now I say again: If anyone is preaching to you a gospel contrary to the one you received, let him be accursed."

That word *accursed* refers to damnation in *hell.* Those who put their trust in a contrary gospel are destined for eternal separation from God. While a Latter-day Saint might find it silly to suggest that those who belong to a church with the name of Jesus in its title might be in jeopardy, to ignore our differences and pretend Mormonism and Christianity are synonymous faiths does nobody any favors. As theologian Norman Geisler puts it, "Truth is 'telling it like it is'":

> Non-Christians often claim that Christians are narrow-minded, because they claim that Christianity is true and all non-Christian systems are false. However, the same is true of non-Christians who claim that what they view as truth is true, and all opposing beliefs are false. That is equally narrow. The fact of the matter is that if C (Christianity) is true, then it follows that all non-C is false. Likewise, if H (say, Humanism) is true, then all non-H is false. Both views are equally narrow. That's the way truth is. Each truth claim excludes contradictory truth claims. Christianity is no more narrow than any other set of beliefs.[14]

If truth matters, then so does doctrine. Theologian Millard Erickson writes:

> To some readers, the word *doctrine* may prove somewhat frightening. It conjures up visions of very technical, difficult, abstract beliefs, perhaps propounded dogmatically. Doctrine is not that, however. Christian doctrine is simply statements of the most fundamental beliefs that the Christian has, beliefs about the nature of God, about his action, about us who are his creatures, and about what he has done to bring us into relationship with himself...Doctrine deals with general or timeless truths about God and the rest of reality.[15]

Theologian R.C. Sproul rightly said, "I am not satisfied to believe just anything simply for the sake of believing. If what I believe is not true—if it is superstitious or fallacious—I want to be liberated from it."[16] Why? Theologian Harold O.J. Brown explained: "For many religions, the cardinal test is right conduct or right observance; for Christianity it is right faith…Creeds played a prominent part in the daily worship and life of early Christians. To a degree that is hard for twentieth-century people to grasp, the early church believed that it was absolutely vital to know and accept some very specific statements about the nature and attributes of God and his Son Jesus Christ."[17]

Current thinking amongst many secular people (and even some Christians) is that truth is whatever a person decides it to be. This generally means that all religious paths lead to God. However, it is impossible for two or more competing *worldviews* to each be true. According to the law of noncontradiction, something cannot be *both* A and non-A at the same time. When two religions are contrasted, such as Mormonism and Christianity, essential beliefs might appear to be similar on the surface. When these teachings are thoroughly inspected, though, irreconcilable differences become evident.

Of course, not everyone is open to the gospel. But some are. In Acts 8:26-40, God told Philip to head southwest from Jerusalem toward Gaza. He ran into a man from Ethiopia—the manager of his queen's financial affairs—who was reading from the book of the prophet Isaiah. Philip asked him, "Do you understand what you are reading?" The man replied, "How can I, unless someone guides me?" Philip proceeded to interpret the passage that he was reading from Isaiah 53 and explained "the good news about Jesus." The man understood and was baptized in this fish-jumps-into-the-boat encounter.

While not every witnessing scenario is this easy, it is vital that every Christian who hopes to be effective in sharing the gospel has a grasp on the basic beliefs of Christianity, as historian Roger E. Olson writes: "There can be no vital, dynamic, faithful Christian discipleship completely devoid of doctrinal understanding. There never has been and there never will be."[18] Brown adds that "it is important to recognize that the very life of Christianity in general as well as the salvation of individual Christians depends on at least a substantial measure of right doctrine, and where right doctrine exists, contrary views must be heresies."[19]

Grasping the essentials of Christianity as well as the basics of LDS theology is crucial or confusion will reign! Only then can Christianity be accurately contrasted with the teachings of Mormonism.

IF THE (LDS) CHURCH ISN'T TRUE, THEN NOTHING ELSE IS?

Those who have been Mormons for a while may be familiar with an in-house LDS phrase that goes something like this: "If the (LDS) church isn't true, then nothing else is." This saying has been used to spur fellow members on, especially those who might struggle in their faith when troubling information about church history or unique doctrines is discovered. The idea is neither rational nor true. Something *must* be true if Mormonism is not. After all, nothing is *not* something. If Mormonism is not true, perhaps Hinduism is. Or Islam. Maybe there is not a god, thus validating atheism. Or possibly we are living in a Matrix-like illusion and reality doesn't exist, as Buddhism teaches. The list of possibilities goes on.

To make an effort to understand what biblical Christianity teaches, Mormons must put away false stereotypes. For example, some mistakenly assume that the Christian doctrine of "salvation by grace alone" minimizes good works. Another assumption is that Christians believe in a boring heaven where everyone strums on their harps while dangling on puffy clouds![20] Many similar misconceptions could be documented.

Corey Miller, a former Mormon who leads a nationwide Christian college campus ministry called Ratio Christi, uses a simple but powerful illustration to show how different Mormonism is from biblical Christianity:

> Many Mormons initially soft-peddle differences until forced to admit them. So I try to engage with them by illustration.
>
> Me: "Let me ask you a personal question. Do you have a mom?"

Mormon: [Smiling, will reply] "Yes, of course."

Me: "I do too! Can you spell that?"

Mormon: "Umm…M.O.M."

Me: "No way, I spell it the same way. Maybe we have the same mom." I ask, "Can you spell it backwards?"

Mormon: "M.O.M."

Me: [Excitedly I blurt out] "Surely, we have the same mom because it is spelled the same!"

Upon further describing our respective moms, if hers is 6 feet tall and mine only 4 feet tall, then they are two different moms. One can then point out that while we all spell "Christ" and "God" the same way the meanings aren't necessarily the same.[21]

Throughout this book, much effort will be extended to distinguish the beliefs taught in Christianity and Mormonism. Some propose that any disagreement is wrong by citing 3 Nephi 11:29 in the *Book of Mormon*, which says "contention…is of the devil, who is the father of contention." However, disagreements are *not* denigrated by the Bible. As scholar J. Gresham Machen once said, "Men tell us that our preaching should be positive and not negative, that we can preach the truth without attacking error. But if we follow that advice we shall have to close our Bible and desert its teachings. The New Testament is a polemic book almost from beginning to end."[22]

Motives must be considered. Yes, I disagree with Mormon*ism*, but let me unequivocally state that I am *not* against the LDS people. Please don't take this wrong, but I love the Mormon people.[23] While I have had many dialogues with Latter-day Saints over the years, I have never equated their disagreement on doctrinal issues as personal attacks on me. I totally concur with J. Reuben Clark—an attorney who served as a member of Mormonism's First Presidency—when he said, "If we have the truth, it cannot be harmed by investigation. If we have not the truth, it ought to be harmed."[24] Taking personal pride out of the equation while considering the facts is necessary to fairly consider both sides of the issue.

The Greek word for *gospel*—literally, "good news"—is where the word *evangelism* originates. Sometimes others will feel like the Christian who presents the truth is maliciously stepping on toes, a fear that paralyzes many Christians from sharing their faith. Commenting on Galatians 4:15-20, Pastor Timothy Keller says:

> If you love a person so selfishly that you cannot risk their anger, you won't ever tell them the truth they need to hear. If, on the other hand, you tell a person the truth they need, but with harshness and not with the agony of a lover, they won't listen to it. But if you speak the truth with lots of love evident at the same time, there is a great chance that what you say will penetrate the heart and heal. A gospel-based ministry is marked by loving honesty, not spin, image and flattery. This kind of gospel ministry is costly to the minister. It is not always easy for those they are ministering to. But it is based on the truth; it is pointing to Christ; and it is eternally worthwhile.[25]

With that said, let me assure you that it is perfectly acceptable for Mormons and Christians to disagree in their beliefs. While I will defend my position rigorously, I do not force anyone to accept my position. And I am open to hearing opposing points of view.

Let no Christian be deceived into thinking that a Latter-day Saint should be despised, ridiculed, mocked, or considered the enemy. And vice versa. My intention in writing this book is *not* to provide information for the Christian to "win debates (at all costs)" while purposely putting people down or minimizing their opinions. There is already enough contention in the world without blindside potshots being taken, so it should be a priority to discuss these issues in a civil manner displaying "gentleness and respect" (1 Peter 3:15). As Keller said, delivering "the truth with lots of love," as taught by Ephesians 4:15, means that cordiality and honesty can both be accomplished in a noncompromising way.

I will stress throughout that Christians must have compassion for the Mormons they know or meet by realizing how costly it could be for them to even consider leaving their religion. For example, departing the faith could cause irreparable damage with their LDS family and friends. One woman wrote in an ex-Mormon Facebook group, "I have a huge fear I could get in trouble for attending a Christian church. I wish I could just have my name removed or leave first but my husband would divorce me and said he can't get into heaven if I leave the church."

What a dilemma for those who wonder what the ramifications would be if they leave Mormonism. Imagine how deciding to leave could even end up causing a failed marriage, as the woman quoted above feared! No wonder some Latter-day Saints decide to stay in their church while pretending to remain faithful even though, in their minds, they have totally rejected this religion. This realistic apprehension must be appreciated by those of us who have never been Latter-day Saints.

Still, no assurance can be made that there won't be fallout for those who leave. What we as Christians can do, however, is promise them that Jesus cares very much. And we care too. While there might not be an immediate replacement of the friendships they currently have in the LDS Church, they can be assured that there is the possibility of finding a place of genuine Christian fellowship in their community where God's authentic Word remains central. We will discuss this issue further in chapter 10.

A spiritual battle is taking place beyond the physical world. The apostle Paul explained in Ephesians 6:12 that Christians "do not wrestle against flesh and blood, but against the rulers, against the authorities, against the cosmic powers over this present darkness, against the spiritual forces of evil in the heavenly places." Because of this, 2 Corinthians 4:4 states that "the god of this world [Satan] has blinded the minds of the unbelievers, to keep them from seeing the light of the gospel of the glory of Christ, who is the image of God."

Once again, let me be clear. Mormons are *not* the enemies of Christians. The religion of Mormon*ism* is. As God told the prophet Isaiah, "Come now, let us reason together" (Isaiah 1:18). Cordial conversations can take place and should always be the goal.

PRESENTING THE CASE FOR CHRISTIANITY TO MORMONS

During the pandemic in late August 2020, my youngest daughter, Hannah, came to me one weekend morning. "Dad, my coworker has left Mormonism and is wondering if there is a resource that could help her better understand what we as Christians believe," she said.

I began to thumb through more than a dozen apologetic books on the shelves of my personal library, all of which do a great job explaining the Christian position. However, I soon realized that it would be far too easy for someone with an LDS background to miss important concepts in these books since they were not written with a Mormon audience in mind.

"A book written for those who think like Mormons is needed," I told my daughter. "It would need to deal with the essential doctrines of Christianity, focusing on issues such as the authoritative role of the Bible, the nature of God, the personhood of Jesus, the concept of the Trinity, and the meaning of salvation." A good resource, I added, would provide responses to common arguments that utilize the *straw man fallacy* to counter Christian teaching.

Little did I know that I had just given myself a writing assignment that would consume my time for the following year!

I should point out that there are other doctrines considered by Christians to be peripheral or secondary issues. These include the mode of *water baptism* (immersion or sprinkling), God's sovereignty or the human free will (Calvinism vs. Arminianism), and teachings on end times. While these are important and do make for interesting discussions, they are topics that Christians are free to disagree on with their fellow believers. While in-house, back-and-forth disagreement is permitted, we must remember that love needs to be emphasized in all conversations (1 Corinthians 13:13). In these days of drive-by slanderous comments made in the faceless twenty-first-century social media realm, the higher road should be taken. Unity in the body of Christ should be preserved despite our differences in these secondary arenas.

Finally, there are opinions based on personal taste, such as the type of music used in church settings on Sunday mornings (hymns or contemporary worship), the freedom to drink alcohol (without getting drunk, as Ephesians 5:18 says), or the preference of a particular Bible translation. It's like pronouncing the word *tomato*. Someone in Britain may say "tah-mah-toe," while an American might say "tuh-may-toe." Is either pronunciation incorrect? In the same way, when it comes to nonessential issues, we can dispense freedom to our brothers and sisters in Christ. Since the essential teachings in Christianity will be our focus, peripheral and personal taste issues will not be emphasized.

SOME THINGS TO CONSIDER

The word *apologetics* comes from the Greek word *apologeia*. It's the same word used in 1 Peter 3:15 to describe how believers should "make a defense to anyone who asks you for a reason for the hope that is in you." Explaining the teachings of Christianity can get quite complicated. Thus, it is necessary for me to offer plenty of evidence to support my case, as many names and numbers will be used.

Some may complain, "Too many details!" However, for me to say, "The Bible is true, just take my word for it" or "Trust me, the Trinity just needs to be accepted" while not providing adequate support is not fair. For many readers, this book may end up becoming a fire-hose presentation. But while the concepts discussed can be deep, they are important. If necessary, take your time and look up the biblical passages. For me to dumb down the material could result in important points being missed.

For many years I coached softball at both the rec-league and high-school levels. My players knew that many post-practice pep talks would include the following encouragement: "Anything worth doing is worth doing well." Whether it was running laps to get into playing shape or fielding ground ball after ground ball in practice, winning games through full effort made it worthwhile when we were successful on the field, whether or not we won every game.

Others may suggest that I should have expounded more on certain teachings. Yes, it is possible to get much deeper with any of the topics discussed in this book, but this book was never meant to be the end-all systematic theology. If you need more details on any doctrine, I have listed some wonderful resources at the end of this (and every) chapter where you can pursue deeper thought.

As far as the intended audience, I have written mainly to lay Christians who would like to better share their faith with those who possess an LDS worldview. A secondary audience is those Latter-day Saints who may know little to nothing about evangelical Christian beliefs. This is a book I hope Christians can confidently give to their inquiring LDS family or friends. While critics may claim that this is an *anti-Mormon* publication, I assure you it's not. There is no slandering or talking down to Mormons in any of the pages. The main goal is to lay out essential Christian beliefs and provide adequate supporting material.

To successfully explain Christianity to those who have an LDS background, I'll need to describe the Mormon position as accurately as possible. Thus, LDS source material will be used, especially the words of church leaders called *general authorities*. These leaders have one of the following positions: 1) the *president*, also called the church *prophet*; 2) the *First Presidency*, made up of the president and his two counselors; 3) *apostles*, of which there are 12; and 4) the *seventies*. When cited, the name of the man's office will be placed in front of the name to indicate his position.

Faithful Mormons believe that these men have been appointed by God and, while not considered infallible, are certainly authoritative. A Mormon may say, "I don't agree with my leader on (fill in the blank)." That is possible, but when it comes to understanding authentic LDS doctrine, I think the positions of these leaders (along with the correlated curriculum they endorse) and how they interpret their church's scriptures ought to take precedence over the opinion of a lay member.[26]

There will also be abundant references from excellent Christian thinkers, pastors, and scholars, many possessing master's or doctoral credentials along with their vast experience. With so many great resources available, these citations are used unashamedly to buttress the case for the historic Christian position. The endnotes provide additional nuggets that ought to be considered.

Someone might wonder why I cite so many biblical verses. It could be argued that such a tactic is overkill and hinders readability. I disagree. Since I am an adamant proponent of the power of God's Word, in-text citations and references will provide the biblical support and help prevent mere opinion from ruling the day. The Bereans were considered noble because they did not take the word of an apostle (Paul) at face value; instead, they were intent on "examining the scriptures" (Acts 17:11).

To show how the information has been used in my own witness, I utilize real-life dialogues I have had over the years. By including these conversations, the goal is to show how Christian principles can be introduced to Latter-day Saints. For practically every dialogue, another believer could use an entirely different strategy that could be better than mine. There is no monopoly on evangelistic tactics.[27]

I want to be clear as well that not all Latter-day Saints will present their case the same way as those described in the dialogues. Conversations are like snowflakes. No two are alike, though they are often similar. Because of this, I have learned never to assume another person's beliefs. If a Latter-day Saint's view contradicts Mormonism, I might ask, "Did you know your church leaders/scripture disagree with your belief(s)?" To find out what an individual Mormon believes—regardless of what the church teaches—I have found two questions to be helpful:

1. "What do you believe about (so and so)?"

2. "What do you mean when you say (so and so)?"

Although I have not attained perfection in sharing my faith (who has?), asking questions like these prevents running over the Latter-day

Saint and forces the Christian to take a step back. Since God has given each person two ears but only one mouth, it is important to remind ourselves that we must listen and not completely dominate the discussion.

As a credentialed teacher in California for many years, I like to utilize educational tools to facilitate learning and retention. Thus, each chapter begins with a one-paragraph preview so the reader can anticipate what will be covered. Five discussion questions are provided at the end of the chapter for those who might like to use the book in a group study setting. The Glossary includes many unique LDS and Christian terms used throughout the book. The first time a unique and important term is used, it is italicized to indicate the word is defined in the glossary.

For additional information and resources, I direct you to the website IntroducingChristianity.com. Among other resources, you will find:

- Links to supplemental articles on mrm.org.

- Additional references for a more complete picture of what LDS scriptures and leaders have said about their religion.

- Possible answers to the discussion questions found at the end of each chapter.

- Short videos on the topics discussed in the chapter.

If you would like to respond to the book, write me at eric@mrm.org and put "Introducing Christianity" in the subject line.

BACKGROUND ON THE AUTHOR

You might wonder if I have ever been a Mormon. The answer is *no*. So why have I spent much of my life researching the religion of Mormonism? It is because I have great concern for the Mormon people, including some friends, family, and neighbors—just as the Jewish-raised Paul devoted himself to the Gentiles.

Here are some bullet points describing my history:

- I grew up as the oldest child in a loving Christian home with parents who converted to Christianity just before I was born.

- I dedicated my life to Christ in January 1972 at the age of nine while watching a Billy Graham crusade on television with my parents.

- My faith was challenged as a junior in a Christian high school when I heard how a thousand people followed the command of a cult leader named Jim Jones and committed suicide by imbibing a poisoned drink in November 1978.

- During the next few years, my faith grew as I studied other religions and compared their beliefs to what I was taught at church as well as at a Christian school.

- From 1983 to 1986, I assisted Jeff Howell, the founder of Making Disciples Ministry who is now in the presence of the Lord. Together we engaged in a public setting with Jehovah's Witnesses as well as New Age and Mormon adherents.

- I graduated from San Diego State University in 1985 and began attending seminary, a postgraduate school for those preparing for Christian ministry.

- I went on a short-term missionary trip to Utah in July 1987, as described in the first part of this introduction. On the team was Terri Bade from Washington state; she agreed to become my wife the following year. In fact, she was the "other missionary" in the evangelism story given at the beginning of this chapter.

- I met Bill McKeever, founder of Mormonism Research Ministry (MRM), in 1989 and accepted his invitation to volunteer with him as a researcher.

- I graduated from Bethel Seminary San Diego in 1991 with a Master of Divinity (MDiv) degree (New Testament).

- I taught English and Bible classes at Christian High School in El Cajon, CA, from 1993 to 2010. For several years, I served as the school's Bible department head. I continue to actively hold a clear secondary English credential in the state of California. I was also an adjunct professor at two San Diego-area colleges as well as at the former Bethel Seminary San Diego.

- In 2010, Terri and I moved to Utah with two of our three children so I could work full-time at MRM.[28]

- This is my fifth book project since 2013.

Enough of the preliminaries. Let's get started!

RECOMMENDED RESOURCES

Systematic theology volumes explain Christian teaching. Do not be intimidated by the fact that these three resources have 1000+ pages. The essential teachings (including scriptural authority, God's nature, Jesus, salvation) are described in much more detail.

Wayne Grudem, *Systematic Theology: An Introduction to Biblical Doctrine* (Grand Rapids, MI: Zondervan Academic, 1994), 1291 pages. (A second edition published in 2020 by the same publisher contains several hundred additional pages.)

John MacArthur and Richard Mayhue, general editors, *Biblical Doctrine* (Wheaton, IL: Crossway, 2017), 1023 pages.

Millard J. Erickson, *Christian Theology* (Grand Rapids, MI: Baker Academic, 2013), 1200 pages. A condensed version of the full edition is *Introducing Christian Doctrine* (Grand Rapids, MI: Baker Academic, 2015), 512 pages.

CHAPTER 1

THE BIBLE

God's Special Revelation

"The grass withers, the flower fades,
but the word of our God will stand forever."

ISAIAH 40:8

CHAPTER PREVIEW

According to Mormonism, the Bible is true only "as far as it is translated correctly." If this claim means that ancient scribes intentionally corrupted the biblical text, then the word translated *is not the correct term. Rather,* transmitted *would be more accurate. While there are no original texts of any Old Testament books, a by-chance archaeological discovery in 1947 eventually led to the uncovering of 11 caves containing hundreds of documents called the Dead Sea Scrolls. In addition, archaeological work undertaken in biblical lands supports the idea that the people, places, and events described in the Bible are historical, not mythological. All in all, the Bible has been properly transmitted and should be considered God's special revelation to help believers understand correct doctrine and behavior.*

D ave approached me on a warm early summer evening while I was passing out Christian information just outside Temple Square in Salt Lake City.

"Do you believe the Bible with its many problems?" he asked as we stood across from each other on the public sidewalk.

He didn't give me a chance to answer before he continued.

"Our church has produced a document called the Articles of Faith. The eighth article states, 'We believe the Bible to be the word of God as far as it is translated correctly.' While the Bible is part of our scripture, we are aware that it cannot be fully trusted."

He was citing from the 13 *Articles of Faith* written by Joseph Smith that is included at the end of the scripture *Pearl of Great Price*. When a biblical verse or passage offered by a Christian appears to conflict with a unique LDS teaching, Article of Faith 1:8 is often cited by Mormons as a counterpoint.

Before we could continue, I needed to distinguish the difference between the meanings of *translation* and *transmission*.

"In your mind, what does 'translation' mean?" I asked.

"It's taking words from one language and putting them into another, like from Spanish into English," he said.

"Exactly," I said. "If that is what is meant, I would agree that a bad translation of the Bible is possible."

I explained how the Bible has been translated into English over the past seven centuries. Those early pioneers who took on this enormous task did so at a great personal cost, as Roman Catholic church leaders opposed efforts to make the Bible accessible to laypeople because it was considered dangerous. Only ordained church officials were deemed to be qualified to properly interpret God's Word. Meanwhile, those who attempted to distribute the Bible to common laypeople were persecuted. For instance, John Wycliffe (1328–1384) and William Tyndale (1494–1536) were each martyred for their translations of the Bible.[1]

While there are many fine English translations, not all are reliable. For instance, the New World Translation (NWT) published by the Watchtower Bible and Tract Society (Jehovah's Witnesses, or JWs) has been discredited by most biblical scholars. One reason is that none of the translators of the NWT had a scholarly grasp on the original biblical languages and therefore forced their presupposed opinions onto their readers.[2] Because JWs deny the *deity* (Godhood) of Jesus, for example, the NWT identifies Jesus in John 1:1 as "a god" rather than "God" as reputable translations do.[3] In Colossians 1:16, the translators added "other" between the words "all things" even though this is neither in the original nor is it implied in the context. The NWT thus reads "all *other* things have been created through him [Jesus]."

Article 8 sheds doubt on the integrity of the monks and other copiers of the biblical text over the centuries. This is a question of the transmission, not the translation, of the biblical text. As LDS Apostle Neil A. Maxwell explained, "By faulty transmission, many 'plain and precious things' were 'taken away' or 'kept back' from reaching what later composed our precious Holy Bible."[4] The First Presidency reported in 1992, "The Bible, as it has been transmitted over the centuries, has suffered the loss of many plain and precious parts."[5]

Referring to Article 8, the late BYU professor Robert J. Matthews made the point clear when he wrote, "Here the word *translated* appears to be used in a broader sense to mean *transmitted*, which would include not only translation of languages but also copying, editing, deleting from, and adding to documents. The Bible has undergone a much more serious change than merely translation from one language to another."[6]

If the Bible cannot be trusted due to "ignorant translators, careless transcribers, or designing and corrupt priests"—as Joseph Smith put it—this would be a serious problem.[7] How can these charges about missing "many plain and precious parts" be countered? This will be the focus of the first two chapters.

SETTING THE TABLE

When it comes to *scripture*, Latter-day Saints typically understand this to refer to any one of four different volumes: the King James Version (KJV) of the Bible, the Book of Mormon, the Doctrine and Covenants, and the Pearl of Great Price. Wayne Grudem accurately explains that when other "scriptures" like these are added to the authority of the Bible, "the result has always been (1) to deemphasize the teachings of the Bible itself and (2) to begin to teach some things that are contrary to Scripture. This is a danger of which the church must constantly be aware."[8]

God has revealed Himself in one of two ways. First, He has made Himself available to all humans through what is called *general* or *natural revelation*, which will be discussed in chapter 3. God is also revealed through what is called *special revelation* as seen in divine miracles (to be discussed in chapter 6) as well as the 66 books of the Bible. Collectively, these books were compiled into an official list called the *canon* and were written:

- in a variety of genres: law, poetry, history, prophecy, gospels, church history, apostolic epistles, and apocalyptic prophecy

- by 40 different authors

- in three languages (Hebrew, Koine Greek, Aramaic)

- on three different continents (Europe, Asia, Africa)

- with one basic story in mind (God's great love for people)

The Old Testament is accepted by both Jews and Christians. Roger Olson writes,

> Although some debate exists about the Council of Jamnia where Jewish rabbis met in [AD] 90, it seems that some important steps toward the official canonization process took place there. The Jewish Bible was defined as twenty-two inspired books: Pentateuch through Lesser Prophets. In later Christian Bibles some of the books of the Jewish canon have been separated so that they make up a total of thirty-nine individual books...By and large, then, it is safe to say that most of the early church fathers of the second and third centuries accepted the Jewish leaders' decision to expand the inspired Scriptures beyond just the Pentateuch (Genesis through Deuteronomy) and to restrict them to the twenty-two (or thirty-nine) books of the Law and Prophets. This then was "the Bible" of the earliest Christian churches after the apostles.[9]

Fifteen books called the *Apocrypha* originated in the Intertestamental Period (from about 300 BC until the time of Christ), including the two books of Esdras and Maccabees as well as the Book of Tobit and the Book of Wisdom. These writings were never considered to be a part of the primary Jewish or Christian canon. Reacting against the teachings of the sixteenth-century Protestant Reformation, the Roman Catholic Church declared that 12 of the apocryphal books were "deuterocanonical" (secondary canonical) during the Council of Trent (1543–1563). It should be noted that Jesus referenced the Old Testament a total of 395 times in the Gospel accounts, yet He never once cited from the Apocrypha.[10]

Besides the four Gospels in the New Testament, there are additional books called gnostic gospels that are not considered authentic scripture. None of these books were written in the first century; with one exception, none were ever cited, read from, or preached by any respected Christian leader during the first three centuries.[11] As New Testament scholar Craig Blomberg notes,

> Given what we know today, are there good reasons for including the gnostic gospels?…The best way to answer this question is to invite readers to access the texts of these documents, read them, and decide for themselves. To begin with, none of them is a narrative of any larger swath of Jesus's life. To call them gospels, therefore, misleads those who have not read them as to their literary genre. Most involve long, rambling discourses attributed to Jesus, supposedly given to one or more of his followers secretly after the resurrection, teaching about the nature of creation and the heavenly worlds, with all sorts of esoteric cosmological speculation.[12]

These writings were never seriously considered for inclusion into the canon by the early church. In the early third century, Origen of Alexandria said there were three categories of books claiming apostolic authority: 1) those that were widely acknowledged, 2) others that were disputed by some, and 3) the rest that were outright rejected by everyone because they taught false doctrine. Those books considered authoritative were the four Gospels along with Acts, the 13 letters penned by the apostle Paul, 1 Peter, 1 John, and Revelation. Because they could not be traced to first-century apostolic writers, disputed books included the *Didache*, the *Epistle of Barnabas*, the *Shepherd of Hermas*, the *Preaching of Peter*, and the *Acts of Paul*.[13]

A total of 21 of the 27 current New Testament books were readily accepted in the first two centuries of the Christian church. During the third and fourth centuries, Christians determined that Hebrews, James, 2 Peter, 2 and 3 John, and Jude were also authoritative. Today the 27 New Testament books that were officially recognized at the Council of Hippo in AD 393 and Carthage in AD 397 are canonical. As New Testament scholar Bruce Metzger told journalist Lee Strobel,

> [T]he canon is a list of authoritative books more than it is an authoritative list of books. These documents didn't derive their authority from being selected; each one was authoritative before anyone gathered them together… For somebody now to say that the canon emerged only after councils and synods made these pronouncements would be like saying, "Let's get several academies of musicians to make a pronouncement that the music of Bach and Beethoven is wonderful." I would say, "Thank you for nothing! We knew that before the pronouncement was made." We know it because of sensitivity to what is good music and what is not. The same with the canon.[14]

THE AUTHORITY OF THE BIBLE

For evangelical Christians, the 66 books of the Bible are scriptural and fully authoritative; no other writings are considered canonical.[15] Let's consider the three *I*'s of scripture: Inspired, Inerrant, and Infallible.

First, *inspired* refers to how the authors of the Bible wrote according to the way God intended them to communicate with humanity.

This idea was recognized during the lifetime of the apostles, including Paul. First Thessalonians 2:13 explains, "And we also thank God constantly for this, that when you received the word of God, which you heard from us, you accepted it not as the word of men but as what it really is, the word of God, which is at work in you believers." Second Timothy 3:16-17 says, "All Scripture is breathed out by God [KJV says "given by inspiration of God"] and profitable for teaching, for reproof, for correction, and for training in righteousness, that the man of God may be complete, equipped for every good work."

When we say God inspired the Bible, this does not mean that He somehow took the hand of each author and forced them to write. Rather, each author's individuality and style are evident. R.C. Sproul explains, "God made it possible for His truth to be communicated in an inspired way while making use of the backgrounds, personalities, and literary styles of these various writers. What was overcome or overridden by inspiration was not human personalities, styles, or literary methods, but human tendencies to distortion, falsehood, and error."[16] As Norman Geisler and Ron Brooks state,

> The net result is that we have the Word of God written by men of God, inspired not only in its concepts, but in the very words used to express those concepts. The human writers are not mere secretaries, but active agents who express their own experiences, thoughts, and feelings in what they have written. It is not simply a record of revelation, but a revelation itself. It is God's message in written form.[17]

The apostle Peter described how the Old Testament prophets wrote with the power of the *Holy Spirit*, the Bible's ultimate author (Hebrews 3:7). Second Peter 1:19-21 states:

> And we have the prophetic word more fully confirmed, to which you will do well to pay attention as to a lamp shining in a dark place, until the day dawns and the morning

star rises in your hearts, knowing this first of all, that no prophecy of Scripture comes from someone's own interpretation. For no prophecy was ever produced by the will of man, but men spoke from God as they were carried along by the Holy Spirit.

Although 2 Timothy 3 and 2 Peter 1 refer primarily to the Old Testament, the New Testament is also considered authoritative. For example, Peter said that Paul wrote "according to the wisdom given him" (2 Peter 3:15). While Paul's theological instruction may have been difficult for some to understand, Peter added in verse 16 that these writings should be considered as authoritative as the "other Scriptures." According to Grudem,

> It is primarily the apostles who are given the ability from the Holy Spirit to recall accurately the words and deeds of Jesus and to interpret them rightly for subsequent generations…The apostles, then, have authority to write words that are God's own words, equal in truth status and authority to the words of the Old Testament Scriptures. They do this to record, interpret, and apply to the lives of believers the great truths about the life, death, and resurrection of Christ.[18]

Second, the Bible is considered the *inerrant* Word of God. Gleason L. Archer stated, "Throughout the history of the Christian church, it has been clearly understood that the Bible as originally given by God was free from error. Except for heretical groups that broke away from the church, it was always assumed that Scripture was *completely authoritative and trustworthy* in all that it asserts as factual."[19]

Jesus had a high view of Scripture, as a tenth of His words in the four Gospels are direct citations from the Old Testament. When He was tempted in Matthew 4:1-11, Jesus referenced the book of Deuteronomy (6:13,16; 8:3) and simply stated that "it is written." He provided historical support for stories in the Old Testament, including the creation of Adam and Eve (Mark 10:6-8), the faith of Abraham, Isaac, and Jacob (Matthew

22:32), and events with Moses, including the burning bush (Mark 12:26), heavenly manna (John 6:31), and the bronze serpent (John 3:14). Jesus even quoted from the Psalms twice while He was on the cross.

After Jesus ascended into heaven, His apostles continued to accept the authority of the Old Testament as well as the words of their Messiah. Claiming in Romans 3:2 that "the Jews were entrusted with the oracles of God," Paul also wrote in 1 Timothy 5:18, "For the Scripture says, 'You shall not muzzle an ox when it treads out the grain,' and, 'The laborer deserves his wages.'" His first citation of "Scripture" comes from Deuteronomy 25:4 while the second references what Jesus said in Luke 10:7.[20]

Finally, the Bible is considered *infallible.* This means that what the Bible teaches about matters of faith and Christian practice is exactly the way God intended. When the sixteenth-century Protestant Reformation took place, the phrase *Sola Scriptura* ("scripture alone") was coined to designate how God's Word trumps human tradition; this idea has been a rallying cry for Protestant Christians ever since. Led by Martin Luther who made a careful study of the books of Romans and Galatians, these Reformers "protested" against the Catholic religious tradition that typically superseded the Bible. Before Johannes Gutenberg's printing press initialized the printing revolution in 1450, many Christians throughout the centuries spent valuable time and resources physically copying and recopying the individual books that were distributed throughout the world. It should be noted that inerrancy and infallibility refer only to the original writings and *not* the copies. As Geisler accurately points out,

> Genuine mistakes have been found—in copies of Bible text made hundreds of years after the autographs. God only uttered the original text of Scripture, not the copies. Therefore, only the original text is without error. Inspiration does not guarantee that every copy is without error, especially in copies made from copies made from copies made from copies. Therefore, we are to expect that minor errors are to be found in manuscript copies.[21]

Critics complain that Christians utilize circular reasoning in their appeal to the authority of the Bible. ("The Bible is true because the Bible says it is true.") What these *skeptics* do not realize is that they are required to argue in a similar fashion when they believe their position is reasonable or logical. According to their position, "My reason is my ultimate authority because it seems reasonable to me." Or, "Logical consistency is my ultimate authority because it is logical." Even Latter-day Saints find themselves in a similar precarious situation when they say, in effect, "Praying about the Book of Mormon or the religion of Mormonism and receiving a personal revelation through prayer is my ultimate authority because my testimony must be true."

While evangelical Christians believe the Bible is true, they have reasons to believe in its authority, including its amazing prophetical accuracy (which we will discuss in chapter 6) as well as its abundant manuscript history. While Christians do appeal to the Bible to support why they believe the way they do, blind faith in God's Word is not required to come to this conclusion.

I told Dave that I wanted to provide him with manuscript evidence for why it is sensible to believe in the Bible, so I decided to describe the amazing twentieth-century discovery of the *Dead Sea Scrolls*.

THE DEAD SEA SCROLLS AND THE OLD TESTAMENT

"Have you ever heard of the Dead Sea Scrolls?" I asked.

"Sure," Dave replied.

When I inquired about how much he understood about this discovery, he replied, "Very little."

"Would it be OK if I explained this important discovery to you?" I asked.

He agreed, so I began by pointing out how approximately 900 different ancient texts were discovered in 11 different caves in the hills along the northwestern shore of the Dead Sea in Israel between 1947 and 1954. About a quarter of the texts were copies of Old Testament books.

The story begins in either late 1946 or early 1947 featuring a Bedouin teen who claimed that he was looking for a lost goat on the side of a hill. Because there was no ground-level entrance, he threw a rock into the hole of a cave seven feet off the ground. Hearing the smashing of pottery, the teen climbed inside and found several 2000-year-old clay jars containing seven ancient manuscripts. This is known as Cave 1.[22]

Over the next decade, copies of approximately 230 texts were discovered, including thousands of fragmentary pieces from all but one of the 39 Old Testament books.[23] The biblical texts dating between the second century BC and the first century AD were written on parchment (untanned sheepskin) as well as papyrus (a paperlike material made from Nile River reeds from Egypt). The original scribes belonged to a Jewish sect known as the Essenes, who lived in that area.

While several of the scrolls found in the caves were stored in pottery jars and wrapped in leather, most of the documents were damaged because they were left exposed to the physical elements. For instance, more than 500 texts discovered in Cave 4 had disintegrated into approximately 15,000 fragments. This cave was first discovered in 1952 by nomadic Bedouin who pirated many of the pieces. Fortunately, the Bedouin never found the bottom level that was later uncovered by archaeologists. Grant money from the Rockefeller Institute was used to reward those who returned their tiny fragments, which were often returned in matchboxes. Over many decades, scholars have worked tirelessly to piece these scrolls back together.

Cave 1 of the Dead Sea Scrolls as seen today in the hills near Qumran in Israel. A Bedouin shepherd threw a rock into the upper hole and heard the smashing of pottery jars containing two Old Testament scrolls of Isaiah. The entrance at the bottom was opened later by archaeologists. Photo by Eric Johnson.

As far as the 230 biblical scrolls found in the caves at Qumran, more than a third were copies of the first five books (Pentateuch, Torah, or Law). Deuteronomy (33 copies) was the largest, followed by Genesis (24), Exodus and Leviticus (18 each), and Numbers (11). This makes sense because these books are the most important for orthodox Jews. Before the Dead Sea Scrolls were discovered, the earliest manuscripts of the Old Testament dated no earlier than the tenth century AD.

This means that the scrolls dating from the second century BC to the first century AD bridge the gap by more than a millennium! Other popular biblical books were the Psalms (39), Isaiah (22), the minor prophets (10), and Daniel (8), all of which contained important eschatological (end-times) passages. The Essenes had developed a specific end-time theology and believed they would overthrow the Jerusalem temple controlled by the Sadducees, another Jewish sect.

The initial discovery in Cave 1 included two complete copies of the book of Isaiah, one of which was a pristine copy known as the Great Scroll of Isaiah. The biblical prophet included many prophesies of the Messiah along with a clear description of God's nature in chapters 43–45. When the Great Scroll of Isaiah (dated 125 BC) is compared to the earliest available text (Aleppo Codex from AD 900), the two are about 95 percent the same! Archaeologist Randall Price explains that "it was evident that, except for minor details (such as spelling) that do not affect the meaning of the text, the two documents were almost identical."[24]

Since most of the discrepancies (called "variants") involve obvious slips of the pen, spelling alterations, and accent marks that had worked their way into the Hebrew language during the 1000-year interim, most scholars do not see a problem with the 5 percent differential. Explaining how textual variants take place in the different biblical manuscripts, Price states,

> Yet we *can* say—and say with greater confidence than ever based on the witness of the Scrolls—that our present text is accurate and reliable, and that nothing affecting the doctrine of the original has been compromised or changed in

any way in the manuscript copies…Those who expected the Scrolls to produce a radical revision of the Bible have been disappointed, for these texts have only verified the reliability of the Old Testament as it appears in our modern translations.[25]

Biblical scholar Gleason Archer adds,

A careful study of the variants of the various earliest manuscripts reveals that *none of them affects a single doctrine of Scripture*. The system of spiritual truth contained in the standard Hebrew text of the Old Testament is not in the slightest altered or compromised by any of the variant readings found in the Hebrew manuscripts…It is very evident that the vast majority of them are so inconsequential as to leave the meaning of each clause doctrinally unaffected.[26]

One scroll containing the Psalms was found in the Cave of the Letters near the Dead Sea Scroll caves and was excavated by archaeologists between 1960 and 1961. Previously, the earliest text of Psalm 22:16 dated about AD 900 can be translated as "like a *lion* are my hands and my feet." However, the Cave of the Letters' scroll shows a slight difference. Even though the words are remarkably close in spelling, the earliest text has the Hebrew verb for "pierced," not the Hebrew noun for "lion." "Lion" makes no sense in that context, while "pierced" is a prophetical reference to the crucifixion of Jesus.

THE EVIDENCE OF ADDITIONAL BIBLICAL ARCHAEOLOGY

After I explained to Dave the discovery of the Dead Sea Scrolls, I wanted to introduce other archaeological discoveries that shed light on the Bible's history.

"Have you heard that there are archaeologists working in countries such as Israel, Turkey, and Italy who research the sites mentioned in the Bible?" I asked.

"I think I have. What exactly do they do?"

"They uncover biblical sites, including those that are being found regularly. Typically, the archaeologists can accurately determine the dates of what they find through such items as pottery and coins."

I pointed out how tells—artificial hills containing multiple civilizations built one on top of the other—are located throughout Israel. These are generally found near transportation (ancient roads) and water sources throughout Israel, both of which were important for a culture to survive. For instance, Bet She'an in northern Israel is where Saul's body was hanged on the city wall (1 Samuel 31:10-12). It was later known as Scythopolis, one of the ten Decapolis cities in the New Testament, and contains several dozen different civilizations going back at least 5000 years. Excavations in dozens of tells found throughout biblical lands have uncovered city walls, buildings, and artifacts—including utensils, arrowheads, and dishes—have made it possible for archaeologists to better comprehend what transpired at these sites.

This tell (artificial hill) at Bet She'an in northern Israel contains more than 20 layers of ancient civilizations. Photo by Eric Johnson.

"Are you saying that archaeology proves the Bible?" Dave asked.

"It's impossible to empirically *prove* the Bible. For instance, it cannot be proven that Jesus fed 5000 people near the Sea of Galilee or that the resurrection of Jesus took place. But the probability of these events increases when we can ascertain the places and people described in the Bible."

Archaeologist John D. Currid says that "the purpose of archaeology (and related fields) is not to prove the Bible. The Bible doesn't need to be proved. It stands well enough on its own...Biblical archaeology serves to confirm, illuminate, and give 'earthiness' to the Scriptures. It helps to demonstrate that the events related in the biblical accounts took place in history."[27] Thus, archaeology is a tool to help document the people, places, and events described in the pages of God's Holy Word.[28]

Archaeologist Joel Kramer provides an excellent illustration of the importance of archeology to understanding the Bible:

> To better grasp the working relationship between the Bible and archaeology, consider the following analogy. A five-hundred-piece jigsaw puzzle box is found with only five pieces inside: one percent of the jigsaw puzzle remains, the rest of the pieces are lost. Those few pieces are important evidence supporting the reality that at one time, the whole puzzle existed. But what can be done with only five pieces out of a five-hundred-piece puzzle? Practically nothing. There is one help, however. The box lid is still intact, and it shows a picture of the whole puzzle. Equipped with this bigger picture, we can now see where the five pieces fit in to their larger context. In biblical archaeology, the five puzzle pieces represent the archaeology—what comes up out of the ground—while the picture on the front of the box represents the role of the Bible.[29]

While many archaeologists in Israel are not believers in God or Christianity, these trained professionals typically use the Bible as their primary source to understand what they are excavating. They realize that this is the best available source to interpret their discoveries.[30] Even though only a small fraction of the possible biblical sites have been fully excavated in countries such as Israel, Turkey, Jordan, Greece, and Italy, the amount of information uncovered throughout the biblical lands is impressive.

I pointed out to Dave my favorite biblical discoveries, including artifacts, uncovered in the twentieth century:

The Pilate Stone. Discovered in 1961 under the theatre at Caesarea Maritima on the western coast of Israel, this first century AD stone inscription contains the name and title of the biblical figure Pontius Pilate who condemned Jesus to the cross (Matthew 27:2; Luke 3:1). Along with a ring owned by Pilate found at Herodium in 1968 and identified in 2018, these are the only two archaeological artifacts uncovered from this otherwise insignificant Roman ruler.

Hezekiah's Tunnel. A 1750-foot tunnel in the City of David in Jerusalem was chiseled out of bedrock by workers who dug from opposite ends during the reign of King Hezekiah. This underground tunnel was built about 700 BC before an expected Assyrian assault, allowing water from a spring located outside the city walls to secretly flow to the city of Jerusalem (2 Kings 20:20). A descriptive marker chiseled in the stone wall at the southern end of the tunnel was discovered more than a century ago. Known as the Siloam Inscription, it was removed and is housed today in the Archaeological Museum in Istanbul, Turkey. Adventurous tourists visiting the City of David can slosh their way through this water tunnel while feeling the chisel marks made on the walls more than 2700 years ago.

The Pilate Stone is displayed in the Israel Museum in Jerusalem and dates about 2000 years ago. This is the first archaeological evidence for the historical figure Pontius Pilate, the procurator who judged Jesus. Photo by Eric Johnson.

The Tel Dan Stele. Discovered in the mid-1990s in northern Israel, this stone contains a triumphal inscription written in Aramaic by Hazael of Aram-Damascus, an important regional figure in the late ninth century BC. The king boasted of his victories over the king of the "House of David." It was the first time David's name was found in any archaeological find, showing that both Israel and Judah were important kingdoms at this time. The artifact is housed at the Israel Museum in Jerusalem.

Pool of Bethesda. This site in the old city of Jerusalem is where Jesus healed a paralyzed man (John 5:2-17). Located a short distance from the Sheep Gate, the pool was excavated in 1956.

Jacob's Well. Originally dug by the patriarch Jacob (Genesis 33:18-19; 48:22), this well in the West Bank of Israel is where Jesus spoke to a Samaritan woman in John 4. It still produces fresh water and can be visited today in the basement of a modern Greek Orthodox church located in the modern city of Nablus.

Magdala. An ancient town near the shore of the Sea of Galilee in Israel, just north of the city of Tiberias, was the hometown of Mary Magdalene, a good friend of Jesus (Luke 8:1-3; John 19:25; 20:11-18). In 2009, the Roman Catholic Church prepared to build a retreat center at this beautiful location. Before builders are allowed to dig in Israel, archaeologists are legally required to search the site. To everyone's surprise, a Jewish town from 2000 years ago was discovered below the ground along with a synagogue that, scholars insist, Jesus would have known. Archaeological discoveries in Israel happen regularly and confirm the history of the Bible!

Names can be another indicator that real people and places are talked about in the Bible. Consider Luke, the author of Luke and Acts who provided many details in his writing. Some antagonists have pointed to Luke 2:1-2 as a historical contradiction. It says, "In those days a decree went out from Caesar Augustus that all the world should be registered. This was the first registration when Quirinius was governor of Syria." This is the only place the Bible mentions Quirinius. Jewish historian Josephus said that Quirinius ruled from AD 5 to AD 6, a decade after the birth of Jesus.

Was Luke wrong? Archaeological evidence, including information from one ancient coin, shows how a "Quirinius" served as governor from 11 BC until the time of Herod. Scholars debate if this was a second man named Quirinius or the same man who served as the governor at two different times. Regardless, Quirinius was the governor at that time, so Luke was correct and his report is accurate.

One more example to support the historicity of Luke's account is found in Acts 18:12-17 when Paul appeared before Gallio, the proconsul of the region of Achaia about AD 51. In the early twentieth century, archaeologists discovered nine fragments of a letter at the temple of Apollo in Delphi, Greece, that was written by the Roman emperor Claudius dated AD 52. Known as the Delphi or Gallio Inscription, one fragment written in Koine Greek mentions the proconsul Gallio, thus fitting the timeline of Acts 18 to a tee! Instead of being shown to be a fraud, Luke accurately described the historical situation of his day.[31]

DID THE EXODUS HAPPEN?

Skeptics often bring up the lack of evidence for the 40-year wandering of more than a million people during the time of the Exodus.

The Magdala synagogue first discovered near the Sea of Galilee in 2009. Photo by Eric Johnson.

Would it even be reasonable to think that any evidence could have survived? A total of 3400 years of desert sand makes it impossible to do archaeology. Besides, the Israelites were a nomadic people during that time and never stayed in any one place long enough to build or leave behind evidence.

Still, archaeology can be used to show how there was an exodus during the second half of the fifteenth century BC. Consider just four discoveries from Egypt as detailed by biblical archaeologist Titus Kennedy:

The Papyrus Brooklyn: A papyrus manuscript discovered in Egypt from the seventeenth century BC—a century or two before the Exodus—contained Hebrew servant names. The list showed how Hebrews lived in Egypt before the Exodus.

Tomb of Rekmire: A mural from the time of the Exodus in 1450 BC discovered in Egypt depicts bricks made with mud and straw. Another text known as the Louvre Leather Roll shows how a certain number of bricks were required to be manufactured even with a lack of materials or the slaves were punished.

Nomads of YHWH: Hieroglyphic inscriptions date to 1400 BC and describe the "land of the nomads of YHWH," the earliest evidence

The Gallio Inscription in the museum at Delphi, Greece. Photo by Loren Pankratz.

of Yahweh, the most intimate name for God. These were written on the walls of two different Egyptian temples as well as a temple pillar and showed how the only people who worshiped Yahweh were the Israelites.

Merneptah Stele: Dated 1219 BC, this is a ten-foot-high Egyptian stone monument with 28 lines of hieroglyphics describing military campaigns by Pharaoh Merneptah. There is a section on the stele that spells "Israel" in Egyptian hieroglyphs referring to a group of people, not a country. According to Kennedy, the Israelites conquered the land of Canaan after the wilderness wandering just as Joshua and Judges detail.[32]

It is realistic to believe that a 40-year exodus of God's people did take place. Of course, faith is required for some biblical events (such as stories involving miracles), but there is so much evidence to make belief in the biblical people and the places reasonable. All things considered, the Book of Mormon has nothing close to the historical attestation so abundantly found to support the historicity of the Bible.

I enjoy leading annual tours to the lands of the Bible, as I have taken more than 500 pilgrims to sites throughout Israel, Jordan, Egypt, Turkey, Greece, and Italy on more than a dozen trips since 2009. As one traveler told me, "I used to read the Bible in black and white, but now I read it in living color!"

In the next chapter, we continue the discussion with Dave as we consider the New Testament copies, the changes made in the Bible, and possible biblical contradictions. We will also have a chance to talk about the "telephone game" illustration often used to criticize the composition of the Bible. Understanding the accuracy of God's Word is vital for the case of Christianity to be made.

DISCUSSION QUESTIONS*

1. The eighth Article of Faith says that the Bible is true "as far as it is translated correctly." Why is the word *transmitted* more precise than *translated* when describing how the text was passed down through the centuries? Why does making this distinction matter?

2. What is the difference between inerrancy and infallibility?

3. What are the Dead Sea Scrolls? How have these proven to be so valuable to scholars in determining the accuracy of the Old Testament?

4. How can biblical archaeology support the case of the people, places, and events described in the Bible? Do you have a favorite archaeological discovery or two? (It doesn't have to be listed in the chapter.) Why do you think that particular discovery is significant?

5. A critic might say there is no evidence for the Exodus led by Moses. Is that true?

---

* Visit IntroducingChristianity.com for possible responses to the discussion questions found at the end of each chapter.

RECOMMENDED RESOURCES

Entry-Level Resources

Josh and Sean McDowell, *Inspired: Experience the Power of God's Word* (Eugene, OR: Harvest House Publishers, 2011).

Lee Strobel, *The Case for Christ: A Journalist's Personal Investigation of the Evidence for Jesus* (Grand Rapids, MI: Zondervan, 1998).

Middle-Level Resources

Titus Kennedy, *Unearthing the Bible: 101 Archaeological Discoveries that Bring the Bible to Life* (Eugene, OR: Harvest House Publishers, 2020).

Randall Price, *Secrets of the Dead Sea Scrolls* (Eugene, OR: Harvest House Publishers, 1996).

Joel P. Kramer, *Where God Came Down: The Archaeological Evidence* (Brigham City, UT: Expedition Bible, 2020).

Advanced Resource

Craig L. Blomberg, *Can We Still Believe the Bible? An Evangelical Engagement with Contemporary Questions* (Grand Rapids, MI: Brazos Press, 2013).

CHAPTER 2

THE NEW TESTAMENT

Trustworthy and Reliable

"For the word of God is living and active, sharper than any two-edged sword, piercing to the division of soul and of spirit, of joints and of marrow, and discerning the thoughts and intentions of the heart."

HEBREWS 4:12

CHAPTER PREVIEW

There are abundant copies of ancient manuscripts containing the New Testament, including more than 5000 written in Greek. This is better evidence than for any other ancient text, including works by Homer and Caesar. A popular skeptic says that there are more variants than there are words in the entire New Testament. Regardless of how these variants are counted, no essential doctrines are affected. Meanwhile, it has been shown that modern Bible translators are honest in their work, especially when certain problematic passages are considered. Just having a good translation is not enough, as the reader must understand the words according to what the original author meant, not what the reader interprets them to mean. Finally, some skeptics like to introduce "contradictions" to show the unreliability of the Bible, but these difficulties generally can be explained when the context is taken into consideration.

As shown in the previous chapter, the Bible is considered scripture in Mormonism, though it is not viewed as being completely trustworthy. Returning to the conversation from chapter 1, Dave decided to refer to Dr. Bart Ehrman, a professor in the department of religious studies at the University of North Carolina at Chapel Hill, whose specialty is the New Testament. If you have watched religious documentaries on television or seen biblical DVD educational courses, you probably have seen him.[1]

"Bart Ehrman says that the New Testament is filled with so many errors that it cannot be trusted," Dave told me. "Here is a scholar with a Christian background and yet he says that the Bible constantly misquotes Jesus. If a New Testament scholar doesn't believe that it is accurate, why should I?"

While his name is popular amongst skeptics, Ehrman is not typically cited by those who call themselves Latter-day Saints. It does not make sense for a Latter-day Saint to attack a scripture that remains a part of LDS canon. As the saying goes, this might seem like cutting off your nose to spite your face. Perhaps this was a sign that Dave—who still claimed to be a faithful Latter-day Saint—had been influenced by skeptical friends. Or maybe he had already mentally checked out of Mormonism. Regardless, it must be understood that some Mormons argue more like agnostics or atheists.

"Just because a person has a doctorate in New Testament does not mean his opinion is correct," I countered. "In fact, it doesn't even mean he is a believer in God."

Ehrman graduated from two reputable evangelical institutions and claimed that he once considered himself a Christian before he decided to become a skeptic. Let's delve into some of his views as expounded in his best-selling 2005 book *Misquoting Jesus: The Story Behind Who Changed the Bible and Why.*[2]

THE COMPILATION OF
THE NEW TESTAMENT

If the New Testament is not accurate, then Mormonism becomes just as irrelevant as Christianity. To attack the accuracy of the entire Bible means that favorite prooftexts often used by Latter-day Saints— James 2:20, 1 Corinthians 15:29, and John 10:34, among many others—should also not be trusted. This is something that many Latter-day

Saints like Dave may have never paused to contemplate. Yet he insisted on disproving the accuracy of the transmitted biblical text regardless.

"There is no way that what we have in our Bibles comes close to what was originally written," Dave said in a determined voice. "If there are no original copies, why should I trust the Bible? Produce the originals and then maybe I can accept it as accurate."

I decided to take a few minutes and provide four reasons to trust the message given in the New Testament.

1. Multiple Copies Are Available

The original biblical manuscripts are called *autographs*. As far as we know, none of the biblical autographs of either the Old or New Testament exist today because each was destroyed or lost. As Christian pastors John MacArthur and Richard Mayhue explain,

> Every book of the Bible was originally composed under the inspiration of the Holy Spirit by a human author. These original works—called *autographs*—were completely without error as the result of divine inspiration. None of these original manuscripts are in existence today. Instead, copies were made and soon thereafter copies of copies. These copies and multitudes of translations have been passed down through the centuries.[3]

Very likely the New Testament autographs would have disintegrated by the third century AD due to wear and tear.[4] I explained to Dave that even if these manuscripts were available today, this would not be enough to convince most skeptics. As New Testament scholar Daniel Wallace stated, "Even if we did have the originals, skeptics who are philosophically committed to their position would try to explain them away…they start where they want to end up and then look at all the evidence selective for their purposes, rather than being open to what the evidence actually reveals."[5]

Even though no original New Testament document exists, many copies (called *apographs*) are readily available to translators. There are not just dozens or hundreds, mind you, but thousands, including more than 5600 Greek manuscripts as described by scholar F.F. Bruce:

> The evidence for our New Testament writings is ever so much greater than the evidence for many writings of classical authors, the authenticity of which no one dreams of questioning. And if the New Testament were a collection of secular writings, their authenticity would generally be regarded as beyond all doubt…There are in existence over 5,000 Greek manuscripts of the New Testament in whole or in part.[6]

While some copies are fragmentary pieces of papyrus, "the average size manuscript is more than four hundred fifty pages long with some fragments dated within the lifetime of the followers of the original apostles!"[7] There are also are more than 24,000 manuscripts written in additional languages such as Latin, Egyptian Coptic, Syrian, and Georgian. As New Testament scholars Darrell Bock and Daniel Wallace write, "All told, the New Testament is represented by approximately one thousand times as many manuscripts as the average classical author's writings. Even the well-known authors—such as Homer and Herodotus—simply can't compare to the quantity of copies enjoyed by the New Testament."[8]

Compared to other ancient literature, scholars point to an abundance of early New Testament writings. In fact, "we have between ten and fifteen manuscripts within one hundred years of the completion of the New Testament, and more than four dozen within two centuries. Of manuscripts produced before AD 400, an astounding ninety-nine still exist—including the oldest complete New Testament, Codex Sinaiticus."[9] The copies circulated during the first two centuries after the time of the apostles. About 15 percent (more than 800) of the available Greek texts were composed before AD 1000. Wallace says this is

> more than forty times the amount of manuscripts from the average classical author in more than two thousand years of copying! The average classical author has zero manuscripts

extant today produced within half a millennium of the composition of his writings. The New Testament has at least two hundred fifty manuscripts—in Greek alone—produced within five hundred years after the composition of the New Testament.[10]

Let's pretend that all the New Testament texts had been commandeered and destroyed by enemies of the Bible. According to Wallace, it still would be possible to refer to the writings of Christians who, "from the late first century to the thirteenth century, quoted from the New Testament in homilies, commentaries, and theological treatises. And they did not have the gift of brevity. More than a million quotations of the New Testament by the church fathers have been collected so far. Virtually the entire New Testament could be reproduced many times over just from the quotations of these fathers."[11]

It is true that there are variants, with the vast majority fitting under the "accidental mistake" category that "include misspellings of words; duplicating or omitting a letter, word, or line of text; dividing words that were originally run together without spacing; or placing punctuation in different places—in short, all the mistakes that even typists today make when typing up someone else's writing instead of merely scanning, copying, or cutting and pasting the original text electronically."[12] Typically, these types of mistakes do not affect the meaning of the text, as Norman Geisler states:

> Whereas there are many variant readings in New Testament manuscripts, there are a multitude of manuscripts available for comparison and correlation of those readings in order to arrive at the correct one. Through intensive comparative study of the readings in 5686 Greek manuscripts, scholars have carefully weeded out errors and additions from "helpful" copyists and discerned which early manuscripts are most accurate.[13]

When a scribe went out of his way to make a change in a manuscript, it appears he may have intended to correct something that he thought needed to be fixed. For instance, if he felt that more of an explanation was needed, he might have added commentary in the column above or below the text. Regardless, it is entirely impractical to suggest that sinister scribes wanted to wreak havoc by creating unauthorized changes to the biblical text.[14] For any "change" to be believable, hundreds of earlier or contemporary texts would have had to be rounded up to make the same change. Copies of the New Testament were scattered throughout the known world, so finding sufficient texts to make these changes would have been unrealistic.

2. Variants Normally Do Not Change the Meaning of a Passage

Ehrman's claim that there are 400,000 "variants" in the New Testament seems curious when it is understood that there are only 138,000 total words in the 27 books. How could there be more variants than there are words? The answer, simply, is that any time there is a difference in multiple texts, a "variant" is counted that many times. For example, the same discrepancy in 50 copies would equal 50 variants. A total of 75 percent of all textual variants involve spelling differences. Even minute or trivial differences are counted.

While tens of thousands of variants may seem overwhelming, this is an overstated charge. Craig Blomberg further explains,

> The vast majority of textual variants are wholly uninteresting except to specialists. When one hears numbers like 400,000 variants (if that number is even accurate), one must remember that they are spread across 25,000 manuscripts. A large percentage of these variants cluster around the same verses or passages. Less than 3 percent of them are significant enough to be presented in one of the two standard critical editions of the Greek New Testament. Only about a tenth of 1 percent are interesting enough to make their way into footnotes in most English translations. It cannot be emphasized strongly enough that *no orthodox doctrine or ethical practice of Christianity depends solely on any disputed wording.*[15]

Daniel Wallace explains that "less than 1 percent of all textual variants are both meaningful and viable."[16] Stated a different way, more than 99 percent of the alternative readings do *not* change any text's meaning. To be clear, no essential Christian doctrine or practice is affected by these variants.

While Dave wanted to argue that discrepancies disprove the Bible's accuracy, F.F. Bruce says many more errors should have been expected:

> When we have documents like our New Testament writings copied and recopied thousands of times the scope for copyists' errors is so enormously increased that it is surprising there are no more than there actually are. Fortunately, if the great number of MSS [manuscripts] increases the number of scribal errors, it increases proportionately the means of correcting such errors, so that the margin of doubt left in the process of recovering the exact wording is not so large as might be feared; it is in truth remarkably small.[17]

3. Set Rules Are Followed

Certain rules are used by biblical scholars to understand what was originally written by the New Testament writers. For instance, priority is given to the earliest copies because it would have been easier to alter later editions. At face value, the copy with the more difficult reading is prioritized over those texts with easier, more polished readings that could indicate changes made by scribes in their attempt to make the passage more understandable or palatable. While the intention may have been honorable, damage was done. When a corrected copy is compared to others, it is generally easy to see.

4. Bible Translators Generally Have Integrity

Finally, much work has been accomplished by the translators to verify their character. My two favorite translations of the Bible are the New International Version (NIV) and the English Standard Version (ESV); both are not only more readable compared to the archaic English of the KJV but also are highly accurate renderings of the original texts.

I had the honor of sitting under the teaching of Dr. Walter W. Wessel (New Testament) and Dr. Ronald Youngblood (New Testament) in seminary classes they taught during the late 1980s, as both were important NIV translators. Each loved to tell stories detailing the responsibility they felt they had in accurately portraying what the biblical writers originally said. What I will never forget is their descriptions of the back-and-forth conversations they had with other scholars on the translation team concerning difficult passages.

Helpful footnotes in modern versions make it possible to consider alternative readings. According to Blomberg,

> Readers of almost any English language translation of the Bible except for the King James Version (KJV) and the New King James Version (NKJV) can look at the footnotes, or marginal notes, of their Bibles and see mention of a broad cross-section of the most important and interesting of these variants. Unfortunately, many readers don't consult these notes often enough. Of course, more and more people are reading their Bible in electronic form, and many electronic versions of the Bible don't even include such notes.[18]

Do these translators always agree on every issue? No. And there are different ways that the original construction of the languages can be translated. But generally, those Christian men and women who have worked on modern English translations, such as my two professors, have taken their job very seriously.

ALTERNATIVE READINGS

When it comes to different readings, scholars work hard to explain why one ought to be preferred over others. Each possibility is graded, with the highest-rated reading being incorporated into the Greek text. As Blomberg explains,

> The United Bible Societies' fourth edition of the Greek New Testament contains 1,438 of the most significant

textual variants in its footnotes and presents the most important manuscript evidence for each reading of the disputed text. Using the letters A through D, the committee that produced the edition also ranks its level of confidence in its decision to adopt a particular reading.[19]

Let's consider Matthew 17:21 in the KJV, a verse citing Jesus who healed a boy with a demon: "Howbeit this kind goeth not out but by prayer and fasting." The United Bible Society (UBS) left this verse— which is found only in the KJV—out of the main text; out of the four ratings (A through D), the omission of the verse is given a strong B grade. The UBS explanation is that the verse may have been added by later copyists to fit the parallel account in Mark 9:29.[20]

Since the evidence supports the case that these words were added by later copyists, modern translations do not include verse 21. Omitting or including this verse has *no* effect on the meaning of the passage. Modern translations explain the verse's omission in a footnote. If there was anything to hide, it would not have made sense to bring up the issue.

In rare cases when there are legitimate alternative meanings, Wallace says that no "cardinal or essential doctrine is altered."[21] For instance, when the deity of Jesus is considered—a crucial Christian doctrine to be discussed in chapter 5—"it's nonsense to say Jesus' deity wasn't invented until the fourth century when you've already got the evidence in earlier manuscripts."[22] F.F. Bruce adds, "The variant readings about which any doubt remains among textual critics of the New Testament affect no material question of historic fact or of Christian faith and practice."[23]

Even the late LDS scholar Lloyd Anderson, who once served as a religion professor at LDS Church-owned Brigham Young University, supported the accuracy of the New Testament:

> One can disagree with the textual assumptions behind some of the modern translations of the New Testament and still not be overly concerned with differences that are

immaterial. For a book to undergo progressive uncovering of its manuscript history and come out with so little debatable in its text is a great tribute to its essential authenticity. First, no new manuscript discovery has produced serious differences in the essential story. This survey has disclosed the leading textual controversies, and together they would be well within one percent of the text. Stated differently, all manuscripts agree on the essential correctness of 99 percent of all the verses in the New Testament. The second great fact that such a survey demonstrates is the progress that has placed the world in possession of manuscripts very near to the time of their writing. One would have to be a student of ancient history to appreciate how much superior the New Testament is to any other book in its manuscript tradition.[24]

CHANGES IN THE NEW TESTAMENT

Another criticism made by Ehrman is how two different passages found in Mark and John are not included in the earliest and most accurate Greek manuscripts. To show this is the case, modern English translations include notes at the front of each of these passages:

Mark 16:9-20 (known as the "longer ending of Mark"): The note in the ESV explains, "Some of the earliest manuscripts do not include [Mark] 16:9-20." More details are provided in the footnote.[25]

John 7:53–8:11: This passage recounts the story of Jesus and the adulterous woman. The ESV note states, "The earliest manuscripts do not include 7:53–8:11."

Wallace writes that "the consensus of New Testament scholars is that these verses were added to the New Testament later, since they are not found in the earliest and best manuscripts and they do not fit with the authors' known syntax, vocabulary, or style. No doctrines are impacted by these variants."[26] The ESV—along with other modern versions—is honest in its assessment. While these two passages remain in the narrative flow, translators do not hide what skeptics might consider to be embarrassing evidence.

Consider 1 John 5:6-8, another passage with a dubious pedigree. It reads:

> [6] This is he who came by water and blood—Jesus Christ; not by the water only but by the water and the blood. And the Spirit is the one who testifies, because the Spirit is the truth. [7] For there are three that testify: [8] the Spirit and the water and the blood; and these three agree.

After verse 7 and before verse 8, the KJV includes these additional words that have become known as the *Comma Johanneum*: "For there are three that bear record in heaven, the Father, the Word, and the Holy Ghost: and these three are one. And there are three that bear witness in earth…"

How did these additional words make it into the KJV? After all, there is no evidence that these were included in early Greek manuscripts but only in the margins of several late copies from the fourteenth century. Despite having no solid source to use in support, the first compiled Greek New Testament (Textus Receptus) published in 1516 and used by the KJV translators included these extra words.[27] Since these verses do not offer legitimate support for the Trinity, knowledgeable Christians should not use them as support for a doctrine easily supported by other passages.

THE TELEPHONE GAME

After I shared much of this information with Dave, it became clear that he would not be easily convinced. He decided to introduce an illustration used by many atheists called the "telephone game" to denigrate the transmissional reliability of the Bible.

"You know that party game we used to play as children where someone whispers a statement to a second person," he said. "Each player communicates with the next person in line, and so on. The last one in line then tells everyone the message he heard, which is usually garbled compared to the original statement." He waited for a few seconds, then asked with a wide smile, "How can you be convinced that the original message written by the biblical writers was accurately copied copy after copy after copy?"

To suggest that the Bible's message became garbled over time is a serious charge. The main difference between this illustration and the way the Bible was transmitted is that the information conveyed in the telephone game is *oral* while the copies of the New Testament were *written*. The game's players are required to rely on what they were verbally told by the previous player, so each person's memory (or lack of it) can affect the outcome. Biblical scholars hold an advantage because they have multiple written records of the text and are not required to rely on anyone's memory.

Christian apologist Greg Koukl presents an illustration of "Aunt Sally's elixir recipe" that provides a valid response to the telephone game illustration:

> Pretend your Aunt Sally learns in a dream the recipe for an elixir that preserves her youth. When she awakes, she scribbles the complex directions on a sheet of paper, then runs to the kitchen to mix up her first batch of "Sally's Secret Sauce." In a few days, she is transformed into a picture of radiant youth.

> Aunt Sally is so excited she sends detailed, handwritten instructions to her three bridge partners (Aunt Sally is still in the technological dark ages—no photocopier or email). They, in turn, make copies for ten of their own friends.

> All goes well until one day Aunt Sally's schnauzer eats the original script. In a panic she contacts her friends who have mysteriously suffered similar mishaps. The alarm goes out to the others who received copies from her card-playing trio in an attempt to recover the original wording.

The Telephone Game vs.
the Transmission of the New Testament Text

 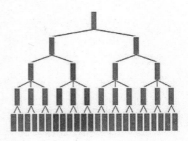

Every person in the chain passes the message on to only one person.	Manuscripts are copied multiple times, resulting in a complex web of relationships.
A **change** introduced by any one person will propagate through the entire chain.	A **change** introduced by any one scribe will affect only a portion of the manuscript tradition.
The message is only reported by the final person in the chain.	The text is attested in over 5,000 extant Greek manuscripts, some from as early as the 2nd century.
The original message is LOST.	The original message is PRESERVED.

Graphic used by permission of Murray Vasser from Asbury Seminary (www.murrayvasser.com).

Sally rounds up all the surviving handwritten copies, 26 in all. When she spreads them out on the kitchen table, she immediately notices differences. Twenty-three of the copies are virtually the same save for misspelled words and abbreviations littering the text. Of the remaining three, however, one lists ingredients in a different order, another has two phrases inverted ("mix then chop" instead of "chop then mix"), and one includes an ingredient not mentioned in any other list.

Do you think Aunt Sally can accurately reconstruct her original recipe from this evidence? Of course she can. The misspellings and abbreviations are inconsequential, as is the order of ingredients in the list (those variations all *mean* the same thing). The single inverted phrase stands out and can easily be repaired because one can't mix something that hasn't been chopped. Sally would then strike the extra ingredient reasoning it's more plausible one person would mistakenly add an item than 25 people would accidentally omit it.

Even if the variations were more numerous and diverse, the original could still be reconstructed with a high level of confidence with enough copies and a little common sense.[28]

In addition, the players in the telephone game are *not* motivated by accuracy. The more garbled the statement made by the final player, the more fun it is for everyone involved. Those scribes who painstakingly copied the words of the Bible were motivated by accuracy, not jocular entertainment. They understood that their work was critical in communicating God's message to humanity. Comparing the game of telephone with the transmission of the Bible, then, is apples and oranges.

Dave did not appear convinced, so I decided to use one more argument to show why the original manuscripts of the New Testament are not necessary.

"If the Bible's autographs existed today, who do you think would own most, if not all, of these?"

He thought for a few seconds, then replied, "The Louvre? Or the British Museum?"

"Perhaps, but wouldn't the more likely candidate be the Roman Catholic Church?"

I explained how the major influencer in Christianity over the centuries was a religious organization that displayed great political and financial strength for hundreds of years. This church might not be as politically powerful as it once was, but it is still the leader of organized Christianity. As far as its wealth, visit Vatican City located in Rome and stroll through the wonderful museums filled with thousands of pieces of priceless artwork, including paintings on the walls and ceilings!

There is no doubt that the leaders of the Roman Catholic Church would have been interested in any of the autographs; in fact, it owns one of the three most accurate New Testament copies in the world, Codex Vaticanus, named after the world's smallest independent state (Vatican City) controlled by the church.

"Let's pretend the Catholic Church owned any of the autographs," I proposed. "Would it be possible that, over the years, corrupt Catholic historians or theologians faithful to their church made their own changes to the originals? Nobody would be able to have full confidence in these manuscripts. On the other hand, having thousands of copies of the New Testament texts available allows for a check and a recheck, which is better than if the autographs were all that were available. Give me a choice between the originals and copies, I will choose the copies every single time."

Although he didn't know it, Dave's assertion that original manuscripts are necessary for the Bible to be trusted results in a major problem for the LDS Church. I decided to make this point.

"Besides, what about the 'Reformed Egyptian' gold plates of the Book of Mormon—its autographs, if you will?" I asked. "These originals are no longer available because Joseph Smith claimed to return the plates to the angel Moroni after he had finished his English translation on June 30, 1829. So how could LDS Church leaders alter several thousand words in the Book of Mormon over the past years without the aid of the autographs contained in the gold plates? It seems quite precarious to do this without any source as support."

He allowed me to finish my argument.

"Since we don't have the gold plates, does this mean that Latter-day Saints should only believe the Book of Mormon 'as far as it is translated correctly'? If you want to criticize the Bible for the lack of autographs, it seems fair that the Book of Mormon should be considered in the same way."

Although I did not bring it up, the Joseph Smith Translation of the Bible could have also been mentioned, as Smith created his own "translation" to fix what he claimed were errors in the Bible. He even added more than a dozen verses to the last chapter of Genesis to include a prophecy about himself, among other additions and subtractions. None of his changes is supported by the textual evidence. Still, Smith claimed that he finished his version on July 2, 1833.[29]

If Smith truly was a prophet who had the ability to translate the Bible without manuscripts, his version should be considered a godsend. However, LDS Church leaders have never officially endorsed nor published it; many Latter-day Saints do not even own a copy.[30] Not actively using or promoting this version seems suspicious if Smith really was a prophet of God who, as Mormons believe, had the ability to translate scripture.

DEALING WITH APPARENT BIBLE CONTRADICTIONS

The discussion with Dave had gone well, but he had one more question.

"What about the contradictions in the Bible?" he asked. "If one passage refutes another, then obviously there must be a problem and the Bible should not be considered trustworthy."

I told Dave that the context of each passage must be considered. When in doubt, the reader will discover that, much of the time, the immediate context answers whatever "contradiction" there may appear to be. Besides, it should be expected that there will be different perspectives from eyewitness accounts. When police detectives are at a crime scene, their job is to separate the witnesses and hear each of their sides of the story. If their testimonies match, this is often a sign of collusion. Instead, it should be expected that their views will slightly differ.

Another consideration is recognizing when language is phenomenal rather than technical. Millard Erickson writes, "When the weatherman on the evening news says that the sun will rise the next morning at 6:37, he has, from a strictly technical standpoint, made an error, since it has been known since the time of Copernicus that the sun does not move—the earth does. Yet there is no problem with this popular expression. Indeed, even in scientific circles the term *sunrise* has become something of an idiom."[31] In addition, numbers in the Bible are sometimes rounded up or down. Erickson reports:

> Suppose a hypothetical case in which the Bible reported a battle in which 9,476 men were involved. What then would be a correct (or infallible) report? Would 10,000 be accurate? 9,000? 9,500? 9,480? 9,475? Or would only 9,476 be a correct report? The answer is that it depends upon the purpose of the writing. If the report is an official military document which an officer is to submit to his superior, the number must be exact. That is the only way to ascertain whether there were any deserters. If, on the other hand, the account is simply to give some idea of the size of the battle, then a round number like 10,000 is adequate, and in this setting is correct.[32]

Skeptics introduce apparent contradictions to trip up Christians. There are several resources at mrm.org that can be helpful when considering common examples:

- "Common Bible Passages Used by the Mormons Index" (*mrm.org/bible-passages*)
- "Why Do You Trust the Bible When It Has So Many Contradictions?" (*mrm.org/bible-contradictions*)

The following books each list problematic passages in biblical order and are helpful tools:

- Josh and Sean McDowell, *The Bible Handbook of Difficult Verses: A Complete Guide to Answering the Tough Questions* (Eugene, OR: Harvest House Publishers, 2013).

- Norman L. Geisler and Thomas Howe, *The Big Book of Bible Difficulties: Clear and Concise Answers from Genesis to Revelation* (Grand Rapids, MI: Baker Books, 2008).

- Walter C. Kaiser Jr., Peter H. Davids, F.F. Bruce, and Manfred T. Brauch, *Hard Sayings of the Bible* (Downers Grove, IL: InterVarsity Press, 1996).

- Norman Geisler and Ron Rhodes, *When Cultists Ask: A Popular Handbook on Cultic Misinterpretations* (Grand Rapids, MI: Baker Books, 1997).

MAKING A REASONABLE CHALLENGE

As discussed earlier, either the Bible is what it claims for itself—the revealed words from the mind of God—or it is a fraud. There is no in between. Everyone should do the research and decide for themselves.

The intended purpose of these first two chapters has been to explain why having a standard for Christian beliefs (the Bible) is crucial to believe and act according to the principles set by God. Unfortunately, many who belong to the media, educational, and entertainment worlds want Christians to eliminate this authority so they can "follow their hearts." Yet Jeremiah 17:9 says,

> The heart is deceitful above all things,
>   and desperately sick;
>   who can understand it?

Trusting in our own ways of thinking merely muddles morals and makes seeking after God a lost priority. God's Word becomes minimized while the biblical worldview is mocked. It is difficult to navigate with a culture so opposed to accepting the Word of God as the standard for how humanity ought to think and live. Thaddeus Williams explains this dilemma:

> One of the cruelest things you can do to young people is tell them to follow their own hearts. Slowly but surely the driving moral of our stories has shifted. It was no longer, don't be self-centered like the witch from *Snow White*, Captain Hook from *Peter Pan*, Jafar from *Aladdin*, or Scar from *The Lion King*. Instead, be courageous for the sake of others, like Pinocchio taking on Monstro or Prince Charming slaying the Dragon. Defeat malevolence with kindness like Cinderella or Snow White. Those timeless truths were replaced with a disorienting false gospel of be true to yourself, follow your heart, and don't let anyone tell you who or how to be. Jesus said, "Whoever causes one of these little ones who believe in me to sin, it would be better for him to have a great millstone fastened around his neck and to be drowned in the depth of the sea," where Pinocchio won't be on his way to save you.[33]

During our time together, Dave and I had covered important topics. As our conversation was ending, I wanted to challenge him.

"Second Timothy 2:15 says that we should 'study' as a 'workman' who 'rightly divides the word of truth,'" I said. "Dave, I challenge you to read the Bible for yourself, without following an LDS reading plan or holding on to preconceived notions. See for yourself what the Bible has to say. This is a very powerful tool."

Many Latter-day Saints I meet admit that they spend much more time reading the Book of Mormon than the Bible. Thus, I recommended that Dave read the Gospel of John, which has a wonderful overview of the life of Jesus. A systematic look at salvation, I said, could be found in the epistle of Romans.[34] It is a powerful apologetic tactic to challenge Mormons to read the Bible on their own, especially the New Testament.

I like to ask Mormons if they have ever read from a modern version of the Bible, as technically they are supposed to use only the KJV. There is nothing wrong with the KJV, but it is difficult for many (myself included!) to understand the language from several hundred years ago.[35] If they don't own a modern translation, consider offering to purchase a copy for them. Or you can invite them to go to BibleGateway.com, which provides free access to a variety of English versions. Explain how the Bible can even be read on a smartphone by using an app. Many serious seekers after the truth have had their lives radically changed by reading with an open mind and heart.[36] I know I have.

When the time is right, I like to offer a person the opportunity to pray with me if a decision is made for Christ, even if we are standing on a public sidewalk in full view of passersby. In 1972, I made a personal decision to follow Christ by responding to a televised crusade invitation offered by the late Billy Graham. As Graham guided, I prayed the "sinner's prayer." Beware, as any prayer—no matter how eloquent it might sound—should never be considered a magical formula or divine requirement. At the same time, there is nothing wrong for a person to pray in acknowledgment of a new belief. Wayne Grudem explains:

> Since personal faith in Christ must involve an actual decision of the will, it is often very helpful to *express* that decision in spoken words, and this could very naturally take the form of a prayer to Christ in which we tell him of our sorrow for sin, our commitment to forsake it, and our decision actually to put our trust in him. Such a spoken prayer does not in itself save us, but the attitude of heart that it represents does constitute true conversion, and the decision to speak that prayer can often be the point at which a person truly comes to faith in Christ.[37]

Although Dave was not ready to make a commitment, I thanked him for the cordial discussion. We said goodbye, and as he walked away, I could only hope that he would ponder the things we talked about.

DISCUSSION QUESTIONS

1. Do you think a skeptic would be convinced about the Bible's reliability if autographs of the biblical books actually existed? Why or why not?

2. While the KJV includes the longer version of 1 John 5:6-8, modern English versions of the Bible put the questionable words in a footnote. Why did these modern translators decide to do this rather than just keep the words as a support for the Trinity?

3. What does the telephone game have to do with the accuracy of the Bible? What is a good response to someone who uses this example to show why the Bible is not trustworthy?

4. A variety of different biblical prooftexts are used to support the LDS position on a variety of doctrines. What are some things to consider when a Latter-day Saint uses a verse to support his or her point of view?

5. Suppose you asked your Mormon friend to read the Bible in a modern translation so it would be easier to understand. What do you think the pushback would be? If your friend agreed, which book of the Bible would be a good place to begin? Why?

RECOMMENDED RESOURCES

Entry-Level Resource

J. Warner Wallace, *Cold-Case Christianity: A Homicide Detective Investigates the Claims of the Gospels* (Colorado Springs, CO: David C. Cook, 2013).

Middle-Level Resources

John Ankerberg and Dillon Burroughs, *Taking a Stand for the Bible* (Eugene, OR: Harvest House Publishers, 2009).

Gordon Fee and Douglas Stuart, *How to Read the Bible for All Its Worth* (Grand Rapids, MI: Zondervan, 1982).

Advanced Resource

F.F. Bruce, *The New Testament Documents: Are They Reliable?* (Grand Rapids, MI: Wm. B. Eerdmans, 1981).

CHAPTER 3

THE EXISTENCE OF GOD

Reasonable Reasons for Belief

"I am the Lord, and there is no other, besides me there is no God."

ISAIAH 45:5

CHAPTER PREVIEW

An atheist is someone who believes that a higher power does not exist while an agnostic is not sure. Unfortunately, many who leave Mormonism become skeptics and abandon their faith in God. Too often, those who reject God do not feel compelled to produce evidence supporting their view, even though their belief cannot be proven. While many will resist, skeptics ought to be willing to provide reasonable explanations for why they believe the way they do—just as they expect Christians to do. When the evidence is considered, belief in God is more sensible than not believing at all. If nothing else, the nonbeliever should be willing to do further research to see where the evidence leads.

Mike walked into the Utah Lighthouse Bookstore in Salt Lake City, Utah, where I occasionally volunteer and asked for material critiquing the LDS position. After a few minutes of looking around, he returned to the front of the store and sat down in a chair across from me. He proceeded to tell me how he had recently left Mormonism after learning details about how the Book of Mormon was translated. According to an essay published on the church's website, Joseph Smith peered at a magical "seer stone" at the bottom of his hat to construct a word-for-word translation.[1] Mike also said he was taken aback when church leaders claimed that the Book of Abraham in the Pearl of Great Price was "translated" in a spiritual, not literal, manner.[2]

"If you don't mind me asking, what do you currently believe about God?" I asked.

"Oh," he replied somewhat hesitantly, "I'm an atheist now."

"Do you know for sure that God doesn't exist?"

"No, I don't know that for sure. I just don't believe in Him."

"Would you believe if the evidence were in favor of God's existence?"

"It depends. Maybe if I could shake God's hand, that would be a good start."[3]

He chuckled at his last comment. Whether he meant it to be humorous, many who claim to be atheists depict a scenario where God is required to answer to them rather than the other way around.

"Mike, everyone has faith to accompany their belief. The theist is a person who maintains that God exists. The atheist believes there is no God. Agnostics say they cannot know for sure that God exists. I think you are a better fit in the agnostic category because it sounds like you're unsure about God's existence."

"You know, you might be right. I think of myself as open-minded. Listen, I've only *not* believed in God for the past few months and I'm in the process of figuring this all out!"

In just a few minutes, Mike had moved from a position of *atheism* to *agnosticism*, which is one step closer to a belief in the existence of God called *theism*. Gauging his body language and tone of voice, Mike seemed hesitant to discuss the topic any further. I try to not force a dialogue with someone who is not ready or interested, as doing this could possibly stifle future conversations. Perhaps our friendly exchange would entice him to return to the UTLM bookstore. Or maybe another Christian would come into his life in the not-so-distant future. After he made his purchase, we said goodbye and he walked out the door.

THE EXISTENCE OF GOD

A chapter on the existence of God may seem out of place in a book explaining Christian doctrines to Latter-day Saints. However, this topic is important because some who leave Mormonism struggle to maintain their belief in God. I have even met people who have decided to remain in the LDS Church as closet atheists while living in fear of being discovered. Admitting to losing their faith in Mormonism could cost them relationships with friends and family members as well as careers and community standing.

Many former Mormons consider themselves atheists or agnostics.[4] Still, I believe many people who have an LDS background remain open to believing in God and would be well-served by talking through the issues with a knowledgeable but patient Christian.

When I talk with skeptical former Mormons, I like to ask, "And how has your decision to leave the LDS Church affected your belief in God and Jesus?" I am no longer surprised when I am told that they quickly abandoned belief in a higher power. I then ask, "Did you once believe in God and Jesus?" The typical answer is, "Of course." My response? "Just because you discovered that the LDS Church is not true, do you think this has to mean that God and Jesus don't exist or care for you?"

My hope is not to overwhelm former Mormons with evidence that they are not willing to hear. One way to counter a possible closed door is using an underutilized tool in the Christian's arsenal, the personal testimony. There are times when someone is open to discuss the issues of God's existence. If so, more than just our personal stories are needed, as powerful as our testimony might be.

While some will criticize Christians for their "gullibility," there is available evidence that can be helpful to those who are objective. Josh and Sean McDowell write that "many Christians use the term 'faith' to mean 'blind faith' rather than biblical faith. But Christianity itself does not demand blind faith." Josh adds, "Christians are often accused of taking a 'blind leap into the dark.' For me, however, I found the evidence for Christianity powerful and convincing. So when I became a Christian, I hadn't leapt blindly into the dark, but stepped into the light."[5]

If this is the case, then it is important to establish a baseline to level the playing field. It must be acknowledged that everyone displays some type of faith, even if no particular deity is acknowledged. This is because empirical (physical) evidence (or lack of it) cannot, on its own, prove or disprove God. Wise people desire to head in the direction where the evidence leads, which is known in philosophical circles as "inference to the best explanation."

The rules for engagement need to be set at the beginning. Unfortunately, some skeptics want Christians to answer their objections while maintaining that they are not responsible to produce evidence for why they reject God's existence. "How can I prove that God is not real?" someone once asked me. "If I take a picture of God *not* in a room, will you stop believing in Him?"

Still, it is a silly argument to suggest that some type of faith is not part of the skeptic's belief system. Norman Geisler and Frank Turek described how the late agnostic scientist Carl Sagan

> made the ultimate statement of *faith in atheistic materialism* when he claimed that "the Cosmos is all that is or ever was or ever will be." How did he *know* that for sure? He didn't. How could he? He was a limited human being with limited knowledge. Sagan was operating in the realm of probability just like Christians are when they say God exists. The question is, who has more evidence for their conclusion? Which conclusion is more reasonable?[6]

Alex McFarland, the director of the Center for Christian Worldview and Apologetics at North Greenville University in South Carolina, writes:

> It is important to realize something about being an atheist that even most atheists fail to acknowledge and that is that atheism requires omniscience (complete knowledge of everything). If you don't believe that, then consider this: An atheist is making a positive assertion that there is no God. The only way that anyone could make such an

assertion would be to presume that he knew everything about everything. Otherwise, there would always be that possibility that God in fact existed, but that He was just outside of knowledge or our ability to know.[7]

Turek describes the responsibility for those who hold to the atheistic position:

> To claim that atheism is not a worldview is like saying anarchy is not really a political position...atheists can say they just "reject God," but they are still confronted with the inescapable problem of how to explain ultimate reality. Just as anarchists affirm the positive belief that anarchy is the best way to organize society, atheists affirm the positive belief that atheistic materialism is the best way to explain ultimate reality...A true atheist is someone who believes there is no God. And atheists have the burden of proof to show how materialism is true and reality can be explained without God.[8]

Let's illustrate the point by discussing the existence of Santa Claus. What makes millions of people (mainly young children) believe in the reality of a jolly old fat man who lives at the North Pole? Faithful believers in Santa could talk about this older bearded man wearing a red suit while sitting in his gingerbread house at the local mall. He can be empirically seen, heard ("ho ho ho"), and even touched. He gets credit for placing billions of presents carefully under a variety of trees on Christmas Eve. Who else could have consumed the glass of milk and cookies left on the corner table? Come on, this certainly must prove the existence of Santa!

Nonbelievers in Santa might counter by saying how many imposters dress up in red suits donning fake beards while sitting on their kingly thrones in malls around the city. Video evidence of parents who were seen placing those presents under the trees might be produced in the case against an authentic Santa. In addition, there is no evidence that any reindeer can fly through the skies.

Imagine the rejoinders of Santa believers. For one, they might insist that the videos showing parents placing presents under the tree only proves what happens at homes where naughty children lived. If the video had been filmed at locations where the nice children lived, the skeptic would be proven false. Besides, how can it be proven that magical reindeer *cannot* fly?

While most rational adults will agree that the case for the existence of a flying-around-the-world Santa Claus is weak, both believer and nonbeliever alike are responsible to produce reasons for their differing perspectives. It *is* possible, then, to present evidence that goes against the existence of a mythical being. In a similar way, the skeptic needs to present evidence to show how God is a fictional concept. Blind faith is not a requirement to either believe or disbelieve in the existence of God.

EVIDENCE FOR GOD'S EXISTENCE

Theists may point to a variety of reasons to support God's existence. In fact, three different books recommended at the end of this chapter provide 20, 31, and even 50 different reasons. It must be understood from the beginning, however, that even a hundred reasons will not sufficiently prove God's existence.

Many skeptics aim their ire at what they believe is a fictional celestial being. Whether they want to point out perceived atrocities in the world, tragic events that took place in their personal lives, or unreasonable prohibitions in the Bible that contradict their preferred way of living, they can be stubborn in their disbelief. As Paul Copan writes, "In defending their faith, Christians must not ignore the personal and moral factors that prevent people from embracing God and that prompt people to obscure important evidences for his existence. Some people simply don't want God in their lives."[9]

Let's suppose that the skeptic is willing to entertain the idea that God exists. If that is the case, here are my three favorite reasons.

1. The Creation of the Universe Points to an Eternal God

Using the finite universe as evidence for a higher power is called a "cosmological argument." This says that there is someone/something beyond the universe who/that created everything. Antony Flew was a twentieth-century atheist philosopher who debated against God's existence for most of his professional life. A few years before he died in 2010, Flew changed his mind and became a theist. Saying he was highly influenced by N.T. Wright, he said that the cosmological argument played a large role in his turnabout. "The only satisfactory explanation for the origin of such 'end-directed, self-replicating' life as we see on earth is an infinitely intelligent Mind," he said.[10]

Although he passed away just three years after his book was published, he said he was open to God's existence: "Some claim to have made contact with this Mind. I have not—yet. But who knows what could happen next? Someday I might hear a Voice that says, 'Can you hear me now?'"[11] If Flew never believed, it's not because God's presence wasn't made known. Indeed, the idea that there is something rather than nothing shows that there must be a higher intelligence beyond this universe. This is an example of what is known as *general (or natural) revelation*. Psalm 19:1 says,

> The heavens declare the glory of God,
>   and the sky above proclaims his handiwork.

Romans 1:18-20 says humans are accountable for believing in God:

> For the wrath of God is revealed from heaven against all ungodliness and unrighteousness of men, who by their unrighteousness suppress the truth. For what can be known about God is plain to them, because God has shown it to them. For his invisible attributes, namely, his eternal power and divine nature, have been clearly perceived, ever since the creation of the world, in the things that have been made. So they are without excuse.

To provide evidence using the cosmological argument, consider the following logical sequence:

1. The universe has a beginning.

2. Anything that has a beginning must have been caused by something else.

3. Therefore, the universe was caused by something else (a Creator).

Here is another way to put it:

1. Everything that began to exist has a cause.

2. The universe began to exist.

3. Therefore, the universe has a cause.

Someone may ask, "Then how was God created?" The key in the first sequence is the second premise, "Anything that has a beginning…" The following sequence fills in the gap:

1. Everything that began to exist has a cause.

2. God did not *begin to exist* since He is self-existent.

3. Therefore, God did not need a cause.

Psalm 90:2 declares, "From everlasting to everlasting you are God." Psalm 93:2 adds that "you are from everlasting." God existed from an eternal past and will continue to exist into an eternal future. Of course, this concept becomes incomprehensible when humans try to fathom this in their finite minds. When I was younger, I used to close my eyes and think of the past as having been "forever and ever and ever…" There would come a point when my brain would suddenly short circuit because this concept did not compute.

Skeptics may feel that the Big Bang theory of evolution and random process is what caused the universe. This takes much more faith than merely believing in God. For one, the person who does not hold to God's existence is limited to just two possibilities:

1. There was nothing before there was something.

2. Matter is eternal.

Neither makes logical sense. For one, something cannot come from nothing since "nothing" (no thing) does not exist. Every seventh grader who has taken a science class knows that "out of nothing, nothing comes." In addition, matter has *not* existed for eternity. Norman Geisler writes,

> Time cannot go back into the past forever, for it is impossible to pass through an actual infinite number of moments. A theoretically infinite number of dimensionless points exists between my thumb and first finger, but I cannot get an infinite number of sheets of paper between them no matter how thin they are. Each moment that passes uses up real time that we can never again experience. Moving your finger across an infinite number of books in a library would never get to the last book. You can never finish an infinite series of real things.[12]

Scientist Stephen Meyer adds, "If the necessary and sufficient conditions for the production of the universe always existed back into the infinite past, then the universe itself should have come into existence an infinitely long time ago (when those conditions 'first' occurred) and we should have evidence of that. But, again, we do not. Instead, we have evidence of a finite, not an infinite universe."[13]

Hence, there had to have been a beginning at some point in the distant past because the universe continues to expand. This means there is a spaceless, timeless, nonmaterial force that philosophers call the First Cause. Christians believe God is the First Cause who has eternally existed and created all finite things.

2. The Design of the Universe Displays the Magnificence of God

I have had many "aha moments" exploring nature where it made perfect sense that God existed. The intricacies of the desert night sky seem to scream for a designer. The argument goes like this:

1. All designs imply a designer.

2. There is great design in the universe.

3. Therefore, there must be a designer of the universe.

A life-permitting universe is infinitesimally rare, as space exploration has given no indication that any life is possible on any other planet. Sir Roger Penrose, who described himself as an atheist, once calculated that there were more possible configurations—in fact, $10^{10^{123}}$—that would generally result in multiple black-hole universes that would never be capable of beginning or sustaining life. Calling this a "hyperexponential number," Meyer describes this as

> 10 raised to the 10th power (or 10 billion) raised again to the 123rd power. To put that number in perspective, it might help to note that physicists have estimated that the whole universe contains "only" 10^{80} elementary particles (a huge number—1 followed by 80 zeroes). But that number nevertheless represents a miniscule fraction of $10^{10^{123}}$. In fact, if we tried to write out this number with a 1 followed by all the zeroes that would be needed to represent it accurately without the use of exponents, then there would be more zeroes in the resulting number than there are elementary particles in the entire universe. Penrose's calculation thus suggests an incredibly improbable arrangement of mass-energy—a degree of initial fine-tuning that really is not reflected by the word "exquisite." I'm not aware of a word in English that does justice to the kind of precision we are discussing.[14]

Suppose the universe had the random building parts to begin with life-sustaining possibility on one of the planets (which we call earth). And for the sake of argument, let's suppose that the universe beat the odds. Still, there are a number of scientific variables that must remain constant for this earth to permit life, including:[15]

- Oxygen comprises 21 percent of the earth's atmosphere. If it were 25 percent, fires would erupt; if only 15 percent, humans would suffocate.

- If the gravitational force were altered by 1 part in 10^{40}, the sun would cease to exist and the moon would crash into the earth.

- If the universe were to expand at a rate one millionth more slowly than it does, the temperature would get as hot as 10,000 degrees C—this would be true global warming!

- The average distance between stars in the galaxy of 100 billion stars is 30 trillion miles. If that distance were altered slightly, orbits would become erratic, and there would be extreme temperature variations. (Traveling at space shuttle speed, 17,000 mph or 5 miles a second, it would take 201,450 years to travel 30 trillion miles.)

- If Jupiter were not in its current orbit, space junk would bombard the earth. Jupiter's gravitational field acts as a cosmic vacuum cleaner, attracting asteroids and comets that would otherwise strike this planet.

Many other examples could be used. What is the possibility that the universe not only had the parts for a beginning but that it continues to run through random chance, not by intelligent design?

Biochemist Michael Behe uses the term "irreducible complexity" to show how Charles Darwin's theory of gradual evolution was impossible, not just improbable. Behe explains how a bacterial flagellum requires parts similar to an outboard motor, as it needs the equivalent of a propellor (flagellum), universal joints, rings, and stators. This simple single-cell organism's transportation system must be put together in an exact manner or the flagellum will be unable to rotate for propulsion. One wrong move in its development and the bacterium will have no ability to move, just as a boat's motor put together the wrong way will mean the fisherman will spend his afternoon at the dock. Thus, the organism needs the exact parts and the proper assembling for those parts to function.

Behe uses the example of an ordinary mousetrap to demonstrate irreducible complexity. Its components are simple: a wooden platform, a metal hammer, a spring, a catch, and a metal bar. He writes, "Suppose while reading one evening, you hear the patter of little feet in the pantry, and you go to the utility drawer to get a mousetrap. Unfortunately, due to faulty manufacture, the trap is missing one of the parts listed above. Which part could be missing and still allow you to catch a mouse?"[16]

Although the instrument seems quite simple, design (and a designer) of this instrument is required. Just like the flagellum, each element of the mousetrap is necessary. Then it is necessary for the trap to be properly assembled. This will not happen by accident. Suppose the trap's parts were placed in a bag and then randomly shaken. How long would it take for this trap to be assembled in exactly the right way? The correct answer is *never*. This is inference to the best explanation.

If a simple bacterium and mousetrap require intelligent design, how much more this earth and universe? Nobody would bet a dollar on the odds for this universe to randomly pop into existence, even if billions of years are allotted for it to happen. The complex universe points to a Designer that is not accounted for in random evolutionary processes.

3. Morality Points to the Justice of God

The moral argument states:

1. There is an objective moral law.

2. Moral laws imply a moral lawgiver.

3. Therefore, there is a moral lawgiver.

Christians agree that both natural and moral evil exist in this sin-tainted universe. Hurricanes, typhoons, and tornados are the result of the natural sin-fallen world. Meanwhile, sinful human beings are free to commit moral wrongdoings. Adam and Eve were perfect beings, but they were given the freedom to disobey God (Genesis 2:16-17). This resulted in the *fall* and introduced *sin* into the world. According to Romans 5:18, this "one trespass led to condemnation for all men." Fortunately, as verse 19 says, Jesus came so that "by the one man's obedience the many will be made righteous."

It needs to be understood that evil cannot exist on its own. Rather, evil is the privation of good. Privation is something that ought to be but isn't. For instance, a new car is made of metal that can be corrupted with rust while a new shirt is damaged when a moth eats a hole in it. Rust and the moth hole do not exist with the original editions. In the same way, evil cannot exist on its own without the original (good).

C.S. Lewis wrestled with the issue of morality before he became a Christian. In his classic book *Mere Christianity*, he wrote, "My agreement against God was that the universe seemed so cruel and unjust. But how had I got this idea of *just* and *unjust*? A man does not call a line crooked unless he has some idea of a straight line. What was I comparing this universe with when I called it unjust?"[17]

Morality is not just a matter of opinion. As Geisler put it,

> Moral laws don't *describe what is, they prescribe what ought to be.* They can't be known by observing what people do. They are what all persons should do, whether or not they actually do...Such statements as "Hitler was wrong" have no force if this is merely an opinion or Hitler's moral judgments are right or wrong depending on the cultural norms. If he was objectively wrong, then there must be a moral law beyond all of us by which we are all bound. But if there is such a universal, objective moral law, then there must be a universal Moral Law Giver (God).[18]

A case can be made that everyone should know that certain things are wrong, including killing or raping innocent people. For the atheistic materialist worldview, morals are difficult to explain because they are not empirically driven. Frank Turek writes, "Morality isn't made of molecules. What does justice weigh? What is the chemical composition of courage? How much hydrogen is in the honesty molecule? Did Hitler just have 'bad' molecules? These are absurd questions because moral standards aren't made of molecules."[19] He adds that "an objective moral value is right even if everyone thinks it's wrong. Since objective morality is grounded in the object known as God's nature, it is unchangeable and authoritative. It is unaffected by our opinions about it."[20]

Morals cannot be manufactured based on a person's feelings or the laws of a society. Instead, something is right or wrong based on God's moral law. In the 1930s, Adolf Hitler instituted legislation in Germany to imprison and murder people in concentration camps based on nothing more than they had the "wrong" heritage, sexual choice, or religion. In the 1950s, laws in the South required Black people to sit in the back of city buses. In 1973, abortion was legalized in the United States based on an overwhelming 7-2 decision in a US Supreme Court case (*Roe v. Wade*). In these three cases, *legality* does not equal *morality*.

There are some things that are immoral because they pervert morality. Genocide, racism, and killing innocent children have been wrong for all people in all periods of history and in all places, regardless of the rationale used in support of these immoral actions. It makes sense, then, that the creator of morals is higher than humans. It is possible to become hardened and suppress the God-given conscience, as Romans 2:14-15 states, "For when Gentiles, who do not have the law, by nature do what the law requires, they are a law to themselves, even though they do not have the law. They show that *the work of the law is written on their hearts.*"

Using the example of killing innocent people for no reason, Geisler and Turek explain,

> We can't not know, for example, that it is wrong to kill innocent human beings for no reason. Some people may deny it and commit murder anyway, but deep in their hearts

they know murder is wrong. Even serial killers *know* murder is wrong—they just may not *feel* remorse. And like all absolute moral laws, murder is wrong for everyone, everywhere: in America, India, Zimbabwe, and in every other country, now and forever. That's what the Moral Law tells every human being.[21]

If morals require a source higher than humans, then God must exist.

WHEN (NOT IF) BAD THINGS HAPPEN

A common objection used against an all-loving, all-powerful God is how bad things happen to "good" people. When Covid-19 swept through the world beginning in 2020, innocent humans suffered and many died. Every day people get hurt or killed in automobile accidents, deteriorate from incurable cancer, and endure family struggles and break-ups. Good friends of mine have had their bodies racked in pain with a variety of ailments. Meanwhile, faithful Christians all over the world are persecuted and even killed for their beliefs.[22]

How do non-Christians deal with calamity and misfortune? Those who hold to the Eastern idea of pantheism claim that evil is illusory. For all other ways of thinking, however, evil is real. Atheists and even agnostics are incapable of comforting someone going through a difficult situation except, perhaps, "My thoughts are with you, but that's just the way the cookie crumbles. Better luck next time." Of course, no atheist would say this out loud, but if there is no purpose when a calamity strikes, what comfort can there be?

Why do bad things happen? The answer is simply this: To bring God glory. While some television preachers proclaim that God desires health and prosperity for faithful believers who donate money to them, this teaching is deception. Verses are snatched out of their context to make it appear God desires Christians to have lives filled with pleasure and happiness.

Instead, the Bible is replete with stories of faithful people who had to endure difficult times. For one, consider the story of Job in the Old

Testament. This godly man lost his family and health along with everything he owned, causing his discouraged wife to tell him to "curse God and die."

Although Joseph's brothers sold him into slavery and Potiphar's wife framed him as a rapist, he played a vital role in preserving God's people. Speaking to his family in Genesis 50:20, Joseph said, "As for you, you meant evil against me, but God meant it for good, to bring it about that many people should be kept alive, as they are today."

And consider the apostle Paul who described in 2 Corinthians 11:16-33 the many bad things that happened in his life, including unjustified beatings, literal stonings, and even a shipwreck. Despite praying three times to have his "thorn in the flesh" removed, Jesus answered Paul in 2 Corinthians 12:9 by promising, "My grace is sufficient for you, for my power is made perfect in weakness."

The Christian is commanded in James 1:2 to "count it all joy, my brothers, when you meet trials of various kinds." I struggle with the "all joy" part, for who likes to go through hard times? But there is a method to the madness. Verses 3 and 4 explain that the "testing of your faith produces steadfastness," which leads to maturity.

In a book written not long after his wife, Joy, passed away from cancer, C.S. Lewis declared that suffering, by itself, serves no good. He said, "What is good in any painful experience is for the sufferer, his submission to the will of God, and, for the spectators, the compassion aroused and the acts of mercy to which it leads."[23] Indeed, hard times can facilitate personal growth and cause one to draw closer to God. It can also help us to see who our real friends are. It may not be easy, but there is a process.

Years ago, a good friend of mine and his wife lost their daughter at her birth. As a nonbeliever at that time, he felt hopeless. A few years later, he became a Christian. His change in faith did not make the pain go away completely, but the support of the body of Christ has been instrumental in his life. Christians are commanded to listen with empathy as the Bible instructs us to "be quick to hear, slow to speak" (James 1:19).

Despite the reality that difficult events in life do take place, it is possible to realize the promise of Romans 8:28, which says, "And we know that for those who love God all things work together for good, for those who are called according to his purpose." Verse 31 adds, "If God is for us, who can be against us?" While it is insensitive to merely cite verses like these to those going through hard times, Christians can be assured that nothing happens unless it first passes through the veil of God's love.[24] As John Piper aptly explains,

> When you read the word "hope" in the Bible (like in 1 Peter 1:13—"set your hope fully on the grace that will be brought to you at the revelation of Jesus Christ"), hope is not wishful thinking. It's not "I don't know if it's going to happen, but I *hope* it happens." That's absolutely *not* what is meant by Christian hope. Christian hope is when God has promised that something is going to happen and you put your trust in that promise. Christian hope is a confidence that something will come to pass because God has promised it will come to pass.[25]

PASCAL'S WAGER AND MORMONISM

The seventeenth-century Christian philosopher and mathematician Blaise Pascal suggested a skeptic should consider the consequences if God does exist. Many believe that the body returns to dust and consciousness ceases. But what if that is wrong and God does exist? What are the consequences if He is rejected? If eternal separation from God throughout eternity is the result, then Pascal said it makes sense to believe.

Don't get Pascal wrong, as he wasn't suggesting that someone should become a Christian merely to gain an insurance policy for eternity. Rather, he admonished people who demanded God to come down from heaven so they could shake His hand. The evidence presented in this short chapter seems to indicate that Something higher than humans exists. If that is true, why not accept Christianity's truth claims?

If a person is willing to consider the possibility of God's existence, I suggest taking James 1:5 literally and praying for wisdom. For someone who desperately wants to know God, such a prayer could be as simple as the following: "God, if You exist, guide me in my search and give me the wisdom to decipher between truth and error."

Applied wisdom is necessary for a person to determine the truth and gain knowledge. J.P. Moreland explains how "wisdom is the fruit of a life of study and a developed mind. Wisdom is the application of knowledge gained from studying both God's written Word and His revealed truth in creation. If we are going to be wise, spiritual people prepared to meet the crises of our age, we must be a studying, learning community that values the life of the mind."[26]

The Latter-day Saint needs to be told that repeating the mantras "I *know* the church is true" and "Joseph Smith *is* a true prophet of God" in a self-convincing way will no longer suffice, as the evidence goes against these claims. Skeptics, too, need to keep an open mind in a pursuit of the truth as God will make Himself available (Deuteronomy 4:29; Jeremiah 29:13). As Acts 17:27 explains, God "is actually not far from each one of us."

DISCUSSION QUESTIONS

1. While there are dozens of arguments used by theists to support a belief in God, just three are detailed in this chapter. Which is the most compelling for you? If you prefer another reason not discussed, what is it? Describe how you would use your tactic with a skeptic.

2. Perhaps the simplest argument is showing how a designer can be inferred for the universe to come together as it did and be capable of life. For you, what is an amazing fact demonstrating the design of the universe?

3. What does the moral argument have to say about the existence of God?

4. What do you think is the main reason why people reject a

belief in God? What can a Christian do to help the average skeptic consider the possibility that there is a God who loves people?

5. If you have a testimony about Jesus, how could this be used to support the existence of God? Are you able to provide a short version of your story in just a few minutes to show how God has personally worked in your life?

RECOMMENDED RESOURCES

Entry-Level Resources

Douglas A. Jacoby, *Compelling Evidence for God and the Bible: Finding Truth in an Age of Doubt* (Eugene, OR: Harvest House Publishers, 2010).

Rick Stedman, *31 Surprising Reasons to Believe in God* (Eugene, OR: Harvest House Publishers, 2017).

Lee Strobel, *The Case for a Creator: A Journalist Investigates Scientific Evidence That Points Toward God* (Grand Rapids, MI: Zondervan, 2004).

J. Warner Wallace, *God's Crime Scene: A Cold-Case Detective Examines the Evidence for a Divinely Created Universe* (Colorado Springs, CO: David C. Cook, 2015).

Middle-Level Resources

Clay Jones, *Why Does God Allow Evil?* (Eugene, OR: Harvest House Publishers, 2017).

Ron Rhodes, *Answering the Objections of Atheists, Agnostics, and Skeptics* (Eugene, OR: Harvest House Publishers, 2006).

William A. Dembski and Michael R. Licona, eds., *Evidence for God: 50 Arguments for Faith from the Bible, History, Philosophy, and Science* (Grand Rapids, MI: Baker Books, 2010).

Norman Geisler and Ron Brooks, *When Skeptics Ask: A Handbook on Christian Evidences* (Grand Rapids, MI: Baker Books, 2013).

Norman L. Geisler and Frank Turek, *I Don't Have Enough Faith to Be an Atheist* (Wheaton, IL: Crossway, 2004).

Kenneth D. Boa and Robert M. Bowman Jr, *20 Compelling Evidences That God Exists: Discover Why Believing in God Makes So Much Sense* (Colorado Springs, CO: David C. Cook, 2005).

Advanced Resources

William A. Dembski and Sean McDowell, *Understanding Intelligent Design: Everything You Need to Know in Plain Language* (Eugene, OR: Harvest House Publishers, 2008).

Stephen C. Meyer, *Return of the God Hypothesis: Three Scientific Discoveries that Reveal the Mind Behind the Universe* (New York: HarperCollins, 2021).

CHAPTER 4

THE NATURE OF GOD

Attributes Worthy of Worship

"This is the message we have heard from him and proclaim to you, that God is light, and in him is no darkness at all."

1 JOHN 1:5

CHAPTER PREVIEW

According to the Bible, some of God's attributes are unique to Him while other characteristics can belong to humans as well. When biblical passages ascribe animal or human characteristics to God, it must be understood that the writers sometimes used symbolic language to make it easier to comprehend the Almighty. As far as His origination, the Bible denies that God was once a sinful human or has a body of flesh and bones. Instead, He existed as God before the creation and will remain as the only God throughout eternity. Among His many attributes, God is both just and holy. As far as God's justice is concerned, humans are unable to enter the presence of the all-holy God unless, somehow, their sins are forgiven. Those who die with unforgiven sin will be separated from God throughout eternity in hell.

Elders Michaels and Sorensen were sitting in our living room holding glasses of ice water my wife, Terri, had given them. The two 19-year-old Mormon missionaries had randomly knocked on our front door. When we invited them inside, they happily obliged on this warm August day.

who had been on his mission for a year and a half,
n in Idaho. He was eager to explain why he was
his life to volunteer for his church.

hear about Heavenly Father and His Son Jesus,"
ng a message that all people need to hear."

appreciate the desire you have to share your faith with others," I
responded. "Could I ask about your belief in 'Heavenly Father'? I have
heard it said, 'As man is, God once was. As God is, man may become.'
Do you believe this is a true statement?"

Elder Michaels nodded. What I had cited is known as the Lorenzo
Snow Couplet, originally created by the man who later became Mormonism's fifth president. It declares that God the Father was once a
human in a previous world and that it is possible for people to become
gods of their own worlds in the next life. The concept of the couplet was
approved by Joseph Smith and remains a part of LDS theology today.[1]

"Could you help me understand what God was like before He came
to this world?" I asked.

The young man looked blankly at me before glancing at his part-
ner, who was also not sure how to answer this question. There has been
much speculation about what God was like, as church leaders have
shied away from this issue. I have spoken to many Mormons who spec-
ulate that God may have been a sinner in an earlier realm. As one lay-
person put it,

> I think that making mistakes is an essential part of a learn-
> ing process. So, if you follow logic and reason, then I def-
> initely think that [God sinning] is a distinct possibility. It
> doesn't make him any less powerful or anything…It makes
> me more comfortable…in the sense that we have hope to
> overcome if he could overcome and become as great as he
> is. Then certainly we have hope to overcome all our trials
> and sinful natures as well.[2]

To suggest that God could have been a sinful human being who
worshiped a "grandfather" God in a previous mortal existence is a

blasphemous concept to Christians.[3] After all, the Bible teaches that God is eternally self-existent and remains unblemished throughout eternity (Psalm 25:8; 92:15). God cannot be tempted by sin (James 1:13).

"*Eternal life* is knowing 'the only true God, and Jesus Christ,'" I continued, citing Jesus's words in John 17:3. "The Old Testament prophets said worshiping the wrong God is idolatry. This idea is supported by Jesus and the apostles."

Since having a proper understanding of God was important in biblical times, it should be important to us today as well. In a book published two years before he passed away, A.W. Tozer wrote,

> What comes into our minds when we think about God is the most important thing about us...Worship is pure or base as the worshiper entertains high or low thoughts of God...A right conception of God is basic not only to systematic theology but to practical Christian living as well. It is to worship what the foundation is to the temple; where it is inadequate or out of plumb the whole structure must sooner or later collapse. I believe there is scarcely an error in doctrine or a failure in applying Christian ethics that cannot be traced finally to imperfect and ignoble thoughts about God. It is my opinion that the Christian conception of God current in these middle years of the twentieth century is so decadent as to be utterly beneath the dignity of the Most High God and actually to constitute for professed believers something amounting to a moral calamity.[4]

Mind you, Tozer wrote this in the early 1960s when he said that the Christian conception of God was a "moral calamity." Imagine what he might say today if he were alive! Defining an attribute of God as "whatever God has in any way revealed as being true of Himself," Tozer added, "The study of the attributes of God, far from being dull and heavy, may for the enlightened Christian be a sweet and absorbing spiritual exercise."[5] Colossians 1:10 talks about "increasing in the knowledge of God." With that said, let's consider the nature of the biblical God.

THE ATTRIBUTES OF GOD

Millard Erickson writes, "Theology is important because correct doctrinal beliefs are essential to the relationship between the believer and God. One of these beliefs deals with the existence and character of God."[6]

There are two types of God's attributes. The first is communicable attributes that can be shared with created beings, especially humans.

COMMUNICABLE ATTRIBUTES	SUPPORTING VERSES
Love	Psalm 86:15; 136:26; Isaiah 54:10; Romans 5:8; 8:39; 1 John 4:7-8
Holy	Exodus 15:11; 1 Samuel 2:2; Isaiah 6:3; Revelation 4:8
Righteous	Psalm 11:7; Romans 3:21; Ephesians 4:22-24
Merciful	Luke 6:36; Romans 9:15-16; Ephesians 2:4-5; Titus 3:5
Faithful	Psalm 36:5; 1 Corinthians 1:9; 10:13; 2 Timothy 2:13; Hebrews 10:23; 1 John 1:9
Wise	Isaiah 28:29; Romans 11:33; James 3:17
Good	1 Chronicles 16:34; Ezra 3:11; Psalm 25:8, 34:8; 145:9; Mark 10:18
Gracious	Exodus 34:6; Psalm 86:15; 103:8; 116:5; 145:8; Joel 2:13
Just	Psalm 75:1-7; 99:4; 146:7-9; Isaiah 30:18; 61:8

Incommunicable attributes cannot be shared with created beings. Though they can be emulated by Christians, they are not shared.

INCOMMUNICABLE ATTRIBUTES	SUPPORTING VERSES
Perfect	Deuteronomy 32:4; Psalm 18:30; Matthew 5:48
Omniscient (all knowing)	Isaiah 46:9-10; Jeremiah 1:5; Acts 1:24; 1 John 3:20

The following list contrasts the Christian and LDS views of God's being:

CHRISTIANITY	BIBLE REFERENCES	MORMONISM	REFERENCES
God is one in essence and is the only God who exists. This is called monotheism (mono = one, theism = belief in God).	Deuteronomy 6:4; Mark 12:29; 1 Corinthians 8:6; 1 Timothy 2:5	Three separate gods (Father/Son/Spirit) who "are one in will, purpose, and love."[7] Tritheism, not monotheism.	Mormons assume that the biblical verses referring to "one God" mean "one in purpose," not "one in essence."
God is spirit.	John 1:18; 4:24; Romans 8:2,14; 2 Corinthians 3:17	God has a body of flesh and bones as tangible as man's.	D&C 130:22
God is omnipresent and is not limited by spatial restraints.	Psalm 139:7-12; Proverbs 15:3; Isaiah 66:1; Jeremiah 23:23-24; Amos 9:2-3	God's body is localized in space and is not bodily omnipresent.	D&C 88:6,7,13
God originated everything out of nothing (Latin: creatio ex nihilo).	Genesis 1:1; Isaiah 37:16; 45:7,18; 66:2; Job 33:4; John 1:3; Colossians 1:15-17	God organized the universe out of preexisting material (Latin: creatio ex materia).	Book of Abraham 4:1; Joseph Smith's King Follett discourse in 1844
God is the only true God in the universe; all other "gods" are false.	Deuteronomy 4:35; 1 Kings 8:60; 1 Chronicles 17:20; Isaiah 43:10-11; 44:6,8; 45:21-22	Multiple true gods existed before Elohim (God the Father) and there will be gods who will follow Him.	Book of Abraham chapters 4 and 5

CHRISTIANITY	BIBLE REFERENCES	MORMONISM	REFERENCES
God is omnipotent (all-powerful) to do all things logically possible, although there are some things He cannot do, including sin or lie (Numbers 23:19; Titus 1:2; Hebrews 6:18).	Genesis 1:1; 18:14; Job 42:2; Isaiah 40:28; Jeremiah 32:17; Matthew 19:26; Luke 1:37; 1 Corinthians 6:14	While He has power over everything, God is limited because He is subject to eternal "natural law." God organized the elements already in existence but He was unable to create out of nothing.	Book of Abraham 3:22 and 4:1 refer to multiple true gods who collaborated on the creation of the universe. Elements, intelligence, and law are coeternal with God (D&C 88:34-40; 93:29,33,35).

One aspect in biblical Christianity not emphasized in Mormonism is how awesome God is. Consider the LDS doctrine of how God (Heavenly Father) once lived in bodily form in a previous realm; it was apparently his righteousness that qualified him to become the God of this world. While few details are provided by LDS leaders, Heavenly Father must have worshiped his god just as Mormons worship him now. In essence, the LDS version of God is just one step ahead of his creation. Qualified Latter-day Saints believe they will be given the right one day to possess godhood in an exalted future state just as God is now; they even think they will be worshiped by their spirit children. This convoluted scheme decimates the majesty of the true God's authentic greatness and truly debases His very being.

In 2017, the Mormon Tabernacle Choir (its name at the time) performed the Christian hymn "How Great Thou Art," which is number 86 in the church's 1985 hymnal. The hymn is based on a poem composed in the nineteenth century by Carl Boberg.[8] A variety of public polls show this to be one of the top-ten hymns of all time. Look it up and see just how powerfully the song declares God's majesty. How is it possible for a Latter-day Saint to sing this hymn with meaning if God is nothing more than a glorified man who may have sinned in a previous existence? To the contrary, biblical Christians are free to sing about God's greatness with gusto! Nobody will *ever* be His equal.

THE FEAR OF THE LORD

Because God is greater than anything that can be imagined, He ought to be feared. Having an appropriate fear of the Lord does not mean looking around every corner and wondering if God is about to pounce. Rather, a healthy fear is having utmost respect. Jerry Bridges explains:

> It is impossible to be devoted to God if one's heart is not filled with the fear of God. It is this profound sense of veneration and honor, reverence and awe that draws forth from our hearts the worship and adoration that characterizes true devotion to God. The reverent, godly Christian sees God first in his transcendent glory, majesty, and holiness before he sees him in his love, mercy, and grace...In our day we must begin to recover a sense of awe and profound reverence for God.[9]

The poetry of the Old Testament describes how important this is. For instance, Proverbs 1:7 says, "The fear of the LORD is the beginning of knowledge," while Proverbs 9:10 and Psalm 111:10 say, "The fear of the LORD is the beginning of wisdom." Concluding his poetic book, Solomon wrote in Ecclesiastes 12:13, "Fear God and keep his commandments, for this is the whole duty of man." Believers with such an attitude are led to life (Proverbs 19:23) and experience "no lack" of anything (Psalm 34:9). Truly God "fulfills the desire of those who fear him" (Psalm 145:19).

The fear of the Lord involves much more than a simple respect for God. According to Proverbs 8:13, it is characterized by hating evil since God abhors pride, arrogance, and perverted speech. Proverbs 3:7 admonishes the righteous to not be "wise in your own eyes" but rather "fear the LORD, and turn away from evil." Proverbs 16:5 adds

n arrogant heart is an "abomination to the Lord"
1. Too many Christians treat God like a cuddly
nonreality ("the big man upstairs") rather than
is.

idea about God eliminates the possibility that
was once a human being or that humans are "gods in embryo," as
Mormonism teaches.[10] Holding false notions about God means there
is not an appropriate fear of the Lord.

THE CONVERSATION CONTINUES

I decided to probe into the thinking of the missionaries in our
home.

"How would you interpret Psalm 90:2 when Moses wrote 'from
everlasting to everlasting you are God'?"

They were not sure how to respond, so I continued.

"The idea that God has never changed is taught in Malachi 3:6.
James 1:17 says that with God 'there is no variation or shadow due to
change.' Even Moroni 8:18 teaches this concept."

The final reference comes from the Book of Mormon, and I asked
if they wouldn't mind looking up the verse. So Elder Sorensen pulled
out his tablet and read Moroni 8:18 out loud: "For I know that God is
not a partial God, neither a changeable being; but he is unchangeable
from all eternity to all eternity."

"What do you think this means?"

"In this realm, God has always been God," Elder Sorensen said.

"By saying 'this realm,' are you suggesting that 'from all eternity to
all eternity' began when God became the God of this world?"

If LDS scripture shows that there never was a time when God was
not God, yet Mormon leaders teach that there was a time when He
was a man, not God (i.e., the Snow couplet's statement that "As man is,
God once was"), then there is a problem. It appeared that the missionary understood the dilemma and decided to change the topic.

"Doesn't the Bible teach that we are made in God's image?" he asked.

Normally, I like to finish the topic of conversation, but since I could tell the missionaries were uncomfortable continuing on the current course, I went with the switch.

"Yes, Genesis 1:26-27 does teach that humans are created in God's image," I said. "Does this mean that God is nothing more than an earlier version of us? Absolutely not, as Christians reject the teaching in D&C 130:22 that God has a 'body of flesh and bones as tangible as man's.'"

Wayne Grudem summarizes Christianity's description of God's image (Latin: *imago dei*) when he wrote, "Both the Hebrew word for 'image' (*tselem*) and the Hebrew word for 'likeness' (*demut*) refer to something that is *similar* but not identical to the thing it represents or is an 'image' of...it simply would have meant to the original readers, 'Let us make man to be *like* us and to *represent* us.'" [11]

Instead of having a fleshly body like ours, God the Father is "spirit" as Jesus taught in John 4:24.[12] Explaining what it means to say God is spirit, Grudem writes:

> *God exists as a being that is not made of any matter, has no parts or dimensions, is unable to be perceived by our bodily senses, and is more excellent than any other kind of existence.* We may ask why God's being is this way. Why is God spirit? All that we can say is that this is the greatest, most excellent way to be! This is a form of existence far superior to anything we know. It is amazing to meditate on this fact.[13]

Elder Michaels chimed in and asked, "What about the time when Moses saw God?"

He was referring to Exodus 33:11, where it says that "the LORD used to speak to Moses face to face, as a man speaks to his friend." To explain the passage, I first needed to show that the Bible should not always be taken literally in its description, which may surprise some readers. But consider how Jesus stated in Matthew 5:29 and 18:9 that if a person's eye caused sin, the eye ought to be plucked out. He also said that an offending hand should be cut off. Did He mean that people should maim themselves? Not at all. Rather, He emphasized the importance of ceasing to sin.

In a similar way, the Bible uses metaphorical language to portray the indescribable God of the universe. While it says that God the Father is "invisible" and that "no one has ever seen God" (John 1:18; 5:37; 1 Timothy 1:17; 6:16), human qualities are used to describe Him. This is called *anthropomorphism* (lit.: in the form of a man). Even though God has no visible form, He is portrayed as having:

- a face (Leviticus 20:6; Numbers 6:25)

- arms (Psalm 89:10; Deuteronomy 4:34; 5:15) with hands (Numbers 11:23) and fingers (Exodus 8:19)

- eyes (Psalm 34:15; Deuteronomy 11:12)

- ears (2 Kings 19:16; Nehemiah 1:6)

- feet (Isaiah 66:1)

- a nose (Deuteronomy 33:10) to smell (Genesis 8:21)

- a mouth (Deuteronomy 8:3) with lips (Job 11:5) and a tongue (Isaiah 30:27)

In addition, God has been personified with traits of an eagle (Deuteronomy 32:11), a shadow (Psalm 91:1), and a temple (Revelation 21:22) as well as having wings as a bird (Psalm 36:7; 91:4). It is said that God has changed His mind (Exodus 32:14), relented (2 Samuel 24:16; Jonah 3:10), remembered (Genesis 9:16), felt sorrow (Genesis 6:6), regretted (1 Samuel 15:35), and rested (Genesis 2:2). Jesus said in John 6:46 that no one "has seen the Father except he who is from God [Jesus]." In Exodus 33, then, God spoke to Moses "face to face" in a figurative, not literal, manner.

Returning to the conversation with the missionaries, I decided to go back to the beginning.

"Mormonism's idea that Heavenly Father once lived as a human in a previous realm concerns me," I said. "After all, whom did God worship? Shouldn't we want to discover that God and worship him too?"

I was taking the first part of Snow's couplet literally. If God had a

God who was true, and if that God had his own God who was true, and so on, going back into an infinite past, then there must be a multiplicity of true Gods. Yet Isaiah chapters 43 through 45 deny the possibility that there can be multiple *true* gods. Consider these verses:

> "Before me no god was formed,
> nor shall there be any after me.
> I, I am the LORD,
> and besides me there is no savior."
> (Isaiah 43:10b-11)

> "I am the first and I am the last;
> besides me there is no god…
> Fear not, nor be afraid;
> have I not told you from of old and declared it?
> And you are my witnesses!
> Is there a God besides me?
> There is no Rock; I know not any."
> (Isaiah 44:6b,8)

> "I am the LORD, and there is no other,
> besides me there is no God."
> (Isaiah 45:5a)

> "I am the LORD, and there is no other."
> (Isaiah 45:18d)

> "Who told this long ago?
> Who declared it of old?
> Was it not I, the LORD?
> And there is no other god besides me,
> a righteous God and a Savior;
> there is none besides me."
> (Isaiah 45:21)

A Mormon may argue that no other god "in this world" ought to be worshiped and that this would not preclude the possibility of gods in *other* worlds. This is reading one's preconceived ideas into the text, as Isaiah made it clear that God does not even *know* about other gods. Could God really have forgotten His own father or those gods who were in existence before Him as well as those who would later follow Him?

"There can only be one true God in existence," I explained. "Known as the Shema, Deuteronomy 6:4 is repeated each Sabbath in every Jewish synagogue around the world. It says, 'Hear, O Israel: The LORD our God, the LORD is one.' The Hebrew word for one is *echad,* which designates the one essence of God and not merely His purpose."

This concept is so important that, when asked about the "most important of all" God's commandments, Jesus recited this statement in Mark 12:29 before summarizing the Ten Commandments. While Latter-day Saints may argue that God is "one in purpose," God's oneness means much more. The polytheistic idea that multiple gods exist—before and after God—is rejected in the Bible. There are serious consequences for not believing in the God who must be worshiped "in spirit and truth" (John 4:24).

A HOLY GOD WHO IS JUST

At this point, Elder Sorensen chose to bring up an issue that would turn Christianity's version of God into an ogre.

"Do you believe your God would send people to hell?"

According to Mormonism, practically everyone will go to one of three *kingdoms of glory*: the *telestial, terrestrial,* or *celestial kingdoms.* This is because each person made the right choice as a spirit in what is known as *preexistence,* thereby siding with Jesus, not Lucifer, during what is called the War in Heaven. We can know this because it is impossible in Mormonism for disobedient spirits in the preexistence to receive a body; these spirits were cast out of what is called the "first estate" and became the demons who follow *Satan.* While *outer darkness* is similar to the biblical version of eternal *hell,* Mormon leaders have taught that this state is basically reserved for these fallen spirits.

I decided to answer his question by asking one of my own.

"Do you think hell—eternal separation from God—is unfair?"

"Of course. How could a loving God eternally punish humans for their temporary sins?"

"Are you suggesting that sin should be forgiven, even if a person doesn't want the sin to be forgiven?"

"If God is love, sending people to hell seems over the top!"

"The Bible teaches that all humans have a major problem. Romans 3:10 says that 'none is righteous, no, not one,' while verse 23 says that everyone was born into sin and 'falls short of the glory of God.'"

Many would like to minimize sin except when that sin goes against them, such as when someone calls them wanting their credit card numbers to fix their computer's Windows problem or having someone cut in line at the grocery store. It has been said that humans are not sinners because they sin, but rather they sin because they are sinners. Contrary to the second Article of Faith originally written by Joseph Smith, it is through Adam's disobedience that all people were tainted with original sin, giving them a corrupt nature that leads to death (Romans 5:12). Besides original sin, everyone commits individual sins by disobeying God's commandments as revealed in the Bible. Each one becomes an expert in "falling short of the glory of God."

I continued.

"God is both holy and just. He cannot allow for sin to come into His presence. In the end, people with unforgiven sins will be eternally separated from God. In essence, people cannot blame God if they reject the gift of forgiveness that He offers."

There are many references to support the idea that God is both holy as well as just. For instance, 1 Samuel 2:2 says,

> "There is none holy like the LORD:
> For there is none besides you;
> there is no rock like our God."

God is praised in Isaiah 6:3:

> And one called to another and said:
> "Holy, holy, holy is the LORD of hosts;
> the whole earth is full of his glory!"

But God is also described in Psalm 33:5 as One who "loves righteousness and justice." Isaiah 61:8 states, "For I the LORD love justice." Proverbs 28:5 teaches that "evil men do not understand justice, but those who seek the LORD understand it completely."

Violators of a nation's laws are generally punished. The thief, murderer, tax evader, or child abuser cannot say, "It is unfair to punish me just because I got caught!" When a crime is committed, justice is due. This was a concept I needed to make clear.

"It is not difficult to show how Adolf Hitler should be banned from heaven," I said.[14] "Let's add Mao, Stalin, Lenin, and Pol Pot to that list of those who deserve to be eternally damned. And let's not stop there. My name needs to be included along with yours."

It was clear I had their attention.

"We may not have murdered, but we have hated. We may not have had sexual relations with anyone outside the bounds of marriage, but we have lusted. If we keep the whole law but fail at just one point, we are guilty of everything.[15] Therefore, you and I deserve hell. It would only be just. As the apostle Paul explained in 1 Corinthians 6, 'the unrighteous will not inherit the kingdom of God.'"

I needed to make it clear that, as fallible humans, we are good at minimizing our own sins and compare ourselves to the Hitlers of the world. The idea of a just God is taught by other religions, including hellfire in Islam for those who reject Allah and his prophet Muhammad. Buddhists and Hindus insist that an awful future state awaits those who have bad karma. And Jehovah's Witnesses warn that the souls of nonmembers will be annihilated. Justice plays a role in Mormonism as well.

"Your scriptures and leaders teach that those who are not considered righteous will be denied godhood in the final state," I said. "Besides, if the preexistence is true as your leaders teach, then one-third of humanity's spirit brothers and sisters were denied bodily tabernacles because of their disobedience, resulting in their being cast out of heaven. These spirits are not qualified for any kingdom of glory and will be destined for outer darkness. You may think that they deserve eternal punishment because of their disobedience, but let me ask you, how many sins have *you* committed?"

Many Latter-day Saints seem to have no problem barring these pre-existent spirits from any of the kingdoms. Yet each person must look in the mirror and understand that punishment for their own sins is deserved, no matter how "good" they may rationalize themselves to be.

There is no doubt that the doctrine of hell is a difficult subject and one that many Christians are hesitant to address, despite the clear teaching given in the Bible. R.C. Sproul says this is not beneficial to the universal Christian church:

> We have an image of God as full of benevolence. We see Him as a celestial bellhop we can call when we need room service or as a cosmic Santa Claus who is ready to shower us with gifts. He is pleased to do whatever we ask Him to do. Meanwhile, He gently pleads with us to change our ways and to come to His Son, Jesus. We do not usually hear about a God who commands obedience, who asserts His authority over the universe and insists we bow down to His anointed Messiah.[16]

Contrary to the perception many have, Greg Koukl brings up an interesting point when he writes, "What was Jesus rescuing us from? Here is the answer. Jesus did not come to rescue us from our ignorance or our poverty or our oppressors or even from ourselves. Jesus came to rescue us from the Father."[17] In Matthew 10:28, Jesus said people should "not fear those who kill the body but cannot kill the soul. Rather fear him who can destroy both soul and body in hell." (Also see Matthew 13:49-50; 24:45-51; Mark 9:43-48.)

When we talk about fairness, what really would be *un*fair is for anyone to get heaven since, as we have discussed, every person deserves hell. It is not a pleasant thought. Hebrews 10:31 says, "It is a fearful thing to fall into the hands of the living God." The apostle John wrote in Revelation 20:15, "And if anyone's name was not found written in the book of life, he was thrown into the lake of fire." God's righteous judgment is described in 2 Thessalonians 1:9: "They will suffer the punishment of eternal destruction, away from the presence of the Lord and from the glory of his might."[18]

Paul also wrote in Romans 2:5-8:

> But because of your hard and impenitent heart you are storing up wrath for yourself on the day of wrath when God's righteous judgment will be revealed. He will render to each one according to his works: to those who by patience in well-doing seek for glory and honor and immortality, he will give eternal life; but for those who are self-seeking and do not obey the truth, but obey unrighteousness, there will be wrath and fury.

Koukl adds this:

> Now, you may debate whether there is real fire in hell or not, but that is hardly the point. I, for one, am not convinced about literal flames or darkness or gnashing teeth. Sometimes eternal things are described in earthly terms because no other options are available. What I am completely convinced of, though, is that the suffering is real and severe, whatever images may be pressed into play to describe it…The conscious torment and suffering of those banished by God will never end. Ever.[19]

The conversation was not over. In chapter 7, we will return to this thoughtful discussion with these two missionaries as the topic turned to the doctrine of the Trinity.

DISCUSSION QUESTIONS

1. Why do Christians consider it blasphemous to suggest that God was once a human who might have sinned in a previous lifetime?

2. What is the difference between a communicable and incommunicable attribute of God? If you could choose only three of God's attributes, which would you say are your favorites and why?

3. What does it mean to say believers should have an appropriate fear of the Lord?

4. What is anthropomorphism? When the Bible uses human characteristics to describe God, how should this be properly interpreted?

5. If someone said that Christianity's God is not fair because not everyone goes to heaven, how could a Christian respond in a biblical manner? Is hell fair?

RECOMMENDED RESOURCES

Entry-Level Resource

Stonecroft Ministries, *What Is God Like?* (Eugene, OR: Harvest House Publishers, 2012).

Middle-Level Resource

A.W. Tozer, *The Knowledge of the Holy: The Attributes of God and Their Meaning in the Christian Life* (San Francisco, CA: Harper and Row, 1961).

CHAPTER 5

JESUS

Savior of His People

*"[Mary] will bear a son, and you shall call his name
Jesus, for he will save his people from their sins."*

MATTHEW 1:21

CHAPTER PREVIEW

Most religions have reserved a special place for Jesus, whether He is considered a prophet, guru, or Messiah. Since divergent views contradict Jesus as He really is, careful consideration must be made. First, the evidence is overwhelmingly in favor that Jesus lived on this earth. While never abandoning His deity, Jesus humbled Himself and became a man who ended up experiencing grief, physical pain, and even a torturous death on a cross. This atoning act provided forgiveness of sins for those who believe in Him. Every person must decide what to do with Jesus: Is He Lord, Liar, Legend, or Lunatic? Even for those who do not call Him "Lord" in this world, there will be a day of reckoning.

Jesus is my Savior, the Son of God, and I have a relationship with Him."

A Mormon missionary named Sister Helgren answered my question about what Jesus meant to her. Her words sound like any number of testimonials given at Christian church services held around the world. Just a few minutes earlier, she and her companion had walked up to me outside Temple Square in Salt Lake City as I was passing out tracts to passersby on the public sidewalk. Getting the missionaries to stop and dialogue outside this iconic Mormon site is not easy to do, but Sister Helgren had a spark in her eyes.

"Some people say we don't believe in Jesus, but that's not true." She pointed to her name badge and added in a hushed and serious tone, "Notice, it says 'The Church of *Jesus Christ* of Latter-day Saints.'"

One thing that Christians have in common with Mormons is the belief that a historical Jesus existed. Biblical scholar Edwin Yamauchi provides a concise list of reasons in support of a historical Christ:

> Even if we did not have the New Testament or Christian writings, we would be able to conclude from such non-Christian writings as [Jewish historian] Josephus, the *Talmud* [a collection of Jewish sayings from the fifth century AD], [first-century Roman historian] Tacitus, and [first-century Roman politician] Pliny the Younger that: (1) Jesus was a Jewish teacher; (2) many people believed that he performed healings and exorcisms; (3) he was rejected by the Jewish leaders; (4) he was crucified under Pontius Pilate in the reign of Tiberius; (5) despite this shameful death, his followers, who believed that he was still alive, spread beyond Palestine so that there were multitudes of them in Rome by AD 64; (6) all kinds of people from the cities and countryside—men and women, slave and free—worshiped him as God by the beginning of the second century.[1]

I decided to better understand Sister Helgren's position by asking a question.

"I can appreciate your enthusiasm. If you don't mind, could you tell me what it means when you call Jesus your Savior?"

"Through the atonement and the grace provided by Jesus, I believe He makes salvation possible for all God's children, including you and me."

"I'm sure you are aware that the majority of religions include Jesus as an important part of their faith. Even most atheists think that Jesus was a real person. How do you know that your prophets and apostles are accurate in their portrayal of Jesus?"

"What do you mean?" she asked.

"Second Corinthians 11:4 says it's possible to believe in 'another Jesus' contrary to the historical version. If you have *another* Jesus, you have the *wrong* Jesus."

J.I. Packer put it this way: "A person who thought that England is ruled today by an ex-go-go dancer named Elizabeth who legislates at her discretion from a wood hut in Polynesia could justly be said to know nothing of the real queen, and similarly it takes more to constitute real, valid saving knowledge of Jesus than simply being able to mouth his name."[2]

Two LDS general authorities would have had no problem with this assessment. Mormon Seventy Bernard P. Brockbank told an April 1977 *general conference* audience, "It is true that many of the Christian churches worship a different Jesus Christ than is worshipped by the Mormons or The Church of Jesus Christ of Latter-day Saints." When asked if Mormons believe in the traditional Jesus, fifteenth LDS President Gordon B. Hinckley answered:

> No, I don't. The traditional Christ of whom they speak is not the Christ of whom I speak. For the Christ of whom I speak has been revealed in this the Dispensation of the Fulness of Times. He together with His Father, appeared to the boy Joseph Smith in the year 1820, and when Joseph left the grove that day, he knew more of the nature of God than all the learned ministers of the gospel of the ages.[3]

In another general conference address given in 2002, Hinckley explained, "As a church we have critics, many of them. They say we do not believe in the traditional Christ of Christianity. There is some substance to what they say."[4] By these leaders' own admission, the Jesus of Mormonism is not the same as the Jesus of Christianity.

I asked the missionaries on the sidewalk outside Temple Square if they would be open to having me present a quick overview on Christianity's perspective of Jesus. They agreed.

THE BIBLICAL JESUS

Let's consider four areas of the person of Jesus:

1. The Origination of Jesus: He Is Eternal God

2. The Incarnation of Jesus: He Became Flesh

3. The Personhood of Jesus: He Is Both God and Man

4. The Purpose of Jesus: He Sacrificed Himself to Save Sinners

For each point, several citations from leaders of the LDS Church are provided along with biblical quotations to show the contrast.

1. The Origination of Jesus: He Is Eternal God

MORMONISM	BIBLE
LDS Seventy Milton R. Hunter: "Jesus became a God and reached His great state of understanding through consistent effort and continuous obedience to all the Gospel truths and universal laws."[5]	John 1:1-3: "In the beginning was the Word, and the Word was with God, and the Word was God. He was in the beginning with God. All things were made through him, and without him was not any thing made that was made."
LDS Apostle Bruce R. McConkie: "Christ attained Godhood while yet in pre-existence, he too stood as a God to the other spirits, but this relationship was not the same one of personal parenthood that prevailed between the Father and his offspring."[6]	Philippians 2:5-6: "Have this mind among yourselves, which is yours in Christ Jesus, who, though he was in the form of God, did not count equality with God a thing to be grasped."

MORMONISM	BIBLE
LDS Apostle Robert D. Hales: "Jesus was born of heavenly parents in a premortal world—he was the firstborn of our Heavenly Father."[7]	Colossians 1:15-17: "He is the *image of the invisible God*, the firstborn of all creation. For by him all things were created, in heaven and on earth, visible and invisible, whether thrones or dominions or rulers or authorities—all things were created through him and for him. And *he is before all things*, and in him all things hold together."
LDS Church teaching manual: "The oldest child in our heavenly family was Jesus Christ. He is our oldest brother."[8]	Jude 25: "To the only God, our Savior, through Jesus Christ our Lord, be glory, majesty, dominion, and authority, *before all time* and now and forever. Amen."

Mormonism proclaims Jesus as being "born of heavenly parents in a premortal world," as Hales put it. Hebrews 13:8 states, "Jesus Christ is the same yesterday and today and forever," so He would have no need of "heavenly parents." The "ruler in Israel" in Micah 5:2 would be "from ancient days," which is another way of saying from the very beginning. In Isaiah 9:6-7, the Messiah is called "Everlasting Father." As Ron Rhodes points out, the ancient Jews considered the phrase "'Father of eternity' as indicating the eternality of the Messiah."[9]

That the Messiah would originate from the line of David is made clear in Isaiah 11:1-3, which was written seven centuries before Jesus was born:

> There shall come forth a shoot from the stump of Jesse,
>   and a branch from his roots shall bear fruit.
> And the Spirit of the LORD shall rest upon him,
>   the Spirit of wisdom and understanding,
>   the Spirit of counsel and might,
>   the Spirit of knowledge and the fear of the LORD.
> And his delight shall be in the fear of the LORD.

John the Baptist declared in John 1:30, "After me comes a man who ranks before me, because he was before me." If John was born six months before Jesus, then how could John say Jesus was before him? Despite what LDS leaders have taught, Jesus was not humanity's oldest brother. He never had to attain godhood because He has always been God and will continue to be God forever (Revelation 1:8,17-18; 21:6; 22:13). In addition, Jesus created all things (John 1:3; Colossians 1:15-17), so it would have been impossible for Him to create Himself (John 1:10; 1 Corinthians 8:6; Hebrews 1:2,10-12).

As Robert Bowman Jr. and J. Ed Komoszewski explain, "Perhaps the most fundamental specific attribute of God that separates him from everything that is not God is that he is *uncreated*. If this attribute is true of Christ, and he is a real, existent being, then he is God. On the other hand, if Christ were by nature a created being, then it would not make much sense to speak of him as God."[10]

Although Jewish readers do not agree, Christian commentators maintain that Jesus appeared throughout the Old Testament as "the angel of the LORD" in what is called a Christophany ("appearance of Christ").[11] Unlike other angels created by God, the angel of the Lord was distinct from the Father (Genesis 31:11,13; Exodus 3:2-6). This name was used in the place of God (Genesis 16:7,13; Exodus 3:2,4). His promises were the same as God's (Genesis 16:10; 22:15-17). Sacrifices were made to the angel of the Lord (Genesis 22:11-13; Judges 6:21)—something reserved for God—and He could forgive sins, something only God can do (Exodus 23:21; Zechariah 3:3-4).

For example, consider Judges 13 and its introduction of Manoah, a man who belonged to the tribe of Dan. Like Abraham and Sarah, Manoah and his wife had no children despite their best efforts. The angel of the Lord appeared to Manoah's wife and announced that she would have a child who would "begin to save Israel from the hand of the Philistines." When Manoah asked for the angel's name, he was told that "it is wonderful" (v. 18). As Manoah sacrificed a young goat and grain offering to Yahweh, verse 20 says that "the angel of the LORD went up in the flame of the altar. Now Manoah and his wife were watching, and they fell on their faces to the ground" in worship. Manoah exclaimed in verse 22, "We have seen God." He was telling the truth, as this was the preincarnate Jesus and the second Person of the Trinity.

Just who was Manoah and his wife? They became the parents of the famous judge Samson.

2. The Incarnation of Jesus: He Became Flesh

MORMONISM	BIBLE
LDS Apostle James Talmage: "In that august council of the angels and the Gods, the Being who later was born in flesh as Mary's Son, Jesus, took prominent part, and there was He ordained of the Father to be Savior of all mankind. As to time, the term being used in the sense of all duration past, this is our earliest record of the Firstborn among the sons of God; to us who read, it marks the beginning of the written history of Jesus the Christ."[12]	Isaiah 7:14: "Behold, the virgin shall conceive and bear a son, and shall call his name Immanuel."
LDS Apostle McConkie: "Christ was Begotten by an immortal Father in the same way that mortal men are begotten by mortal fathers."[13]	Matthew 1:18: "Now the birth of Jesus Christ took place in this way. When his mother Mary had been betrothed to Joseph, before they came together she was found to be with child from the Holy Spirit."
Thirteenth LDS President Ezra Taft Benson: "The Church of Jesus Christ of Latter-day Saints proclaims that Jesus Christ is the Son of God in the most literal sense. The body in which He performed His mission in the flesh was sired by that same Holy Being we worship as God, our Eternal Father. Jesus was not the son of Joseph, nor was He begotten by the Holy Ghost."[14]	Luke 1:35: "And the angel answered [Mary], 'The Holy Spirit will come upon you, and the power of the Most High will overshadow you; therefore the child to be born will be called holy—the Son of God.'"

Regarding the birth of Jesus, the term *incarnation* means that Jesus (as God) was born to Mary through the power of the Holy Spirit. John 1:14 says that Jesus "*became flesh* and dwelt among us." In other words, He had characteristics that every human possesses with the exception of a sinful nature (2 Corinthians 5:21). Ron Rhodes writes, "Obviously, if Christ was not God *before* his human birth in Judea, then he was not God *afterward*."[15] He makes an astute observation that, even though it is called the *virgin birth*, "it was the conception of Jesus in Mary's womb that was supernatural, not his birth."[16]

Millard Erickson says that "the influence of the Holy Spirit was so powerful and sanctifying in its effect that there was no conveyance of depravity or of guilt from Mary to Jesus."[17] He adds that

> Jesus' conception in the womb of Mary was not the result of sexual relationship. Mary was a virgin at the time of the conception, and continued so up to the point of birth, for the Scripture indicates that Joseph did not have sexual intercourse with her until after the birth of Jesus (Matt. 1:25). Mary became pregnant through a supernatural influence of the Holy Spirit upon her, but that does not mean that Jesus was the result of copulation between God and Mary. It also does not mean that there was not a normal birth.[18]

John MacArthur and Richard Mayhue point out that "without a virgin conception of Jesus, there can be no guarantee of his sinlessness. The descendants of Adam are sinners because Adam sinned; the descendants of Adam die."[19] They explain that "the elimination of the virgin birth would jeopardize the entirety of Jesus's life and ministry and the attendant doctrines. These include his being both truly God and truly man, his sinless life, his miraculous deeds, his truth-filled teaching, his voluntary sacrifice as a substitute for sinners, his bodily resurrection, his bodily ascension, and his future return."[20]

Mormon leaders have taught that God the Father had a "literal" (their word) physical relationship with Mary to conceive Jesus, which is not a biblical concept. Luke 1:35 says the Holy Spirit "overshadowed" Mary in a powerful yet nonsexual and nonphysical way.[21]

3. The Personhood of Jesus: He Is Both God and Man

MORMONISM	BIBLE
LDS President Ezra Taft Benson: "To qualify as the *Redeemer* of all our Father's children, Jesus had to be perfectly obedient to all the laws of God. Because He subjected Himself to the will of the Father, He grew 'from grace to grace, until he received a fulness' of the Father's power. Thus He had 'all power, both in heaven and on earth' (D&C 93:13,17)."[22]	Philippians 2:5-11: "Have this mind among yourselves, which is yours in Christ Jesus, who, though he was in the form of God, did not count equality with God a thing to be grasped, but emptied himself, by taking the form of a servant, being born in the likeness of men. And being found in human form, he humbled himself by becoming obedient to the point of death, even death on a cross. Therefore God has highly exalted him and bestowed on him the name that is above every name, so that at the name of Jesus every knee should bow, in heaven and on earth and under the earth, and every tongue confess that Jesus Christ is Lord, to the glory of God the Father."
LDS Apostle Richard G. Scott: "Jesus Christ possessed merits that no other child of Heavenly Father could possibly have. He was a God, Jehovah, before His birth in Bethlehem. His beloved Father not only gave Him His spirit body, but Jesus was His Only Begotten Son in the flesh. Our Master lived a perfect, sinless life and therefore was free from the demands of justice. He was and is perfect in every attribute, including love, compassion, patience, obedience, forgiveness, and humility."[23]	John 20:26-29: "Eight days later, his disciples were inside again, and Thomas was with them. Although the doors were locked, Jesus came and stood among them and said, 'Peace be with you.' Then he said to Thomas, 'Put your finger here, and see my hands; and put out your hand, and place it in my side. Do not disbelieve, but believe.' Thomas answered him, 'My Lord and my God!' Jesus said to him, 'Have you believed because you have seen me? Blessed are those who have not seen and yet have believed.'"

Jesus was fully God and fully man. The following chart offers a summary of His characteristics:

JESUS AS GOD	JESUS AS MAN
One with the Father (John 10:30)	Had human ancestry (Genesis 3:15; Matthew 1; Luke 3; Romans 1:3)
He knew (omniscient) (Matthew 9:4; Mark 2:8; John 4:16-18)	Did not "know" (Mark 13:32)
Recognized as God (Romans 9:5; 1 John 5:20; Hebrews 1:8) with the same name (John 8:58 with Exodus 3:14)	Was tempted (Matthew 4:1; Hebrews 4:15)
Fulness of deity lives in Jesus (Colossians 2:9; Titus 2:13)	Cried (Luke 19:41; John 11:35)
Creator of all things (John 1:3; Colossians 1:15-17)	Had a human birth (Mark 6:3; Luke 2:7; Galatians 4:4)
Raised Himself from the dead (John 2:19)	Increased in wisdom and stature (Luke 2:52)
The image of God (2 Corinthians 4:4; Colossians 1:15; Hebrews 1:2-3)	Became tired (Matthew 8:24; John 4:6)
Salvation found in His name (John 14:6; 17:3; Acts 4:12)	Became hungry (Matthew 4:2)
Forgiver of sins (Mark 2:5-7)	Became thirsty (John 19:28)
Worshiped (Matthew 2:11; 14:33; 28:9,17; Luke 24:52; John 9:38; Hebrews 1:6)	Died (John 19:33-34)—one cannot be much more human than that!

From the time He was born until He suffered an excruciating death, Jesus lived the perfect human life. He was tempted but did not sin (Hebrews 4:15; 7:26; 1 Peter 2:22; 1 John 3:5). The apostle John wrote that those who deny Jesus's humanity possess the "spirit of the antichrist" (1 John 4:2-3; 2 John 7). Grudem explains, "Was Jesus fully human? He was so fully human that even those who lived and worked with him for thirty years, even those brothers who grew up in his own household, did not realize that he was anything more than another very good human being. They apparently had no idea that he was God come in the flesh."[24]

While most religions teach that Jesus was a real person, only Christians worship Him as God. In the Gospels, the Jewish leaders were ruffled when Jesus called Himself God, including in John 10:33: "It is not for a good work that we are going to stone you but for blasphemy, because you, being a man, make yourself God" (also see John 8:58-59). Jesus maintained His deity when, in John 20:26-29 (cited above), He commended the apostle Thomas for recognizing Him as "my Lord and my God." Some argue that perhaps Thomas was startled, but why would Jesus compliment him in verse 29 for taking the Lord's name in vain? To be sure, there are at least eight other instances where Jesus is worshiped:

- A healed leper (Matthew 8:2)

- A ruler (Matthew 9:18)

- Jesus's disciples (Matthew 14:33)

- A Canaanite woman (Matthew 15:25)

- Mother of James and John (Matthew 20:20)

- A Gerasene demoniac (Mark 5:6)

- A healed blind man (John 9:38)

- Again, the disciples (Matthew 28:9,17)[25]

The first of the Ten Commandments says nobody should be worshiped except God. The Greek word for worship (*proskuneo*) is "used to designate the custom of prostrating oneself before a person and kissing his feet, the hem of his garment, the ground, etc."[26] In the New World Translation (Jehovah's Witnesses), the word *obeisance* is used for the passages listed above, which means "honor" rather than "worship." In the right context, obeisance is a possible translation, but this is *not* the case in the examples given above. Instead, these passages are offered "to Jesus, who is revered and worshiped as Messianic King and Divine Helper."[27]

In Isaiah 45:22-23, the prophet declared how God will be worshiped:

> "Turn to me and be saved,
>   all the ends of the earth!
>   For I am God and there is no other.
> By myself I have sworn;
>   from my mouth has gone out in righteousness
>   a word that shall not return:
> 'To me every knee shall bow,
>   every tongue shall swear allegiance.'"

Then, in Philippians 2:9-11 (cited earlier), Paul cites this same passage and says everyone will bow to Jesus. He really must be God to receive everyone's worship!

Bowman and Komoszewski raise an excellent point when they write,

> If we are to experience a healthy relationship with God, we need to be intimately acquainted with the biblical teaching about the divine identity of Jesus. This involves more than merely knowing about, and agreeing with, the doctrine of the deity of Christ, though that is certainly essential. It must become more to us than a line we say in a creed. We need to know what it means to say that Jesus is God and why it matters. We need to see Jesus as God. We need to think about Jesus and relate to him in the full light of the truth of his identity. We need to appreciate the significance of his divine identity for our relationships with God and others.[28]

It may sound confusing to some that Jesus is fully God and fully man. How does that work? Norman Geisler and Peter Bocchino explain:

> The New Testament clearly points to Jesus as being one person who has two natures, human and divine. A quick

glance at this truth may bring about the misunderstanding that the often-touted phrase—"God became man"—means that the infinite became the finite. This is not a technically accurate description of the Incarnation...the Incarnation should be understood to mean that, "Jesus, God the Son, existing as the second person of the triune God, *united* His divine nature to a human nature and through it came into the world." Meaning, He didn't stop being God when He added humanity to Himself.[29]

Christian leaders at the Council of Chalcedon (near Istanbul, Turkey) gathered in AD 451 to discuss the personal unity of Jesus and ended up calling this doctrine the *hypostatic union*. Because Jesus was human, He fully experienced humanity as we all do. However, He is not two persons but rather one person with two natures: divine and human. In essence, Jesus is fully God and fully human, or 100 percent of each. This is a divine mystery and yet, like the doctrine of the Trinity that will be discussed in chapter 7, it is an essential truth.

Wayne Grudem states, "The assertion that 'Jesus was fully God and fully man in one person,' though not a contradiction, is a paradox that we cannot fully understand in this age and perhaps not for all eternity, but this does not give us the right to label it 'incoherent' or 'unintelligible.'...If we are to submit ourselves to God and to his words in Scripture, then we must believe it."[30] Grudem goes on to say,

> When we are talking about Jesus' human nature, we can say that he ascended to heaven and is no longer in the world (John 16:28; 17:11; Acts 1:9-11). But with respect to his divine nature, we can say that Jesus is everywhere present...So we can say that both things are true about the *person* of Christ—he has returned to heaven, *and* he is present with us. Similarly, we can say that Jesus was about thirty years old (Luke 3:23), if we are speaking with respect to his human nature, but we can say that he eternally existed (John 1:1-2; 8:58) if we are speaking of his divine nature.[31]

Another helpful term is *communicatio idiomatum*, Latin words for "communication of properties." Jesus's divine nature was not communicated, or transferred, to His human nature, and vice versa. MacArthur and Mayhue write that "whatever can be said of one of Christ's natures can be rightly said of Christ as a whole person. For example, Paul's comment in Acts 20:28 does not mean that the divine nature has blood, for God is spirit (cf. John 4:24). But because 'blood' is a property of Christ's human nature and 'God' is a property of his divine nature, Paul can say of Jesus that God purchased the church with his own blood."[32]

Christians worship Jesus as the ultimate God-man, a much higher view than our LDS friends who believe that Jesus is a secondary god when compared to God the Father.

4. The Purpose of Jesus: He Sacrificed Himself to Save Sinners

LDS Apostle Richard G. Scott: "His mercy pays our debt to justice when we repent and obey Him."[33]	1 Timothy 1:15: "The saying is trustworthy and deserving of full acceptance, that Christ Jesus came into the world to save sinners, of whom I am the foremost."
Seventeenth LDS President Russell M. Nelson: "Thanks to the Atonement, the gift of immortality is *unconditional*. The greater gift of eternal life, however, is *conditional*. In order to qualify, one must deny oneself of ungodliness and honor the ordinances and covenants of the temple."[34]	Hebrews 4:15-16: "For we do not have a high priest who is unable to sympathize with our weaknesses, but one who in every respect has been tempted as we are, yet without sin. Let us then with confidence draw near to the throne of grace, that we may receive mercy and find grace to help in time of need."

For a millennium, God preserved the line of David through some tumultuous times. The result is that Jesus came from this line according to the genealogies given in the Gospels of Matthew and Luke. John the Baptist recognized Jesus as the "Lamb of God, who takes away the sin of the world" (John 1:29), a reference to the sacrificial animal described in the Old Testament (Exodus 12:1-13; Isaiah 53:7). Jesus fulfilled the prophecies in Psalm 22 and Isaiah 53 by forgiving sins in what is called substitutionary atonement.

As the book of Hebrews explains, "For if the blood of goats and bulls, and the sprinkling of defiled persons with the ashes of a heifer, sanctify for the purification of the flesh, how much more will the blood of Christ, who through the eternal Spirit offered himself without blemish to God, purify our conscience from dead works to serve the living God" (9:13-14). Comparing Jesus with the Old Testament sacrificial animals, Hebrews 9:22-23 teaches that "without the shedding of blood there is no forgiveness of sins" and that a "better sacrifice" was needed, which verse 26 says Jesus "put away sin by the sacrifice of himself." Hebrews 10:4 explains how temporary animal sacrifices in the Old Testament needed to be continually repeated since they were incapable of cleansing sins. Verse 14 adds that only someone who lived a perfect life would suffice.

When Jesus died on the cross (1 Corinthians 15:1-3), it meant that "by the one man's [Jesus] obedience the many will be made righteous" (Romans 5:19). Believers are then "reconciled to God" (Romans 5:10) "through faith in Christ, the righteousness from God that depends on faith" (Philippians 3:9). The New Testament teaches that all people need to turn to Jesus to be saved (John 3:18,36; 10:7-15; Acts 16:31; Romans 10:9-13; 1 John 5:10-13). This allows believers to have "the right to become children of God" (John 1:12; Romans 8:14). And because He is God, Jesus can be addressed by Christians in prayer (Acts 7:59-60; 1 Timothy 2:5), which is something Mormons do not do (even though they may pray "in Jesus's name" at the end of their prayers).[35]

When it comes to the atonement, LDS leaders emphasize the events in the Garden of Gethsemane rather than the cross.[36] This makes no sense because the sacrificial victim described in the Bible needed to die; without death, there was no efficacious sacrifice. As cruel as the cross might seem to some, it was necessary, and those who do not comprehend it are missing this important concept.

LORD, LIAR, LUNATIC, OR LEGEND

Going back to the conversation with the missionaries outside Temple Square, I took a moment to summarize the four points I had just shared.

"Sisters, we both agree that Jesus is a special person. But I believe the version of Jesus accepted by Christians all over the world for close to two millennia is more accurate than the LDS version."

Their body language made it appear they were getting ready to leave.

"Before you go, I'm wondering how you view Jesus. Is He just your 'eldest brother,' as your leaders have taught? If that is true, Jesus is not worthy of our worship."

Some who may not be familiar with LDS theology might think I am exaggerating about Mormonism's teaching that Jesus is humanity's "eldest brother," but this idea finds plenty of support in Mormon sources. For instance, tenth President Joseph Fielding Smith referred to God the Father and explained how "Jesus Christ, his first Begotten Son in the spirit creation and his Only Begotten Son in the flesh, is our Eldest Brother."[37]

I continued.

"On the other hand, if biblical Christianity is correct, Jesus is the true capital-G God who became flesh and dwelt among people. C.S. Lewis laid out the 'great trilemma' by saying how everyone must make a choice: Is Jesus Lord, liar, or lunatic?"

While I was unable to quote Lewis verbatim, here is what he said in his classic work *Mere Christianity*:

> I am trying here to prevent anyone saying the really foolish thing that people often say about Him: "I'm ready to accept Jesus as a great moral teacher, but I don't accept his claim to be God." That is the one thing we must not say. A man who was merely a man and said the sort of things Jesus said would not be a great moral teacher. He would either be a lunatic—on a level with the man who says he is a poached egg—or else he would be the Devil of Hell. You must make your choice...But let us not come with any patronizing nonsense about His being a great human teacher. He has not left that open to us. He did not intend to...Now it seems to me obvious that He was neither a lunatic nor a fiend: and consequently, however strange or terrifying or unlikely it may seem, I have to accept the view

that He was and is God. God has landed on this enemy-occupied world in human form.[38]

A case could be made for a fourth possibility, which is that a legend grew over time, turning Jesus into God.

I continued: "Jesus said in Matthew 11:28-29, 'Come to me, all who labor and are heavy laden, and I will give you rest. Take my yoke upon you, and learn from me, for I am gentle and lowly in heart, and you will find rest for your souls.' For those who take Him up on His offer, Jesus provides complete freedom through the forgiveness of sins, and there is nothing you do for it. You just need to receive the gift that He extends."

The conversation with the missionaries was cordial and noncombative. They smiled, we said our goodbyes, and the two ladies walked away. The chances were good that they would talk about these issues together when they returned home, which is why I like to use as many biblical passages as possible. After all, Isaiah 55:11 states that God's Word does not return "empty."

DISCUSSION QUESTIONS

1. If the Jesus of Mormonism is different from the Jesus of the Bible, what is the implication? In other words, why is understanding the correct version so important?

2. According to the Bible, Jesus was fully God and man. Why would it be wrong to say Jesus was merely half man and half God?

3. What are some of the differences between Mormonism and Christianity concerning the origination and incarnation of Jesus?

4. Jesus is priest, prophet, and king. What is the significance of Him holding these offices?

5. How do you respond to the claim that Jesus is a good moral teacher but nothing more?

RECOMMENDED RESOURCES

Entry-Level Resource

Josh McDowell and Dave Sterrett, *Who Is Jesus...Really?* (Chicago, IL: Moody Publishers, 2011).

Middle-Level Resources

Robert M. Bowman Jr. and J. Ed Komoszewski, *Putting Jesus in His Place: The Case for the Deity of Christ* (Grand Rapids, MI: Kregel Publications, 2007).

Lee Strobel, *The Case for the Real Jesus: A Journalist Investigates Current Attacks on the Identity of Christ* (Grand Rapids, MI: Zondervan, 2007).

J. Warner Wallace, *Person of Interest: Why Jesus Still Matters in a World that Rejects the Bible* (Grand Rapids, MI: Zondervan, 2021).

Ron Rhodes, *Christ Before the Manger: The Life and Times of the Preincarnate Christ* (Grand Rapids, MI: Baker Book House, 1992).

Advanced Resource

Mark Strauss, *Four Portraits, One Jesus: An Introduction to Jesus and the Gospels* (Grand Rapids, MI: Zondervan, 2007).

CHAPTER 6

THE RESURRECTION

The Cornerstone of Christianity

"But the angel said to the women, 'Do not be afraid, for I know that you seek Jesus who was crucified. He is not here, for he has risen, as he said.'"

MATTHEW 28:5-6

CHAPTER PREVIEW

Instead of being a distant deity, God involves Himself in the affairs of humanity. Because God is all-powerful, it is possible for Him to break natural law and do anything He wills. Unlike a magician's sleight of hand, miracles are real and meant to glorify God. If miracles can happen, then it is possible for a dead man to raise Himself from the dead. Indeed, the evidence shows that the man Jesus died an excruciating death on the cross, as prophesied in the Old Testament, and then rose again from the dead. While a variety of theories have been created to account for what happened to the body of Jesus, none are plausible besides the miraculous resurrection account detailed in the Bible.

The Islamic cleric (called an imam) was addressing students from my Christian high school Bible classes who had accompanied me on an optional field trip to his San Diego, California, mosque. After giving an hour-long presentation, he wanted to know if any of the three dozen teenagers had questions. One student decided to ask him to describe his view of Jesus.

"You must understand that Isa [Jesus]—Peace Be Upon Him[1]—is very important to us," he replied. "Yet we do not hold that he should be considered the same as God. That is a wrong view. A person who says such a thing commits *shirk* [blasphemy]. He was not killed on the cross as you may have been taught, and he certainly didn't rise from the dead."

He continued, "The Christian beliefs on this topic are lies coming from corrupted scripture. Our scripture, the Qur'an, is Allah's [God's] perfect revelation for us today."

Another student raised her hand.

"What evidence do you have that Jesus was *not* killed on the cross?" she asked.

The imam recited Surah 4:157 in the Qur'an, first in Arabic before restating it in English. It reads, "That they said (in boast), 'We killed Christ Jesus the son of Mary, the Messenger of Allah'—but they killed him not, nor crucified him, but so it was made to appear to them, and those who differ therein are full of doubts with no (certain) knowledge, but only a conjecture to follow, for of a surety they killed him not."[2]

He continued. "Isa probably lived for several more years in Egypt before Allah called him to heaven. But he did *not* die on the cross."

The student remained undeterred.

"How do you account for the Bible saying that both the disciples and His mother saw Jesus hanging on the cross?" she asked.

"Nobody knows. Maybe Allah wanted to fool the ignorant and ungodly by making a traitor appear to look like Isa."

The imam was theorizing that the apostle Judas—best known for his betrayal of Jesus the night before—might have been the one who really was crucified.[3] According to this Islamic leader, Christians were blasphemously worshiping a traitor, not a Savior. He also made an off-topic reference to the crusaders from the Middle Ages who, he said, committed many atrocities against Muslims and whose emblem on their shields was the cross.

It is a shame that Muslims so readily reject Christianity because of a series of complicated events that took place a thousand years ago.[4] Regardless of fault, no Christian I know would say that Christianity should be advanced through violent means. Jesus said in John 18:36,

"My kingdom is not of this world. If my kingdom were of this world, my servants would have been fighting, that I might not be delivered over to the Jews. But my kingdom is not from the world."

If the death and *resurrection* of Jesus were historical events, then the evidence should be considered by every seeker after truth. This will be the focus in this chapter.

A LAYOUT OF THE FACTS

Concerning the death, burial, and resurrection of Jesus, the apostle Paul summarized the events in 1 Corinthians 15:3-8, which were probably composed in an early church creed "*within the first five years after Jesus' death*,"[5] before AD 40 when no New Testament book had yet been composed! The recorded facts include:

- "Christ died for our sins in accordance with the Scriptures"

- "he was buried"

- "he was raised on the third day in accordance with the Scriptures"

- "he appeared to Cephas [Peter], then to the twelve"

- "he appeared to more than five hundred brothers at one time, most of whom are still alive, though some have fallen asleep"

- "he appeared to James, then to all the apostles"

- "he appeared also to me"

If the resurrection didn't happen, the story of Christianity could not be sustained. Like a snag on a sweater, it would quickly unravel. In verse 14, Paul wrote that "if Christ has not been raised, then our preaching is in vain and your faith is in vain." He said in verses 15-18 that he would "be misrepresenting God, because we testified about God that he raised Christ, whom he did not raise if it is true that the dead are not raised. For if the dead are not raised, not even Christ has been raised. And if Christ has not been raised, your faith is futile and you are still in your sins. Then those also who have fallen asleep in Christ have perished." Verse 19 adds that if the resurrection of Jesus is fraudulent, Christians are "of all people most to be pitied."

In a sermon given on March 29, 1891, Charles Spurgeon proclaimed,

> If you ask where God's glory most is seen, I will not point to creation, nor to providence, but to the raising of Jesus from the dead. It is true that in the silence of the tomb there were no spectators, but God himself was there. After the deed was done, there were many who beheld his glory; and when at the close of his sojourn below he ascended beyond the clouds all heaven came forth to meet him, and to behold the conqueror of death and hell. In his resurrection the glory of God was laid bare.[6]

The consequences are immense if Jesus did not rise from the dead, as described by scholars Gary Habermas and Michael Licona:

> Anyone can claim anything. Jesus asserted that he was speaking truth from God. When someone makes such a lofty claim, critics rightly ask for the evidence. Jesus' critics asked him for a sign, and he said he would give them one— his resurrection. It is the test by which we could know that he was telling the truth. Such a historical test of truth is unique to Christianity. If Jesus *did not* rise from the dead, he was a false prophet and a charlatan whom no rational person should follow. Conversely, if he *did* rise from the dead, this event confirmed his radical claim.[7]

The historicity of the resurrection of Jesus, then, is crucial for Christianity to be taken seriously. When Latter-day Saints leave their church and turn to atheism or agnosticism, I find this topic to be powerful in confronting their disbelief. If the resurrection is true, then Christianity is validated. If it is not, then Christianity can be disregarded. It's that simple.

THE POSSIBILITY OF MIRACLES

Before we can proceed, it is important to determine if *miracles* are even possible. Wayne Grudem defines a miracle as "*a less common kind of God's activity in which he arouses people's awe and wonder and bears witness to himself.*"[8] Supernatural biblical events confirm the messages of prophets, apostles, and other representatives of God.

In the Old Testament, the ten plagues brought forth by God haunted the Egyptians and culminated in the death of all first-born animals and children (Exodus 11 and 12). The walls of Jericho fell after the Israelites marched around the city (Joshua 5:13–6:27). Elijah was victorious on Mount Carmel when God accepted his sacrifice while rejecting the offering given by the false prophets of Baal (1 Kings 18:16-46). Many similar events could be cited.

Miracles also played an important role in the ministry of Jesus. As Norman Geisler says, "Those in the New Testament particularly capture our attention, because they are well-attested and reveal Jesus Christ in his power over Satan, sickness, and the grave. The New Testament shows that the ongoing power of Christ was present in the young church."[9] The Jewish rulers acknowledged in John 3:1-2 that miracles confirmed Jesus's divine authority.

In Acts 2:22, Peter preached that Jesus was "a man attested to you by God with mighty works and wonders and signs that God did through him in your midst, as you yourselves know." And Hebrews 2:3-4 states, "It was declared at first by the Lord, and it was attested to us by those who heard, while God also bore witness by signs and wonders and various miracles and by gifts of the Holy Spirit distributed according to his will."

Not every miracle done by Jesus was recorded. John 20:30-31 says, "Now Jesus did many other signs in the presence of the disciples, which are not written in this book; but these are written so that you may believe that Jesus is the Christ, the Son of God, and that by believing you may have life in his name." Dozens of miracles in the early church, including the healings of sick people (Acts 3:1-10; 5:12-16), the opening of prison doors (Acts 5:19; 12:7; 16:25-26), and even resurrection from the dead (Acts 20:7-12), are recorded.

Miracles were denied by the eighteenth-century skeptic David Hume, who felt the events were just too incredible to be believed. Those who reject miracles like to pose this challenging question: "If God can do *all* things, could He build a rock so large that He could not move it?" Be careful in falling for this catch-22. As Millard Erickson writes, "He can do only those things which are proper objects of his power. Thus, he cannot do the logically absurd or contradictory."[10] There are, in fact, some things God cannot and will not do, including:

- break His promises (Romans 4:20-21; Hebrews 10:23)

- lie (Numbers 23:19; Hebrews 6:17-18)

- be tempted by evil (James 1:13)

- cease to be God (Psalm 90:2)

- sin (1 John 1:5; 3:3-5)

- create another true God (Isaiah 44:6-8)

Asking if God can build a rock so big that He could not move it is a categorical error. It is like asking what the color blue smells or tastes like. Blue is something seen, not smelled or tasted. To play with the skeptic's mind, I have responded more than once, "Yes, God *could* make a rock so big that He couldn't move it. And then He'd move it!" After all, two can play this mind-numbing game!

The belief that God is unable (or unwilling) to do whatever He deems necessary to bring Himself glory is an example of deism. This view says God is beyond this world (transcendent) but does not involve Himself in the world's affairs (immanent). While Thomas Jefferson, the third president of the United States, believed in the general history of the Bible, he rejected miracles and even took a pair of scissors to literally cut out the miraculous stories to create *The Jefferson Bible*.

While he included the crucifixion and death of Jesus at the end of his compilation, Jefferson left out the story of the resurrection. The Gospels end with John 19:41-42 and Matthew 27:60, which in

Jefferson's version reads, "Now in the place where he was crucified, there was a garden; and in the garden a new sepulchre, wherein was never man yet laid. There they laid Jesus, and rolled a great stone to the door of the sepulchre, and departed."[11] If this were the end of the story, all hope would be lost. Left alone, humanity would forever sit behind the proverbial eight ball.

Contrary to deism, God has involved Himself throughout human history. If an omnipotent God exists, then supernatural events must be possible, and humanity is better for it. Norman Geisler and Ron Brooks explain:

> Deism is inconsistent on its most basic premise. Deists believe in the biggest miracle of all (Creation) but reject what they consider to be all the little miracles. If God was good enough and powerful enough to create the world, isn't it reasonable to assume that He could and would take care of it too? If He can make something out of nothing, then He can certainly make something out of something; as for example, Jesus made wine out of water.[12]

As described in Genesis 1, time, matter, space, and energy were created instantaneously out of nothing (*creatio ex nihilo*), as contrasted to Mormonism's creation out of preexisting material (*creatio ex materia*), which contradicts Hebrews 11:3. It says, "By faith we understand that the universe was created by the word of God, so that what is seen was not made out of things that are visible." In other words, God spoke *all* things into existence. As Josh McDowell and Dave Sterrett write, "Now, if God does exist in reality, and created everything as we know it—all of the *water*, for instance—then it's not a problem for God to part the *waters* of the Red Sea, or for Jesus to turn *water* into wine, calm the *waters* of the storm, or walk on *water*. If the first miracle of Genesis 1:1 took place, then other miracles are possible."[13]

Without the possibility of miracles, the Bible offers nothing more than feel-good stories, banal platitudes, and powerless promises. The result is nothing less than a complete abandonment by God. But if miracles are possible, then it makes perfect sense for the Creator to become intimately involved with humanity and offer Himself as a ransom (Matthew 20:28; 1 Timothy 2:5-6).

BIBLICAL PROPHECIES ABOUT JESUS

Historically, faithful believers have been able to anticipate God's future work through prophecy. As far as Jesus is concerned, the Old Testament provides specific descriptions of the Messiah. For one, it teaches that He would be born of a virgin (Isaiah 7:14) from the seed of Abraham (Genesis 12:1-3), and, more specifically, from the tribe of Judah (Genesis 49:10) and the house of David (2 Samuel 7:12-17). This event was predicted to take place in Bethlehem (Micah 5:2), with a messenger (John the Baptist) preceding Him (Isaiah 40:3).

Isaiah 35:5-6 says,

> Then the eyes of the blind shall be opened,
>   and the ears of the deaf unstopped;
> then shall the lame man leap like a deer,
>   and the tongue of the mute sing for joy.

Jesus fulfilled this prophecy according to Matthew 9:35: "And Jesus went throughout all the cities and villages, teaching in their synagogues and proclaiming the gospel of the kingdom and healing every disease and every affliction."

Perhaps no single prophecy from the Old Testament is clearer than what is revealed in Isaiah 53. Among other things, it teaches in the first six verses that the Messiah would be:

- despised and rejected
- a man of sorrows
- afflicted and suffer greatly
- pierced and crushed

Verse 7 says,

> He was oppressed, and he was afflicted,
>> yet he opened not his mouth;
> like a lamb that is led to the slaughter,
>> and like a sheep that before its shearers is silent,
>> so he opened not his mouth. [14]

In addition, it was predicted that He would be buried in a rich man's tomb (v. 9),[15] "bear their iniquities" (v. 11),[16] be "numbered with the transgressors" (v. 12),[17] and make "intercession for the transgressors" (v. 12).[18] Other descriptions of Jesus's humiliating death include:

- People would mock Him (Psalm 22:7-8; Matthew 27:31,39-44).

- His hands and feet would be pierced (Psalm 22:16; Luke 23:33) along with His side (Zechariah 12:10; John 19:34).

- Soldiers would cast lots for His garments (Psalm 22:18; John 19:23-24).

It was also predicted that Jesus would rise from the dead (Psalm 16:10; Mark 16:6; Acts 2:30-31), ascend into heaven (Psalm 68:18; Acts 1:9), and sit at the right hand of the Father (Psalm 110:1; Hebrews 1:3). These prophecies were composed centuries before Jesus was born, taking away the possibility that they were nothing more than lucky or educated guesses. Just to prove that He was who He claimed to be, Jesus predicted His own death and resurrection as recorded in John 2:18-21 (also see Matthew 12:40, Mark 8:31, and John 10:17-18):

> So the Jews said to him, "What sign do you show us for doing these things?" Jesus answered them, "Destroy this temple, and in three days I will raise it up." The Jews then said, "It has taken forty-six years to build this temple, and will you raise it up in three days?" But he was speaking about the temple of his body.

After Jesus was crucified, the disciples had forgotten His prophetic words, even though the Jewish religious leaders remembered. According to Matthew 27:62-63, the Pharisees approached Pontius Pilate following the death of Jesus and said, "Sir, we remember how that impostor said, while he was still alive, 'After three days I will rise.'" Imagine the shock of the disciples when they finally realized what Jesus had been saying all along!

THE DEATH OF JESUS

To have a resurrection, a death must first take place. How can it be known if Jesus really died on the cross? Some skeptics claim that Jesus was taken off the cross before He had a chance to die and that the damp air in the tomb along with the fragrant spices revived Him. This "swoon" or "apparent death" theory claims that Jesus had the opportunity to escape so He could make appearances to the disciples before He died.

A police detective television series in the 1970s starred actor Peter Falk, who played Lieutenant Frank Columbo. In the first fifteen minutes of each two-hour episode, the audience watched a murder take place. After the commercial break, the lieutenant arrived on the scene. Wearing a wrinkled rain jacket while holding a stub of a cigar in his right hand, the bumbling detective appeared to be anything but a threat to the actual murderer whom the audience knew had set up a more likely suspect to be the fall guy.

"Something doesn't look right," Lt. Columbo would typically say in his Italian New York accent while asking the actual killer question after question. By the end of the show, the murderer was exposed through having to answer so many questions.[19]

Regarding the death of Jesus and in refutation of the swoon theory, here are questions a detective like Lt. Columbo might ask (with answers using information from the biblical accounts):

What happened to Jesus before He was nailed to the cross? He was exhausted and did not sleep the night before; even His disciples could not stay awake in the Garden of Gethsemane on Thursday night/Friday morning. It is here where He bled (Luke 22:44). Jesus was arrested on Friday morning before the soldiers mocked and beat Him (Matthew 27:30). They also flogged Him with a whip with three leather strips embedded with pieces of bone, rocks, and metal. This torture instrument ripped the flesh, setting the stage for circulatory shock. There was a great loss of blood, another reason why Jesus was so weak that He could not carry the cross (Matthew 27:32).

What is known about the results of crucifixion? There is no evidence that any victim ever survived crucifixion. The word *excruciate* comes from *crucifixion*, as *ex* (out of) and *crux* (cross) literally means "out of the cross." The nails pounded into a person's wrists and feet would have severed nerves and arteries. Again, there would have been a great loss of blood, with no chance for a modern-day transfusion. No victim escaped death.

What evidence was there that Jesus had not been drugged and fainted? While Mark 15:36 says He was given sour wine, this would not be enough to intoxicate.

What did the soldiers do when Jesus appeared to be dead on the cross? According to the account in John 19:34, a soldier took a spear and pierced Jesus's side. Blood and water flowed out, testifying to the death of Jesus.

Where did they put the body after taking it off the cross? A Jewish leader (Joseph of Arimathea) donated his own tomb and laid Jesus there after wrapping His body in a linen shroud (Matthew 27:57-61).

It appears unlikely that Jesus could have pretended to die only to later escape. If the swoon theory is supposed to be taken seriously, these additional questions should be asked:

- How did Jesus untangle Himself from the cloths in which He was wrapped (Matthew 27:59)?

- With major wrist and foot injuries (nails through the wrists and ankles), how could Jesus stand up or move the large stone placed at the tomb's entrance, especially when He had no leverage from the inside?

- Would the Roman soldiers who were placed at the tomb (Matthew 27:62-66) have risked their lives by letting Jesus escape, especially since the penalty for letting this happen could have been death?

- How did Jesus get to Emmaus, which is located six miles away, to converse with two followers later that Sunday afternoon (Luke 24:13-35)?

- How did Jesus return to Jerusalem that same evening (Luke 24:36-49)?

There is no way that Jesus could have survived the cruelty that took place on the cross. As the *Journal of the American Medical Association* reported,

> Clearly, the weight of historical and medical evidence indicates that Jesus was dead before the wound to His side was inflicted and supports the traditional view that the spear, thrust between His right ribs, probably perforated not only the right lung but also the pericardium and heart and

A rolling rock stone tomb located in northern Israel. Photo by Eric Johnson.

thereby ensured his death. Accordingly, interpretations based on the assumption that Jesus did not die on the cross appear to be at odds with modern medical knowledge.[20]

THE CROSS AND AN EMPTY TOMB

The symbol of the cross is controversial with Latter-day Saints, as church leaders have appeared repulsed by any mention of blood and the death of Jesus. For instance, LDS President Gordon B. Hinckley wrote, "But for us, the cross is the symbol of the dying Christ, while our message is a declaration of a Living Christ."[21] Instead of the cross, Mormonism emphasizes the Garden of Gethsemane. For example, LDS Apostle Bruce R. McConkie wrote,

> Where and under what circumstances was the atoning sacrifice of the Son of God made? Was it on the Cross of Calvary or in the Garden of Gethsemane? It is to the Cross of Christ that most Christians look when centering their attention upon the infinite and eternal atonement. And certainly the sacrifice of our Lord was completed when he was lifted up by men; also, that part of his life and suffering is more dramatic and, perhaps, more soul stirring. But in reality the pain and suffering, the triumph and grandeur, of the atonement took place primarily in Gethsemane.[22]

Even wearing a decorative cross was considered offensive by tenth LDS President Joseph Fielding Smith:

> Because our Savior died on the cross, the wearing of crosses is to most Latter-day Saints in very poor taste and inconsistent to our worship. Of all the ways ever invented for taking life and the execution of individuals, among the most cruel is likely the cross. This was a favorite method among the Romans who excelled in torture. We may be definitely sure that if our Lord had been killed with a dagger or with a sword, it would have been very strange indeed if religious

people of this day would have graced such a weapon by wearing it and adoring it because it was by such a means that our Lord was put to death.[23]

Paul countered such an argument in 1 Corinthians 1:22-25:

> For Jews demand signs and Greeks seek wisdom, but we preach Christ crucified, a stumbling block to Jews and folly to Gentiles, but to those who are called, both Jews and Greeks, Christ the power of God and the wisdom of God. For the foolishness of God is wiser than men, and the weakness of God is stronger than men.

The 2004 film *The Passion of the Christ* shocked many moviegoers. Some theater managers reported that popcorn and drinks were left under their seats, practically untouched by the audience that was shaken by the disturbing scenes. Indeed, director Mel Gibson's portrayal depicted in vivid detail the final gruesome hours in the life of Jesus.

While the LDS leadership would like to distance themselves from the powerful image of what took place on the cross, the Bible says it is only through the shed blood of Jesus that atonement becomes efficacious. Leviticus 17:11 says, "For the life of the flesh is in the blood, and I have given it for you on the altar to make atonement for your souls, for it is the blood that makes atonement by the life."

According to Hebrews 9:11-28, the blood of animal sacrifices foreshadowed what happened to Jesus. Verse 22 says that "without the shedding of blood there is no forgiveness of sins." J.C. Ryle, a nineteenth-century bishop of Liverpool, England, stated, "We can never attach too much importance to the atoning death of Christ. It is the leading fact in the word of God, on which the eyes of our soul ought to be ever fixed. Without the shedding of his blood, there is no remission of sin. It is the cardinal truth on which the whole system of Christianity hinges."[24]

As Robert Bowman put it,

The importance of Jesus' resurrection for Christianity can hardly be exaggerated. It is a basic presupposition of the Christian faith: As the risen Lord, Jesus has conquered sin and death on our behalf, has been exalted to the throne of heaven at the Father's right hand, and has sent the Holy Spirit to give us new life and to make us God's people through faith in Christ. This is why the resurrection of Christ is a key element in the Apostles' Creed, the Nicene Creed, and most of the other confessions and statements of faith that Christians have written throughout church history.[25]

Someone might ask why God couldn't have just snapped His fingers and forgiven everyone's sins. Millard Erickson says that those who make this appeal fail "to consider who God really is...But for God to remove or ignore the guilt of sin without requiring a payment would in effect destroy the very moral fiber of the universe, the distinction between right and wrong. An additional problem is that God is a being of infinite or perfect holiness and goodness. An offense against him is much more serious than an offense against an ordinary sinful human."[26]

Those who participated in the killing of Jesus played an integral role in God's plan. In his first sermon recorded in Acts 2:22-23, the apostle Peter told a Jewish audience, "Men of Israel, hear these words: Jesus of Nazareth, a man attested to you by God with mighty works and wonders and signs that God did through him in your midst, as you yourselves know—this Jesus, delivered up according to the definite plan and foreknowledge of God, you crucified and killed by the hands of lawless men."

He also said in Acts 4:27-28, "For truly in this city there were gathered together against your holy servant Jesus, whom you anointed, both Herod and Pontius Pilate, along with the Gentiles and the peoples of Israel, to do whatever your hand and your plan had predestined to take place." This event was predicted by Jesus at the Last Supper in Luke 22:22 when He prophesied, "The Son of Man goes as it has been determined."

Paul said in 1 Corinthians 1:18 that "the word of the cross is folly to those who are perishing, but to us who are being saved it is the power of God." He added in 1 Corinthians 2:2 that he "decided to know nothing among you except Jesus Christ and him crucified." And Paul said in Galatians 6:14 that he would not "boast except in the cross of our Lord Jesus Christ." John MacArthur and Richard Mayhue explain how "Herod, Pilate, Judas, and the Jews conspired to bring about the crucifixion because they wanted to be rid of this man who indicted them for their sin. But God ordained the evil of the cross *for the good* that it would bring, namely, the salvation of his people from their sin."[27]

There is no getting around the cross, as Ryle pointed out that "unless you know the power of Christ's cross by experience, unless you know and feel within that the blood shed on that cross has washed away your own particular sins, and unless you are willing to confess that your salvation depends entirely on the work that Christ did on the cross, Christ will profit you nothing." Then he warned, "As long as you live, *beware of a religion in which little is said of the cross.* You live in times when this warning is sadly needful. Beware, I say again, of a religion without the cross."[28]

Because of its symbolic importance, many churches feature a cross inside their sanctuary. In addition, many Christians wear crosses around their necks and proudly display this symbol in their homes. For believers, there is powerful symbolism in the cross, with just as much meaning as a pin of Moroni or a temple attached to their clothing might be for some Mormons. Paul Copan explains how he answered one Muslim who mocked the cross:

> "How can Christians wear with pride the instrument of torture and humiliation? If your brother were killed in an electric chair, would you wear an electric chair around your neck?" I replied that it depends: "If my brother happened to be Jesus of Nazareth and his death in an electric chair brought about my salvation and was the means by which evil was defeated and creation renewed, then he would have transformed a symbol of shame and punishment into something glorious."[29]

This symbol represents what Jesus did "in order that the world might be saved through him" (John 3:17).

FOUR FACTS SUPPORTING THE BODILY RESURRECTION

Fortunately for Christianity, the story of Jesus did not end at the cross. The resurrection is the claim that Jesus literally rose to life from the dead. Here are four reasons that support this theory as accurate:[30]

1. After His crucifixion, Jesus was buried in the tomb of the Jewish religious leader Joseph of Arimathea.

- The tomb's location was known.

- It does not seem likely that a Jewish religious authority would have been included in the resurrection story unless it was factual.

- There are no other ancient burial stories to compete with this story.

2. On the Sunday following the crucifixion, Jesus's tomb was found empty by a group of female followers.

- The oldest Gospel account (Mark) includes this material.

- Practically all biblical scholars—conservative and liberal alike—accept the empty tomb.[31]

- Females (second-class citizens in that region) were the first to see Jesus.

- The disciples considered a bodily resurrection (Luke 24:10-11) a most unlikely outcome.

- If the tomb were not empty, it would make no sense for the Jewish leaders to bribe the soldiers to lie and say the body was stolen (Matthew 28:11-15).

3. On multiple occasions and under various circumstances, different individuals and groups of people claimed to encounter the resurrected Jesus (1 Corinthians 15:1-8).

- Jesus appeared to several individuals (Peter, James, Paul).

- He also made appearances to "the Twelve" and a group known as "all the apostles."

- There was an appearance to more than 500 believers.

- Jesus was physically handled by Thomas in John 20:24-29. A spirit does not have flesh and bones.

- To show that He had a physical body, Jesus ate food on four difference occasions, as described in Luke 24:30,42-43; John 21:12-13; and Acts 1:4.

4. The twelve apostles insisted that Jesus rose from the dead.

- While the apostles are portrayed as doubters who easily got confused, they were not typically deceptive or immoral.

- There was no motive for them to steal the body (as originally claimed by the Jewish leadership in Matthew 28:13). None of the three reasons why people typically deceive (financial greed, sexual or relational desire, or pursuit of power) were realistic motives for the apostles.[32]

- If these men did not believe the resurrection was true, it is highly unlikely they would have risked imprisonment or death by publicly proclaiming the resurrection just a few weeks after Jesus died.

- According to church tradition, all but one of the 12 apostles went to their deaths as martyrs. People are generally willing to die for something they think is true but *not* for what they know is not true.

FOUR ALTERNATIVE THEORIES

Besides the swoon theory, skeptics have offered additional theories over the past two millennia, especially during the past three centuries. William Lane Craig, who spent two years of his life studying the resurrection, writes, "Ever since the disciples began to proclaim that Jesus was risen from the dead, some have denied the historical resurrection and have tried to come up with ways of explaining away the evidence through alternative theories."

Craig adds that most "have proved to be blind alleys and have been unanimously rejected by contemporary scholarship." Still, he believes that it is worthwhile to consider these debunked theories because "the average person today, Christian or non-Christian, is largely unaware that they are in fact blind alleys. Many non-Christians still reject or at least claim to reject Jesus' resurrection because of arguments that have been decisively refuted time and again and which no modern scholar would support."[33]

Due to limited space, let's consider just four of these theories while raising pertinent detective-like questions:

1. Unknown Tomb. Jesus was buried in a common pit grave unknown to the disciples. The "resurrection" happened because nobody knew where the tomb was located.

- Wasn't this Joseph of Arimathea's tomb? This makes it a *known* tomb.

- Wasn't the location of the tomb known by the Roman soldiers? By the women who prepared Jesus's body? By the Romans who stationed a guard there? By the Jewish leaders who ordered the soldiers to be placed at the tomb? If so, then the authorities merely needed to investigate the tomb where the body was laid.

- Why would the Jewish leaders concoct a lie about what happened to the body (i.e., saying the disciples stole it)? Wouldn't they be motivated to find the body?

- If the body were never found, why did the disciples claim that Jesus was resurrected? To believe Jesus had not resurrected and make up stories about this would make them liars.

- If they knew Jesus had not resurrected, why did all the disciples except one (John) suffer torturous deaths that could have been avoided? Some might die for something they believe is true, but rarely will a person die for a lie.

Conclusion: Too many people knew where Joseph's tomb was located. Jesus's enemies would have been motivated to find the right tomb and produce the body. If the body was lost and never found, the disciples had no motive to preach a bodily resurrection.

2. Hallucination. The followers of Jesus became so emotionally involved with Jesus's messianic expectation that their minds projected visions or hallucinations of a risen Jesus. This theory is often tied in with the suggestion that the resurrection was nothing more than a legend created much later.

- How is it possible for multiple people to have simultaneous visions or hallucinations?

- Since a hallucination is based on a person's prior knowledge and understanding, and since Jesus's closest followers had no hope for a resurrection (e.g., hiding out in fear after Jesus had died), how could they all have had a hallucination of the same unexpected event?[34]

- What about the 500 witnesses (1 Corinthians 15:6)? If the event were a hallucination, it would have been risky for Paul to encourage his readers to contact the "witnesses" and find out that the resurrection was not real.

- Why would the Gospel writers include the embarrassing detail that women were the first witnesses (John 20:1-18)? Craig explains, "The early believers would have no motive in humiliating its leaders by making them into cowards and the women into heroes...It would be pointless for early believers to manufacture a story of an appearance to legally unqualified women."[35]

- Why did John report that Jesus was not just seen but also physically handled (John 20:24-28)?

- Doesn't it take many years after the fact for a legend to become believable?

Conclusion: The evidence strongly suggests that the early Christians believed they experienced the resurrection, which would negate any legendary story that would have taken many years to develop.

3. Existential Resurrection. A historical resurrection can never be proven, but it is not necessary. What is most important is that Christ is raised in a person's heart.

- Why was Paul so adamant in 1 Corinthians 15 that a physical, not spiritual, resurrection *is* important?

- What good is a warm, fuzzy feeling if the resurrection is not historical?

- What about the testimony of 500 people who claimed to see Jesus in a resurrected state?

- Why were the disciples willing to die when they would have known their feelings were based on emotions and not reality?

Conclusion: The disciples were not interested in a "feel good" ending. They were more interested in following the truth.

4. The Jesus Tomb. This is a newer theory developed by movie director James Cameron (*Titanic*) and publicized in a 2007 documentary that aired on the Discovery Channel. It claims that Jesus was only temporarily buried in Joseph of Arimathea's tomb before His body was moved to another tomb less than a mile away in a suburb of Jerusalem (Talpiot). Originally discovered in 1980, six of the ten first-century ossuaries (bone boxes made of limestone) containing 17 skeletons had inscriptions on the side of the boxes such as "Jesus, Son of Joseph," "Judah, son of Jesus," "Matia," "Maria," and "Mariamne Mara," which, as the theory goes, may have been Mary Magdalene the wife of Jesus.

- Why would Jesus have been buried in Jerusalem? He was from Nazareth in Galilee, a more logical place for a family burial.

- Why would the guard outside the tomb allow the body to be taken to another tomb?

- How do we know these ossuaries contained the bones of Jesus and His relatives? In fact, 75 percent of all names in first-century Israel involved only 16 different male and

Three of the ossuaries originally discovered in a Jerusalem neighborhood and displayed at the Israel Museum in Jerusalem. These ossuaries were featured in a 2007 film by James Cameron and were claimed to once contain the bones of Jesus and His family. Photo by Eric Johnson.

female names. Jesus, Joseph, Mary, and Matthew were some of the most used names in that culture. The chance of this cluster of names being found in one tomb is about 1 in 600, which are not impossible odds.

- Why should the differing DNA found in the "Mariamne Mara" ossuary even suggest any connection to Jesus since the idea of Him having had a wife is pure conjecture?

- What about the early tradition that points to the Church of the Holy Sepulcher in Jerusalem as the site where Jesus was crucified and buried? It seems unlikely that the tomb of Joseph of Arimathea would have had any meaning if there was no resurrection that took place in that particular tomb.

Conclusion: Circumstantial evidence is dangerous. Several archaeologists who were interviewed for the Discovery Channel documentary, including agnostic Shimon Gibson, do not agree with the movie producer's conclusion. They claimed their taped interviews were manipulated to make it appear they agreed with this producer when they did not.[36]

CONCLUSION

Those theories that insist Jesus did not resurrect from the dead lack historical support and, as Craig explains, it "takes more faith to believe in those theories than it does to believe that Jesus really rose from the dead."[37] He adds, "One of the greatest weaknesses of alternative explanations to the resurrection is their incompleteness: they fail to provide a comprehensive, overarching explanation of all the data. By contrast the resurrection furnishes one, simple, comprehensive explanation of all the facts without distorting them. Therefore, it is the better explanation."[38]

First Peter 1:3 says that God "has caused us to be born again to a living hope through the resurrection of Jesus Christ from the dead." There is power in the cross and the victory over death Jesus accomplished by rising from the dead. Nineteenth-century singer Ralph E. Hudson wrote the chorus to "At the Cross" penned by Isaac Watts (1674–1748) and made this salient observation:

> At the cross, at the cross where I first saw the light,
> And the burden of my heart rolled away,
> It was there by faith I received my sight,
> And now I am happy all the day![39]

Let your LDS friend know that there is hope beyond the walls of the LDS Church, but it can be found only in Jesus. For those who believe, the resurrection is nothing less than a game changer.

DISCUSSION QUESTIONS

1. Why is God's ability to intervene in the world crucial to the case for Christianity?

2. The swoon theory describes how Jesus was not dead when placed in the tomb. Provide three reasons why Jesus must have died. Why is the death of Jesus required for Christianity to be true?

3. Why does it not make sense that the disciples stole the body of Jesus?

4. Do you agree with J.C. Ryle when he said, "As long as you live, *beware of a religion in which little is said of the cross*"? Why is this symbol so important to Christian believers?

5. Most Latter-day Saints believe in the death and resurrection of Jesus. Why, then, do you think this chapter was included in a book describing basic Christian doctrines when Mormons and Christians generally agree? (Hint: Think about the mindset of a person who leaves Mormonism and is contemplating truth.)

RECOMMENDED RESOURCES

Entry-Level Resources

Josh and Sean McDowell, *Resurrected: Experience Freedom from the Fear of Death* (Eugene, OR: Harvest House Publishers, 2012).

John Piper, *The Passion of Jesus Christ* (Wheaton, IL: Crossway, 2004).

Middle-Level Resources

Robert M. Bowman Jr., *Jesus' Resurrections and Joseph's Visions: Examining the Foundations of Christianity and Mormonism* (Tampa, FL: DeWard Publishing, 2020).

Gary R. Habermas and Michael R. Licona, *The Case for the Resurrection of Jesus* (Grand Rapids, MI: Kregel, 2004).

William Lane Craig, *The Son Rises: Historical Evidence for the Resurrection of Jesus* (Eugene, OR: Wipf & Stock Publishers, 2001).

CHAPTER 7

THE TRINITY

One God, Three Persons

*"The grace of the Lord Jesus Christ and the love of God and
the fellowship of the Holy Spirit be with you all."*

2 CORINTHIANS 13:14

CHAPTER PREVIEW

The Trinity is an essential doctrine in the historic Christian church. Unfortunately, many people who object to this teaching have an improper understanding of what it says. Simply put, the Trinity describes one God as revealed in three Persons: the Father, Son, and Holy Spirit. The three Persons are not only one in purpose but also one in essence, as each is fully God. The biblical evidence to support this important teaching provides clarity. Undoubtedly, any rejection of the Trinity is a rejection of God Himself.

In chapter 4, I spoke with two LDS missionaries—Elders Michaels and Sorensen—about the nature of God. We continue that conversation in this chapter as the two young men decided to introduce a topic considered by many Latter-day Saints as the coup de grace in dismissing biblical Christianity.

"Do you believe in the Trinity?" Elder Michaels asked.

When I said I did, he sighed softly and reacted as if he felt pity for me. Perhaps this is because Mormonism's leaders have traditionally mocked this important Christian teaching.[1] For example, Joseph Smith stated,

> Many men say there is one God; the Father, the Son and the Holy Ghost are only one God. I say that is a strange God anyhow—three in one, and one in three! It is a curious organization...All are to be crammed into one God, according to sectarianism. It would make the biggest God in all the world. He would be a wonderfully big God—he would be a giant or a monster.[2]

Mormon Apostle Dallin H. Oaks told a general conference audience, "We maintain that the concepts identified by such nonscriptural terms as 'the incomprehensible mystery of God' and 'the mystery of the Holy Trinity' are attributable to the ideas of Greek philosophy. These philosophical concepts transformed Christianity in the first few centuries following the deaths of the Apostles."[3] Speaking at another general conference, LDS Apostle Jeffrey R. Holland stated,

> Our first and foremost article of faith in The Church of Jesus Christ of Latter-day Saints is "We believe in God, the Eternal Father, and in His Son, Jesus Christ, and in the Holy Ghost." We believe these three divine persons constituting a single Godhead are united in purpose, in manner, in testimony, in mission. We believe Them to be filled with the same godly sense of mercy and love, justice and grace, patience, forgiveness, and redemption. I think it is accurate to say we believe They are one in every significant and eternal aspect imaginable *except* believing Them to be three persons combined in one substance, a Trinitarian notion never set forth in the scriptures because it is not true.[4]

"I get so confused when I try to understand what Christians mean when they say 'Trinity,'" Elder Sorensen said.

"Could you define what you think this doctrine teaches?" I asked.

"It's like having one God in three gods," he said. "This is contradictory and makes no sense. The Trinity was created many years after the Bible was written."

Right away, I knew some education would be needed to correct his straw man fallacy, as the doctrine of the Trinity does *not* teach there is "one God in three gods." Unfortunately, when the topic is brought up by a Mormon, some Christians automatically retreat. Perhaps it is because biblical doctrine is not emphasized as much as it should be in Christian churches, as many believers have not been properly instructed. While the *word* is not found in the Bible, the *concept* of the Trinity certainly is! To reject this teaching is to deny God as He is. As James White writes,

> If we have defective knowledge, or worse, if we have *wrong* information and have been deceived, our worship is either lessened (due to simple ignorance), or it is completely invalid, as the worship of idols and false gods. That is not to say that we have to have perfect knowledge to worship God—none of us do. But our desire must be to grow in the grace and *knowledge* of God, and we must always remember that Jesus taught that eternal life was the possession of those who *know* the one true God. Knowledge does not save (that is the error of Gnosticism); but true worship does not exist without knowledge.[5]

Wayne Grudem adds,

> The doctrine of the Trinity is one of the most important doctrines of the Christian faith. To study the Bible's teachings on the Trinity gives us great insight into the question that is at the center of all of our seeking after God: What is God like in himself? Here we learn that in himself, in his very being, God exists in the persons of the Father, Son, and Holy Spirit, yet he is one God.[6]

"Based on your definition, I don't think you really understand the meaning of this teaching," I gently told the missionaries. "Would you mind if I explained it to you?"

"Give it a shot," Elder Sorensen replied. "No Christian has ever been able to make any sense of it to me."

To deny the Trinity means "the heart of the Christian faith is at stake."[7] Thus, it is important for Christians to be ready to defend this vital teaching to Latter-day Saints who are willing to listen. They may not be convinced in just one conversation, but at least they can be encouraged to think through the issue while ceasing attacks on the teaching with fallacious arguments.

PRESENTING THE BIBLICAL CASE FOR THE TRINITY

Before I had a chance to begin my explanation, Elder Michaels wanted to introduce an argument of his own.

"How can the Trinity be true if the word is *never* used in the Bible?" he asked.

As Oaks said earlier, Mormonism denies the Trinity because it is not "set forth in the scriptures." This is a common objection offered by critics, so I decided to use Elder Michaels's question to help me move into the topic. For one, the word is constructed of the Latin prefix *tri* (three) and the suffix *unity* (one). Since the authors of the New Testament wrote in Koine Greek, not Latin, it makes perfect sense the word is missing in the Bible! Contrary to the teaching of an LDS general authority, R.C. Sproul wrote, "It really is naïve to object that the word itself is not found in Scripture if the concept is found in Scripture and is taught by Scripture."[8]

I decided to answer the missionary's question by pointing out an inconsistency in the LDS worldview.

"There are many unique LDS doctrines not specifically named in Mormonism's ancient scriptures (Bible and Book of Mormon), including *telestial kingdom*, *patriarchal blessing*, and *preexistence*. While none of these terms can be found in Mormonism's ancient scriptures, each is an important theological concept. If you are going to criticize the Christian term *Trinity*, then why does *your* church use theological terms never used in these ancient scriptures?"

Another example I could have added was Mormonism's doctrine of Heavenly Mother, as it is never named in any of the *standard works*. A *Gospel Topics Essay* published by the LDS Church admits that "our present knowledge about a Mother in Heaven is limited."[9] Talk about mystery! It seems hard to believe that a doctrine with neither precedence nor mention in the LDS scriptures is readily accepted by faithful Mormons.

Many Latter-day Saints will want to switch the topic when something comes up that they would rather not address. For example, when I challenge Mormons about historical or archaeological problems with the Book of Mormon, my concern is normally dismissed. More than once I have been told, "You just have to pray about it and have faith."[10] Instead of avoiding the doctrine of the Trinity because it may appear to be "difficult," I think it is important for the Christian to not run away from the topic, especially when the Mormon will expect most Christians to become quickly flustered.

While the missionaries held disdain for the word *Trinity*, they provided an incorrect definition. Without trying to embarrass them, I began by saying the doctrine of the Trinity teaches that there are three *Persons* but one God, not three gods in one God as was stated. As someone has put it, there are three *who's*—the Father, Son, and Spirt—yet one *what*, or the essence of God.

"One Christian theologian devised the simplest definition of the Trinity in just one sentence," I said. "Are you ready?"

Both missionaries nodded.

"Within the one Being that is God," I said, "there exists eternally three coequal and coeternal persons, namely, the Father, the Son, and the Holy Spirit."[11] I then listed the five points that characterize the Trinity:

1. There is one eternal God (Deuteronomy 6:4; Mark 12:29; 1 Corinthians 8:4; Galatians 3:20).

2. The Father is God (John 6:27; Ephesians 4:6).[12]

3. The Son is God (John 1:1-14; 8:58; 10:30; 20:28; Philippians 2:5-11; Colossians 1:15-17; 2:9).[13]

4. The Spirit is God (Genesis 1:2; Psalm 139:7-8; Acts 5:3-4; 2 Corinthians 3:17-18; Ephesians 4:30).[14]

5. The Father is not the Son or the Holy Spirit, the Son is not the Father or the Holy Spirit, and the Holy Spirit is not the Father or the Son.

I explained how the Trinity describes one God as revealed in the three Persons of the Father, Son, and Holy Spirit. As Genesis 1:26-27 says, "Then God said, 'Let *us* make man in our image, after our likeness." The plural pronoun is used since the Hebrew word for God (*Elohim*) is plural.[15] Matthew 28:19-20 states, "Go therefore and make disciples of all nations, baptizing them in the name of the Father and of the Son and of the Holy Spirit, teaching them to observe all that I have commanded you." Notice the intentional use of the singular noun ("name") with the three who comprise that name. I decided to provide several examples to show how each person of the Trinity possesses the full attributes of God.

"Who created the universe?"

"God," they said in unison.

"You are correct, as Genesis 1:1 says that God (referring to the Father) made the heavens and the earth. But did you know that Genesis 1:2 says that the "Spirit of God" was involved in creation? And Jesus is crowned the creator of all things according to John 1:3 along with Colossians 1:15-17 and Hebrews 1:2."[16]

I decided to provide another example.

"Who resurrected Jesus from the dead?"

The two looked at each other.

"All of them," Elder Sorensen said sheepishly.

"Wow, you're ahead of me," I said with a chuckle. "Yes, all three *were* involved in the resurrection of Jesus. In John 2:19, Jesus said that He would raise Himself from the dead. But Acts 3:15 says the Father raised Him, and Romans 8:11 credits the Holy Spirit with this accomplishment."

I could see the wheels turning in their heads.

"Help me to understand, then, to whom was Jesus praying in the Garden of Gethsemane," Elder Sorensen said. "If there is one God, and the Father is God, why did Jesus pray to Himself?"

He was referring to Jesus's prayer in the garden before He was betrayed and arrested, which is described in Matthew 26:36-56. Another example often brought up is how John baptized Jesus in the Jordan River. As Jesus stood in the water, the voice of the Father came out of heaven and a dove representing the Holy Spirit descended (Matthew 3:13-17). Those who reject the Trinity sarcastically inquire if Jesus might have been a ventriloquist who was throwing His voice.

"Jesus was praying to the Father," I said. "The Father did not send Himself to pay for the sins of people. Instead, He sent Jesus. Christians reject the idea that the Father is the same as the Son."

Immediately, Elder Sorensen brought up another biblical passage.

"So why did Jesus say the Father was greater than He was? This makes it appear Jesus is less than the Father."

He was referring to John 14:28. To understand this passage, several points must be understood. As we discussed in chapter 5, Philippians 2:5-11 teaches how Jesus—though He never gave up His divine nature—humbled Himself to become human. If the president of the United States walked into the room and someone said, "Here is a man greater than all of us," would this statement be true? Notice that the word used is *greater*, not *better*. It is a reference to authority, as the president has more power than anyone else in the United States. As White points out, "Difference in function does not indicate inferiority of position."[17] In the same way, we can say that Jesus submitted Himself to the Father while not giving up His claim to deity.

Elder Michaels had waited his turn to ask a question.

"I have heard that the Trinity was a doctrine made up at a church council. Is it possible you are accepting a false teaching created by corrupted men?"

Just because the Trinity was not overtly taught before the fourth century, the basics for the teaching were already implicit in Christianity. Talking about the deity of Jesus, Harold Brown writes that "one of the values of Christian heresy—which sometimes appears older than orthodoxy—is that it suggests that orthodox doctrine, against which it reacts, was present from a very early date, even though not expressly formulated."[18]

When Arius brought forth a disagreement by declaring Jesus to be human but not God, it caused the church leaders to wrestle with orthodox teaching. The issue of Jesus's deity had never been challenged in this way. The Roman emperor Constantine, who had declared Christianity to be the state's religion, decided to assemble a group of church bishops in AD 325 to debate it. The Council of Nicaea (located in modern-day Turkey) became the first ecumenical gathering of Christian leaders.

In contrast to the beliefs advocated by Arius, the vast majority of the 318 bishops concluded that Jesus was fully God as well as fully man. It was not a political decision but rather a biblical conclusion, as they believed that the version of Jesus offered by the Arians was heretical. Referring to Bishop Eusebius, who was a follower of Arius, Roger Olson writes how he

> stood before the council and read a clear and blatant denial of the deity of the Son of God, emphasizing that he is a creature and not equal to the Father in any possible sense... Before Eusebius finished reading it, some of the bishops were holding their hands over their ears and shouting for someone to stop the blasphemies. One bishop near Eusebius stepped forward and grabbed the manuscript out of his hands, threw it to the floor and stomped on it. A riot broke out among the bishops and was stopped only by the emperor's command. Apparently, in spite of circulating letters written by Arius and Alexander before the council, most of the bishops were naïve about how clear-cut the issue really was.[19]

The version of Jesus proposed by the Arians (as a created being) is not much different from the Jesus of Mormonism, as described by Olson:

Thus Arius and his colleagues—the Arians—affirmed a kind of Trinity made up of three "divine" beings (Father, Son and Holy Spirit), only one of whom is truly God. He continued in his profession of faith to affirm unequivocally that only the Father is "without beginning" and that the Son, though a great creature who shares many of God's attributes, did not exist before he was begotten by the Father...For only if Jesus Christ is God are we saved...Even before there was a New Testament to appeal to as the written authority for Christian faith and practice, the implicit apostolic faith of early Christianity revolved around the scandal of the deity of Christ...If it were removed in any way, then the hope for eternal participation in God's own life and for forgiveness and restoration to the image of God would fall apart. The gospel itself would be wrecked.[20]

The Nicene Creed is still recited 17 centuries later by Christians across the world. In its revised form, it states,

We believe in one God, the Father almighty, maker of heaven and earth, of all things visible and invisible. And in one Lord Jesus Christ, the only Son of God, begotten from the Father before all ages, God from God, Light from Light, true God from true God, begotten, not made; of the same essence as the Father. Through him all things were made. For us and for our salvation he came down from heaven; he became incarnate by the Holy Spirit and the virgin Mary, and was made human. He was crucified for us under Pontius Pilate; he suffered and was buried. The third day he rose again, according to the Scriptures. He ascended to heaven and is seated at the right hand of the Father. He will come again with glory to judge the living and the dead. His kingdom will never end. And we believe in the Holy Spirit, the Lord, the giver of life. He proceeds from the Father and the Son, and with the Father and the Son is worshiped and glorified. He spoke through the prophets. We believe in one holy catholic [universal] and apostolic church. We affirm one baptism for the forgiveness of sins. We look forward to the resurrection of the dead, and to life in the world to come. Amen.

Notice how the creed says that Jesus was "*begotten, not made*." This is what theologians call "eternal generation." A human has a beginning. However, while He became human, Jesus remains eternally God. John 1:1 definitively states, "In the beginning was the Word, and the Word was with God, and the Word was God." Verse 14 makes it clear that "the Word [Jesus] became flesh and dwelt among us." This creed fits right in line with biblical teaching. As James White writes,

> Each of the persons is said to be eternal, each is said to be coequal with the others as to their divine nature. Each fully shares the one *Being* that is God. The Father is not 1/3 of God, the Son 1/3 of God, the Spirit 1/3 of God. Each is fully God, coequal with the others, and that eternally. There never was a time when the Father was not the Father; never a time when the Son was not the Son; never a time when the Spirit was not the Spirit. Their relationship is eternal, not in the sense of having been for a *long* time, but existing, in fact, outside the realm of time itself.[21]

Theology professor Matthew Barrett explains more:

> God's one essence is indivisible; it has no parts. The divine essence does not break into three parts to form three persons. Introducing such a separation results in a God compounded of parts. Rather, the three persons are one in essence, each a subsistence of the identical, self-same essence, wholly possessing that one essence, not merely a portion of it. Although we distinguish the persons from the essence, we dare not think the essence is some fourth thing that the persons divvy up to hold in common...Nor should we look at the persons and think that if we put two

of them together, we have more "God" than if we only stick with one of them.[22]

The third member of the Trinity—the Person of the Holy Spirit—was never a discussion point at the Council of Nicaea. Only the deity of Jesus—certainly crucial for the doctrine of the Trinity—was debated. Later, the Holy Spirit was discussed at the second ecumenical council at Constantinople (modern Istanbul in Turkey) held in AD 381 and He was affirmed as God. While Mormons are told to have disdain for creeds, what they certainly do not realize is how many aspects of the Nicene Creed are found in Doctrine and Covenants 20![23] If creeds teach false doctrine, as LDS leaders have said, then how can this be explained?

IS THE MYSTERY OF THE TRINITY ILLUSTRATABLE?

Three points must be clearly conveyed to someone who rejects the Trinity. First, it must be understood that God revealed more of Himself as we move from the Old Testament to the New. This is called progressive revelation. Norman Geisler explains that "the Old Testament revealed only hints of the Trinity taught in the New Testament (for example, Matt. 3:16-17; 28:18-20). The New Testament declares explicitly what was only implicit in the Old Testament."[24] Those who lived in the days of the Old Testament had a basic concept of God even if they had not had everything revealed to them. With the coming of Jesus, Christians have a fuller concept, though it is not complete.

Second, it must be understood that the doctrine of the Trinity will never be fully comprehended by the human mind. It's like heaven and having a basic concept of what this state will be like. However, a full comprehension of the splendor prepared by God awaits the believer for a future day. So it is with the Trinity. To fully grasp the true essence of God would require omniscience, a trait possessed only by God Himself. Christians accept this teaching by faith because this is how God is revealed in the Bible. Grudem writes:

[I]t is not correct to say that we cannot understand the doctrine of the Trinity at all. Certainly we can understand and know that God is three persons, and that each person is fully God, and that there is one God. We can know these things because the Bible teaches them...Scripture does not ask us to believe in a contradiction. A contradiction would be "There is one God and there is not one God," or "God is three persons and God is not three persons," or even (which is similar to the previous statement) "God is three persons and God is one person." But to say that "God is three persons and there is one God" is not a contradiction. It is something we do not understand, and it is therefore a mystery or a paradox, but that should not trouble us as long as the different aspects of the mystery are clearly taught by Scripture, for as long as we are finite creatures and not omniscient deity, there will always (for all eternity) be things that we do not fully understand.[25]

Louis Berkhof wrote, "*The Church confesses the Trinity to be a mystery beyond the comprehension of man.* The Trinity is a mystery, not merely in the Biblical sense that it is a truth, which was formerly hidden but is now revealed; but in the sense that man cannot comprehend it and make it intelligible."[26] Harold Brown said the Trinity "has proved impossible for Christians actually to *understand* the doctrine or to explain it in any comprehensive way. The doctrine of the Trinity speaks of the inner nature of the transcendent God, a matter that certainly surpasses our human ability to understand and that must be respected as a divine mystery."[27]

Unfortunately, Latter-day Saints are taught that it *is* possible to understand God's nature. The first Article of Faith states that there are three beings who make up the Godhead: God the Father, Jesus, and the Holy Ghost. As the church's website puts it, "although the members of the Godhead are distinct beings with distinct roles, they are one in purpose and doctrine. They are perfectly united in bringing to pass Heavenly Father's divine plan of salvation."[28] This is an example of tritheism (belief in three separate gods) and should not be mistaken for the Trinity.

Such a God is devoid of mystery. Isn't it better to have a true God with mystery than a false version that can be better comprehended?

Finally, the Trinity cannot be illustrated in a way that will be satisfactory to many nonbelievers. Since New Testament times, several illustrations have been used to try to explain this incomprehensible doctrine, yet they typically break down. As John MacArthur and Richard Mayhue state, "Theologians have attempted to find a perfect illustration of the Trinity, but all these attempts have either divided the essence [of God], compromised the distinction between the three persons, or lost sight of God's *personal* essence...No illustration can communicate the Trinity because the Trinity is God and always transcends the created order in essence, persons, and relationships."[29]

One common illustration describes how the egg is made up of three parts: shell, white, and yolk. This is a better portrayal of the tritheistic view that there are three gods who are one in purpose only. As discussed in chapter 4, Deuteronomy 6:4 declares that God is not only one in purpose but also one in being. Grudem explains,

> To say, for example, that God is like a three-leaf clover, which has three parts yet remains one clover, fails because each leaf is only part of the clover, and any one leaf cannot be said to be the whole clover. But in the Trinity, each of the persons is not just a separate part of God, each person is fully God. Moreover, the leaf of a clover is impersonal and does not have distinct and complex personality in the way each person of the Trinity does.[30]

Other examples used to illustrate the Trinity include water (steam/liquid/ice) or the roles of a man (father/son/husband). These better illustrate the false teaching called Sabellianism, also known as modalism, that says God is one person who reveals Himself through three different "modes" (or "manifestations"). Thus, illustrations like these have the potential to do more harm than good.

There are two examples I do like to use. One, I ask what "1 and 1 and 1" equals. The answer typically given is *three* (1 + 1 + 1), as most tackle the equation in a linear fashion. Yet those three numbers could just as well result in the answer *one* (1 x 1 x 1). It is somewhat of a mystery to say that three ones equal one when no subtraction has taken place. Depending on how the equation is viewed, one and three can each be considered correct answers.

A second possibility is to utilize the triangle (illustrated here) to show how there are equal angles (representing equality with God) while each angle remains separate (representing the uniqueness of each Person). Thus, the Father is fully God, the Son is fully God, and the Spirit is fully God, yet the Father is not the Spirit, the Spirit is not the Son, and the Son is not the Father. This goes together well with the five points listed above describing the Trinity.

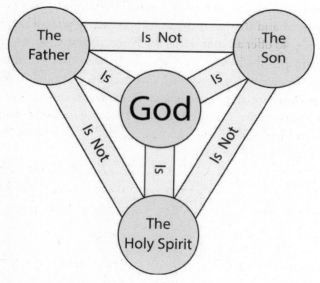

According to the Trinity, God eternally exists as three separate persons (Father, Son, Holy Spirit). Each is fully God yet there are not three gods but one.

WRAPPING UP THE CONVERSATION

It was obvious that the missionaries wanted to fully comprehend this teaching but were frustrated about its mysterious nature.

"I know you both would like me to just flesh out the doctrine in a way that makes logical sense," I told them. "But, as I have said, Christians believe the Trinity because the concept is taught in the Bible. For close to 2000 years, Christians have accepted the basic tenets. Without the Trinity, there would be confusion for Christians to claim that there is one God while maintaining that they should worship Jesus as God, as the New Testaments teaches should be done."

I went on to describe how Christ's atonement would have no meaning unless the Trinity is true. If Jesus had been a perfect man but was *not* God in the flesh, He would have been powerless to provide full payment for the sins of believers. John Piper stated it well when he wrote, "The punishment owing to our sin could be paid by another because God sent his Son in the likeness of sinful flesh. He was the *divine* Son, and he was sinless in his *human* nature. Therefore he had both the divine worth and the human mortality to accomplish what no one else could—to offer an infinitely valuable sacrifice and die for the sins of his people (Heb. 2:14)."[31]

It appeared the missionaries had reached information overload, which is perfectly understandable when so many concepts of a difficult-to-understand doctrine are presented. I waited for a few seconds to let what I had said sink in, but I still needed to show how "mystery" played a role in their own faith.

"Elders, do you believe God the Father (*Elohim*) was once a human in another realm?" I asked, referring to the first part of the Lorenzo Snow couplet that we had discussed earlier (see chapter 4).

"Of course we do," Elder Michaels said.

"Can you explain that doctrine to me?"

He paused before answering, "We just don't know very much about this teaching."

"OK, fair enough," I said. "So you believe God the Father lived previously as a man in another world, but you can't really explain that in words? And yet you have no passages in your ancient scriptures to support your idea? You just believe it is true and accept it by faith?"

He nodded.

"I have biblical support to accept the Trinity as true even though I cannot fully comprehend the teaching," I said. "Accepting this teaching is not a wish-and-a-prayer jump in the dark; rather it's a leap in the light. I believe I have much more reason to accept the Trinity as a true concept in contrast to the LDS idea that God the Father once lived as a fleshly man on another world."

The missionaries did not accept the doctrine of the Trinity that day. However, they had been presented with the Christian concept about God's nature. Now they needed to do more research and consider the things that were said. They were free to deny the Trinity, but instead of creating their own false version of the Trinity, they needed to counter the five points emphasized in this chapter:

1. There is one eternal God.

2. The Father is God.

3. The Son is God.

4. The Spirit is God.

5. The three Persons are unique and are not each other.

I recommend that you memorize these five points—use the triangle illustration to help—and have no fear about discussing this (or any other) biblical doctrine. I think it can also be important to learn about church history, especially why the Council of Nicaea was held and what the bishops concluded.[32] Correcting the LDS conception of Christianity's view of God could be the cause for a revolution in any Mormon's worldview.[33]

DISCUSSION QUESTIONS

1. What is the problem with illustrations that attempt to explain the nuances of the Trinity?

2. Suppose someone suggests that the Trinity is not true because the word is not found in the Bible. Is this a good argument? How can this idea be countered?

3. James White said, "Knowledge does not save; but true worship does not exist without knowledge." What did he mean? Do you agree or disagree with this assessment? Why?

4. Someone may complain about the Trinity because the concept cannot be understood. How would you answer this objection?

5. Some people have suggested that the Trinity teaches that God was the Father in the Old Testament. He then became Jesus in the New Testament and today God is revealed through the Holy Spirit. What is the problem with this thinking?

RECOMMENDED RESOURCES

Check out mrm.org/trinity-index for a variety of articles and videos. These two books are also recommended:

E. Calvin Beisner, *God in Three Persons* (Eugene, OR: Wipf & Stock Publishers, 2004).

James R. White, *The Forgotten Trinity: Recovering the Heart of Christian Belief* (Minneapolis, MN: Bethany House, 2019).

CHAPTER 8

JUSTIFICATION

Forgiveness of Sins by Faith Alone

"And there is salvation in no one else, for there is no other name under heaven given among men by which we must be saved."

ACTS 4:12

CHAPTER PREVIEW

Christianity is all about the complete forgiveness of sins, which the Bible says is available only through faith alone in the work accomplished by Jesus on the cross. This is a different concept than having to perform certain works/duties for eternal life. A person's efforts are not enough to pay any portion of sin's debt. While adherents of other religions ask what must be done for the forgiveness of sins, the Christian asks, "What did God do for me?" And that makes all the difference in the world.

On November 9, 2019, I stood across the street from Lavell Edwards Stadium in Provo, Utah. It was a couple of hours before the LDS Church-owned Brigham Young University (BYU) Cougars were scheduled to play a football game against my oldest daughter's alma mater, Liberty University (Lynchburg, VA). I held up a copy of *The Miracle of Forgiveness*, a popular book written in 1969 by Spencer W. Kimball who later became the church's twelfth president. Ten additional copies were stacked neatly in a cardboard box nearby.

"Free copy of *The Miracle of Forgiveness,*" I called out to several dozen

BYU fans as they walked by me. My wife held a sign with a large picture of the book with "Free Copy" emblazoned across the top.

"This is a book every Latter-day Saint ought to read. Come get a free copy."

Since the fall of 2014, I have purchased more than 1300 copies of the book in local Utah thrift stores for a dollar or two each and highlighted several dozen pertinent quotations in each one. When asked why I give away the book, I explain how Kimball accurately interpreted unique LDS scriptural passages to describe the requirements necessary to go to the *celestial kingdom*. While some Mormons disagree with a deceased leader such as Kimball, it is impossible to ignore these references since their religion is supposed to be based on these scriptures.

Standing on public property while giving away books written by an LDS general authority is a tactic that has allowed me to publicly engage a Mormon audience. Many older Latter-day Saints already have a copy, so I may hand out only 12-15 of the books during any evangelistic session. Even if I don't give away many books, dozens of short

The author (in the center, wearing a baseball cap and talking to a Latter-day Saint couple) speaks to a couple outside the stadium where the BYU Cougars play football games. Photo by Terri Johnson.

conversations are initiated, especially with younger Mormons. The best part, though, is that I am rarely called an anti-Mormon, in stark contrast to the many times I have distributed Christian newspapers or tracts.[1]

As Kimball attested in his book, the gospel of Mormonism is contrary to what is taught in biblical Christianity.

THE MIRACLE OF FORGIVENESS AND MORMONISM'S IMPOSSIBLE GOSPEL

Because *The Miracle of Forgiveness* is not a part of Mormonism's scriptural canon, some Latter-day Saints quickly dismiss the book as "outdated," even though several million copies have been distributed. Local church leaders (known as bishops) were known for handing out copies to disobedient members as a reminder of the stringent requirements necessary to qualify for eternal life. The book has been lauded at several general conference sessions. For example, LDS Apostle Richard L. Evans called it a "wonderful work" in April 1970 while another apostle, Richard G. Scott, said it provided a "superb guide to forgiveness" in April 1995; five years later, Scott called the book "inspired."[2]

For many years, a copy has been prominently displayed on the second floor of the Church History Museum in Salt Lake City under Kimball's portrait. In 1998, the First Presidency produced a leatherbound version that was given away as a Christmas present to church employees.[3] A card accompanying the book states, "We are pleased to present to you this classic edition of President Spencer W. Kimball's book *The Miracle of Forgiveness*. President Kimball's enlightening teachings on the Atonement of Jesus Christ are a precious treasure for all who follow the Savior." In 2006, the church published the manual *Teachings of Presidents of the Church: Spencer W. Kimball*, which was studied by the church membership the following year. It cited *The Miracle of Forgiveness* 69 times, including 22 times in chapter 4 titled "The Miracle of Forgiveness."

Standing on that street corner across from the stadium, I spotted a young man—a sophomore at the LDS Church-owned school, I later found out—who was waiting for the crosswalk light to turn green.

"Free copy?" I said while holding out the book in his direction.

"I already read it. It's excellent," he replied confidently.

"Since you have read it, may I ask if you are successfully doing everything that President Kimball said you're supposed to do?"

He looked at me with a smile before replying, "Are you suggesting we have to be *perfect*?"

Before I had a chance to respond, the crosswalk light turned green and the crowd began making its way across the street. I watched as the young man motioned for his friends to go on, and said he would meet them inside the stadium.

As he approached me, I introduced myself and he told me his name was Marcus. I decided to answer his question about having "to be perfect" with a question of my own.

"Marcus, did you know President Kimball said it was *possible* to be perfect?" I turned to page 286 in the copy I was holding and showed him where Kimball wrote,

> In the context of the spirit of forgiveness, one good brother asked me, "Yes, that is what ought to be done, but how do you do it? Doesn't that take a superman?" "Yes," I said, "but we are commanded to be supermen. Said the Lord, 'Be ye therefore perfect even as your Father which is in heaven is perfect.' (Matt. 5:48.) We are gods in embryo, and the Lord demands perfection of us."[4]

This is not the only time Kimball said perfection was possible. I showed Marcus, on page 209, where this general authority claimed "to be perfect means to triumph over sin. This is a mandate from the Lord. He is just and wise and kind. He would never require anything from his children which was not for their benefit and which was not attainable. Perfection therefore is an achievable goal."

Marcus took his time thinking through what I said before he responded, "President Kimball did *not* say you have to be perfect in *this* lifetime, only in the next."

I turned to the next page where Kimball wrote, "As I have indicated previously, the time to do this is now, in mortality." I could have pointed out other quotes in the book. For instance, he cited Alma 34:32 in chapter 1—titled "This Life Is the Time"—which says, "For behold this life is the time for men to prepare to meet God." Commenting on that, Kimball wrote on page 10 "that *the time to act is now, in this mortal life*." On page 168, he said that "we should not wait for the life beyond but should abandon evil habits and weaknesses while in the flesh on the earth," adding on page 201 that "the time to do this is now, in mortality." On page 248, he stated, "*While in this probation* and *in this life* certainly means the period of our mortal lives." The evidence against Marcus's denial was strong.

In fact, Kimball said that those who get baptized in the LDS Church and regularly attend services but die without "perfect[ing] their lives" will receive no second chances in the hereafter. He wrote on pages 313-14:

> One cannot delay repentance until the next life, the spirit world, and there prepare properly for the day of judgment while the ordinance work is done for him vicariously on earth. It must be remembered that vicarious work for the dead is for those who could not do the work for themselves. Men and women who live in mortality and who have heard the gospel here have had their day, their seventy years to put their lives in harmony, to perform the ordinances, to repent and to perfect their lives.

I have found that Latter-day Saints are among the hardest-working and most sincere people of any religion. Still, Kimball wrote a chapter titled "Abandonment of Sin." I turned to page 163 where Kimball cited Doctrine and Covenants 58:43, which says, "By this ye may know if a man repenteth of his sins—behold, he will confess them and forsake them."

"How many sins does D&C 58:43 infer must be forsaken?" I asked Marcus.

"All of them."

"How often must they be forsaken?"

"All the time."

Faithful Mormons strive to become "exalted" and receive "eternal life" in the celestial kingdom, which is what Kimball referenced on page 207 when he said that "the gracious gift of salvation (is) offered on condition of obedience." This includes getting baptized in water by a man with priesthood authority from the LDS Church, getting married ("sealed") for eternity in an LDS temple, doing work on behalf of ancestors, and remaining faithful until the end of life. Kimball explained on page 325 that

> forgiveness is not granted merely for the asking. There must be works—many works—and an all-out, total surrender, with a great humility and a "broken heart and a contrite spirit." It depends upon you whether or not you are forgiven, and when. It could be weeks, it could be years, it could be centuries before that happy day when you have the positive assurance that the Lord has forgiven you. That depends on your humility, your sincerity, your works, your attitudes.

Throughout his book, Kimball used the unique LDS scriptures to show how a person can be cleansed of sin through obedience. In the second chapter, titled "No Unclean Thing Can Enter," he cited 1 Nephi 15:34 ("There cannot any unclean thing enter into the kingdom of God") as proof that all people are culpable unless they have been able to cleanse themselves. On page 201, he referenced D&C 1:31-32, which says, "For I the Lord cannot look upon sin with the least degree of allowance; Nevertheless, he that repents and does the commandments of the Lord shall be forgiven."

If keeping *all* the commandments is what qualifies a person for eternal life in Mormonism, then *all* sin needs to cease. Kimball went so far as to say on page 355 that a "transgressor must have reached a 'point of no return' to sin wherein there is not merely a renunciation but also a deep abhorrence of the sin—where the sin becomes most distasteful to him and where the desire or urge to sin is cleared out of his life."

"Marcus, have you reached a 'point of no return' where you always turn your back to sin?" I asked.

He shook his head.

"Where do Latter-day Saints with unforgiven sins go when they die?"

He said that he "hoped" it would be the celestial kingdom, even though he admitted that he was incapable of fulfilling Kimball's requirements.[5] Then he added, "I know I'm not perfect, but God knows that I'm *trying*. I really am doing my very *best*."

Realizing their dire straits, many Latter-day Saints have convinced themselves that they will be fine even when sin is not cleared out of their lives. Kimball disagreed. On page 164 under the subheading "Trying Is Not Sufficient," Kimball wrote, "Nor is repentance complete when one merely *tries* to abandon sin. To try with a weakness of attitude and effort is to assure failure in the face of Satan's strong counteracting efforts. What is needed is resolute action." On page 165, he added, "To 'try' is weak. To 'do the best I can' is not strong. We must always do *better* than we can. This is true in every walk of life." Kimball added the italics in those sentences to emphasize his points.

"Marcus, the bar set by your own scriptures as interpreted by your church's twelfth president is high. Would it be OK if I explained Christianity's view of salvation?" He agreed.

AN ESCAPE FROM HELL

As we discussed in chapter 4, hell is an eternal reality for those who do not have a relationship with God. I wanted to explain the situation to Marcus.

"Rebellion against God deserves punishment," I said. "There is no way a human can undo this dilemma through good works. According to Romans 3:23, every person is a sinner who has broken God's law. Isaiah 64:6 explains that a person's righteous deeds are like filthy rags in God's sight."

I stopped for a second to let these verses sink in.

"You deserve hell, Marcus, and so do I. That is bad news. But there is also good news! Right after Romans 3:23 says everyone has sinned, verse 24 adds that believers 'are justified by his grace as a gift, through the redemption that is in Christ Jesus.' Romans 6:23 has bad news too, saying 'the wages of sin is death.' Fortunately, there is a comma rather than a period after the word *death*. Verse 24 says that 'the free gift of God is eternal life in Christ Jesus our Lord.'"

It appeared Marcus was following what I was saying, so I continued.

"Marcus, Jesus explained in John 3:36 that 'whoever believes in the Son has eternal life; whoever does not obey the Son shall not see life, but the wrath of God remains on him.' Wrath is not for Christians, because Romans 5:9 describes how believers 'have now been justified by his blood, much more shall we be saved by him from the wrath of God.'"

The word *gospel* means "good news," for good reason. There is "victory through our Lord Jesus Christ" and hope can be claimed by the Christian (1 Corinthians 15:57). Though believers in Jesus have nothing to offer to purchase this gift, there is "now no condemnation for those who are in Christ Jesus" (Romans 8:1). I'll take this over the alternative any day of the week!

It is possible to misinterpret the Bible by not grasping the context. A person who reads Titus 3:5 where it says that believers are saved "not because of works done by us" could become easily confused by flipping over to Philippians 2:12 where it commands Christians to "work out your own salvation with fear and trembling." Which is it, by works or *not* by works? When it comes to "salvation," there are past, present, and future aspects that need to be considered. To put it simply, *justification* connotes past tense, while *sanctification* describes a present tense, and *glorification* is a future state completed in heaven.

Let's start with justification.

JUSTIFICATION: A GIFT FROM GOD

Justification is a legal term that declares a person "not guilty" in the sight of God based on the work accomplished by Jesus, not on the efforts of the individual (Galatians 2:15-16). As Romans 3:28 puts it, the believer "is *justified* by faith apart from works of the law." Let's consider some terms that fit under the justification umbrella.

Redemption: The deliverance from sin in its guilt, defilement, power, and liability through Christ's sacrifice (Ephesians 1:7; Colossians 1:13-14; Titus 2:14; Hebrews 9:11-12).

Grace: Unmerited favor from God provided to those who believe (John 1:16; Romans 3:24; 6:14; 11:6; Titus 2:11).

Mercy: The penalty for sin—eternal death—is eliminated by God with no liability to the believer (Lamentations 3:22-23; Luke 6:36; Hebrews 4:16; James 5:11; 1 Peter 1:3).

Imputation: Righteousness credited to a sinner's account not earned through good works (Romans 4:5; Philippians 3:9; 1 Peter 2:24).

Forgiveness: The complete putting away of sin and its consequences with no strings attached (Colossians 3:13; 1 John 1:9; 2:12).

According to Mormonism, an individual can qualify for the best this religion has to offer through successful effort, which includes getting baptized, attending church services, and qualifying for temple participation. While the Book of Mormon teaches in 2 Nephi 10:24 "that it is only in and through the grace of God that ye are saved," this is not a verse many Mormons cite. Instead, they are more likely to bring up 2 Nephi 25:23, which says "for we know that it is by grace that we are saved, after all we can do."

What does "after all we can do" even mean? Taken literally and as it has been historically interpreted by LDS general authorities, grace becomes efficacious only when someone has become fully obedient to the rules of Mormonism.[6] Thus, good works are required for any chance to obtain what is called "celestial glory" and life forever with one's family.

In recent years, some LDS leaders and scholars have toyed with the language to make the difference between Mormonism and biblical Christianity appear minimal. For instance, the late Stephen Robinson, who served as a professor at LDS Church-owned Brigham Young University, taught in 1990 that it is necessary for people to just *do their best and Jesus will do the rest*.[7] He described how he had "prodded" his wife when she was experiencing depression before she shared her true feelings with him:

> "You want to know what's wrong? I can't do it anymore. I
> can't get up at 5:30 in the morning to bake bread and help

my kids with their homework and do my own homework. I can't do my Relief Society stuff and get my genealogy done and sew and go to the PTA meetings and write the missionaries…"

She added, "I don't have the talent that Sister Morrell has. I can't do what Sister Childs does. I try not to yell at the kids, but I do. I'm not perfect, and I'm never going to be perfect. I'm afraid I'm not going to make it to the celestial kingdom."

I said, "Janet, I know you have a testimony…"

"Of course I do! That's what's so terrible. I know the gospel's true. I just can't do it. I've tried and I've tried, but I can't do it all, all of the time."[8]

While Robinson wanted to believe that his wife had misunderstood Mormonism's teaching, the fact is she comprehended the dilemma better than he did. Just read *The Miracle of Forgiveness*, among many other works written by LDS leadership. Contrary to this concept, nobody is worthy to earn God's favor and good works have *nothing* to do with justification. Consider what the apostle Paul wrote in Romans 4:1-5:

What then shall we say was gained by Abraham, our forefather according to the flesh? For if Abraham was justified by works, he has something to boast about, but not before God. For what does the Scripture say? "Abraham believed God, and it was counted to him as righteousness." Now to the one who works, his wages are not counted as a gift but as his due. And to the one who does not work but believes in him who justifies the ungodly, his faith is counted as righteousness.[9]

When Jesus was asked in John 6:28 what was required for salvation, He answered in verse 29, "This is the *work of God*, that you believe in him whom he has sent." God desires a relationship with those who approach Him with empty hands, as justification is a "work of God." Faith is the result of God's redeeming work and is not something that can be figured out. Wayne Grudem explains,

> If the *ultimate* determining factor in whether we will be saved or not is our own decision to accept Christ, then we shall be more inclined to think that we deserve some credit for the fact that we were saved; in distinction from other people who continue to reject Christ, we were wise enough in our judgment or good enough in our moral tendencies or perceptive enough in our spiritual capacities to decide to believe in Christ. But once we begin to think this way then we seriously diminish the glory that is to be given to God for our salvation.[10]

Imputation means the Christian is made righteous through the power of God. As 2 Corinthians 5:21 says, "For our sake he made him to be sin who knew no sin, so that in him we might become the righteousness of God." Speaking to Christians, Paul explained in Romans 5:8 that "God shows his love for us in that while we were still sinners, Christ died for us." Citing Isaiah 53:5, 1 Peter 2:24 declares that "by his wounds you have been healed."

Millard Erickson writes, "Thus, when looking at the believer, God the Father does not see him or her alone. He sees the believer together with Christ, and in the act of justification justifies both of them together. It is as if God says, 'They are righteous'…Justification, then, is a three-party, not a two-party matter."[11] It is as if "Jesus has taken us off death row and then has hung around our neck the Congressional Medal of Honor. We are received and welcomed as heroes, as if we had accomplished extraordinary deeds."[12]

There is a difference between a sinful attempt to accomplish the impossible and allowing God to do the work. As R.C. Sproul wrote,

> The good news of the gospel is that we don't have to wait until we become perfectly righteous *in ourselves* before God

will consider us and declare us righteous or accept us in His sight as justified people. God makes a provision for justification whereby people who are sinners, while they are still sinners, can be reconciled to Him and declared just in His sight…The basis or the ground of our justification, by which God declares us just, is not because He looks at us and sees our righteousness, but because He sees the righteousness of Christ.[13]

I decided to recite for Marcus two verses memorized by many Christians. Ephesians 2:8-9 states, "For by grace you have been saved through faith. And this is not your own doing; it is the gift of God, not a result of works, so that no one may boast."

"The apostle Paul insisted that there is nothing wrong with works," I said. "But when it comes to being made right with God and receiving undeserved mercy and forgiveness, no amount of works will suffice. A person can come into relationship with God only by grace through faith."[14]

I pointed out how Kimball had mocked this concept when he wrote, "One of the most fallacious doctrines originated by Satan and propounded by man is that man is saved alone by the grace of God; that belief in Jesus Christ alone is all that is needed for salvation."[15] When we use words such as faith or believe, it could be easily misunderstood as a wish and a prayer, such as, "You just gotta have *faith* the San Diego Padres will win the World Series," or "You can get an A in biology only if you *believe*."

Grudem believes the word *trust* is "closer to the biblical idea, since most people are familiar with trusting persons in everyday life. The more we come to know a person, and the more we see in that person a pattern of life that warrants trust, the more we find ourselves able to place trust in that person to do what he or she promises, or to act in ways that we can rely on."[16] As Keller states, "Religious people are rejecting Jesus as Savior, because all their religious works are efforts to merit God's favor. Their savior is their own achievements; Jesus may be an example or a helper, but He is not Savior."[17]

On the other hand, Christianity teaches that one's efforts are not capable to cleanse sin. Protestant Reformer Martin Luther made an excellent observation when he said, "For if I obtain grace by my own endeavors, what need have I of the grace of Christ for the receiving of my grace?"[18] As John MacArthur and Richard Mayhue write,

> There have only ever been two religions: the religion of human achievement, by which man works to contribute to his own righteousness, and the religion of divine accomplishment, whereby God accomplishes righteousness by the holy life and substitutionary death of the Son of God and then freely gives that righteousness as a gift through faith alone...Because Christians are justified by faith alone, their standing before God is not in any way related to personal merit. Good works and practical holiness are not the grounds for acceptance with God.[19]

Roger Olson describes the dichotomy between the "theology of glory" and the "theology of the cross":

> The theology of glory, then, is a human-centered theology that leads to an overestimation of natural human power and ability. The theology of the cross shows the true condition of humans as helpless sinners alienated from God in mind and heart and desperately in need of God's rescue mission, the cross of Christ. The theology of glory implies that humans can pull themselves up to God by their own bootstraps, so to speak, and leads to projects of self-salvation and theological speculation. The theology of the cross proclaims that humans are totally dependent and unable to figure out anything about God apart from God's own self-disclosure and leads to discipleship marked by suffering for God and others.[20]

I decided that a parable could help me explain to Marcus the incredible power of the gospel message.

A GRANDFATHER'S
BIRTHDAY PRESENT

A high school boy was celebrating his sixteenth birthday with family and friends in attendance. After opening most of his presents, his grandfather handed him a card. The boy ripped open the envelope and quickly read the words that were penned inside: "Dear Grandson, I love you so much. I have deposited ten into your bank account. Happy birthday."

The boy looked at his grandfather, and then smiled before he lifted a half-hearted thumbs-up. "Thanks, Grandpa," he said before grabbing the next present. The boy may have hidden his discouragement at what he considered to be a "cheap" gift, but probably not.

A few weeks later, this grandson was driving the family car when he happened to notice the gas gauge arrow pointing to "E." "Great, now what do I do?" he asked himself, knowing full well he was broke. Suddenly, he remembered the ten dollars his grandfather had deposited in his bank account, so he drove to the nearest branch, parked the car, and walked inside. Handing his debit card to a teller, the boy said, "Give me my ten dollars." She punched a few buttons on her register, opened her cash drawer, and handed him a crisp ten-dollar bill along with the receipt.

As the boy returned to his car, he glanced at the receipt and became agitated. He ran back into the bank and made a beeline for the teller, knocking into the older female customer she was helping and not apologizing.

"What a cruel joke!" he shouted while waving the receipt in the teller's face.

"Excuse me, just what *is* the matter?" she asked, obviously shocked at his behavior.

"Oh, like you don't know? You manipulated the receipt to read $9,999,990. How would you like it if I played that joke on you?"

She smiled and then began to quietly chuckle.

"Oh, I'd love it if you did this to me," she said. "You had ten million dollars before you took out your ten dollars, so this is what you have left over."

Suddenly, the boy's face became beet red as he dropped the receipt and it fluttered to the floor.

"You've got to be kidding me," he whispered.

Those in the bank lobby were mesmerized watching the spectacle. What a difference six extra zeros make! Even if this boy worked for 40 years, he would need to earn an average of $250,000 each year to make this much money over four decades. Few people make $5 million in wages during their lifetimes, let alone $10 million!

What this boy didn't know is that his grandfather had sold everything to gift him with this much money. The elderly man showed his love by sacrificing all he owned. For several weeks, the "ten" gift had meant nothing to the boy because he did not view the gift as having value. Now it all made sense. This was a gift with no strings attached, even if he didn't *deserve* it.

I told Marcus this illustrates the sacrifice made by Jesus on the cross and how it satisfied "the positive demands of the law by imputing Christ's righteousness to us...His perfect righteousness is thus the ground on which we stand before God."[21] Jesus said in John 15:13, "Greater love has no one than this, that someone lay down his life for his friends." In the next verse, He called believers "friends." First John 4:9-10 adds these words of hope: "In this the love of God was made manifest among us, that God sent his only Son into the world, so that we might live through him. In this is love, not that we have loved God but that he loved us and sent his Son to be the propitiation for our sins."

Propitiation refers to how justice is fully satisfied through the sacrifice of Jesus. Nineteenth-century pastor Charles Spurgeon—known as the Prince of Preachers—put it this way:

> When Christ redeemed his people, he did it thoroughly; he did not leave a single debt unpaid, nor yet one farthing for them to settle afterwards. God demanded of Christ the payment for the sins of all his people; Christ stood forward, and to the utmost farthing paid whatever his people owed. The sacrifice of Calvary was not a part payment; it was not a partial exoneration, it was a complete and perfect payment,

and it obtained a complete and perfect remittal of all the debts of all believers that have lived, do live, or shall live, to the end of time.[22]

Christians rejoice when the incredible concept of this gift is grasped as contrasted with the idea that obedience on the part of the individual is required. John Stott describes this misunderstanding:

> We insist on paying for what we have done. We cannot stand the humiliation of acknowledging our bankruptcy and allowing somebody else to pay for us. The notion that this somebody else should be God himself is just too much to take. We would rather perish than repent, rather lose ourselves than humble ourselves.[23]

Outside of Christianity, adherents of every other religion, including Mormonism, ask, "What must I do for eternal life?" On the other hand, Christians ask, "What did God do for me?" Jesus said in John 3:16, "For God so loved the world, that he gave his only Son, that whoever believes in him should not perish but have eternal life."

The story of the boy receiving ten million dollars seemed to resonate with Marcus, but it was obvious that he was not convinced.

"It sounds way too easy," he complained.

I replied that it was *not* too easy for Jesus, who unselfishly gave up everything to provide salvation to those trusting in Him. Second Corinthians 8:9 states, "For you know the grace of our Lord Jesus Christ, that though he was rich, yet for your sake he became poor, so that you by his poverty might become rich." The cost was great, but the reward for His children is priceless.

BECOMING A CHILD OF GOD

In Christianity, it is possible to become righteous only through faith. Jesus said in John 3:3 that "unless one is born again he cannot see the kingdom of God." First Peter 1:23 states that the believer is born "not of perishable seed but of imperishable." A person who is *born again* cares "for the things of God and desires to seek God. Now there is an affection for God that was not there before."[24]

In a spiritual way, the believer becomes "a new creation," as the apostle Paul described the experience in 2 Corinthians 5:17. He wrote, "The old has passed away; behold, the new has come," adding in verse 18 that this experience is provided "from God...through Christ" who reconciles believers to Himself while not counting "their trespasses [sins] against them" (v. 19). Where do these sins go? Psalm 103:12 explains "as far as the east is from the west, so far does he remove our transgressions from us." As nineteenth-century theologian Charles Hodge explained, "We are not justified because we are holy; but being justified, we are rendered holy."[25]

Mormonism teaches that humans are literal children of God who once existed as spirits in a previous life called the *preexistence*. Christianity disagrees by teaching that a person becomes a *child of God* by faith through *adoption,* as supported by these verses:

- John 1:12-13: "But to all who did receive him, who believed in his name, he gave the right to become children of God, who were born, not of blood nor of the will of the flesh nor of the will of man, but of God."

- Romans 8:14-17: "For all who are led by the Spirit of God are sons of God. For you did not receive the spirit of slavery to fall back into fear, but you have received the Spirit of adoption as sons, by whom we cry, 'Abba! Father!' The Spirit himself bears witness with our spirit that we are children of God, and if children, then heirs—heirs of God and fellow heirs with Christ, provided we suffer with him in order that we may also be glorified with him."

- Galatians 3:26-29: "For in Christ Jesus you are all sons of God, through faith. For as many of you as were baptized into Christ have put on Christ. There is neither Jew nor Greek, there is neither slave nor free, there is no male and female, for you are all one in Christ Jesus. And if you are Christ's, then you are Abraham's offspring, heirs according to promise."

- Galatians 4:6: "And because you are sons, God has sent the Spirit of his Son into our hearts, crying, 'Abba! Father!'"

- 1 John 3:1-2: "See what kind of love the Father has given to us, that we should be called children of God; and so we are. The reason why the world does not know us is that it did not know him. Beloved, we are God's children now, and what we will be has not yet appeared; but we know that when he appears we shall be like him, because we shall see him as he is."

Jesus made the following offer in Matthew 11:28-30: "Come to me, all who labor and are heavy laden, and I will give you rest. Take my yoke upon you, and learn from me, for I am gentle and lowly in heart, and you will find rest for your souls. For my yoke is easy, and my burden is light." The gift comes through acceptance by the individual, not through coercion or force.

Some people will refuse the gift and assume that they are undeserving of this type of love. Yet Ephesians 1:3-14 explains how a person can be adopted as a child of God. Contrast those who are called "children of wrath" (Ephesians 2:3) and "sons of disobedience" (Ephesians 2:2; 5:6)!

While Mormonism has priesthood offices for its male members, Christianity offers a "royal priesthood" (1 Peter 2:9) to all believers, regardless of their age, sex, or status. This doctrine, called "the priesthood of the believer," played a major role in the Protestant Reformation five centuries ago.

AN INVITATION TO THE GOSPEL

It must *never* be thought that additional evidence will cause a person to turn to Christ. While I like to provide plenty of support for my beliefs, the work of the Holy Spirit is the primary factor. As William Lane Craig explains, "Therefore, when a person refuses to come to

Christ it is never just because of lack of evidence or because of intellectual difficulties: at root, he refuses to come because he willingly ignores and rejects the drawing of God's Spirit on his heart. No one in the final analysis really fails to become a Christian because of lack of arguments; he fails to become a Christian because he loves darkness rather than light and wants nothing to do with God."[26]

Sometimes, though, an opportunity to receive Jesus as Savior needs to be given.

"Marcus, there are many like the teenage boy from my story who have no idea the value of the gift offered by Jesus, whom the Bible calls 'the author and the finisher of our faith.' I encourage you to stop relying on your own works and begin trusting in what Jesus has done. He offers something much more valuable than ten million dollars, as He can cleanse you from your sins and provide you with eternal life. Is that something you would like to consider?"

Marcus smiled but shook his head no. Thanking me, he said that he needed to head to the stadium and meet his friends. Understanding that I am responsible only for "sales" and that God is in charge of "production," I knew I had done everything possible to present the gospel clearly. Converting a person is beyond our pay grade. I said a quick prayer for Marcus and thanked God for the productive conversation as he walked away. Even with the rejection, Marcus had been presented with the Christian gospel.

Earlier I mentioned Philippians 2:12 and how the Christian is to "work out your own salvation with fear and trembling." How does that work? In the next chapter, we'll discuss the role of sanctification in the Christian's life. After all, if Christians are saved by grace, then what motive could there be to do good works?

DISCUSSION QUESTIONS

1. Someone might argue that *The Miracle of Forgiveness* is not scripture, so this book should not be considered authoritative. How could this argument be countered? Do you personally think using an LDS book to evangelize Mormons is a good or bad idea? Explain.

2. Spencer W. Kimball wrote, "We are gods in embryo, and the Lord demands perfection of us." Does the Bible agree with this assessment?

3. Christianity teaches that justification is a gift of God. For some like Marcus, receiving this gift sounds too easy. Why does this concept seem to be so difficult for those outside of Christianity to accept?

4. What is the "bad news" of the gospel? Should this bad news ever be introduced into a conversation when presenting the gospel?

5. How is the biblical concept of becoming a child of God different from what is taught in Mormonism? Have you become a child of God? If you have, describe your life with Jesus. If you haven't made that decision, what holds you back?

RECOMMENDED RESOURCES

Entry-Level Resource

John Ankerberg and John Weldon, *How to Know You're Going to Heaven* (Eugene, OR: Harvest House Publishers, 2014).

Middle-Level Resource

John Piper, *God Is the Gospel: Meditations on God's Love as the Gift of Himself* (Wheaton, IL: Crossway Books, 2005).

Advanced Resource

James R. White, *The God Who Justifies: The Doctrine of Justification* (Minneapolis, MN: Bethany House Publishers, 2001).

CHAPTER 9

SANCTIFICATION

A Life Marked by Good Works

"Keep your conduct among the Gentiles honorable, so that when they speak against you as evildoers, they may see your good deeds and glorify God on the day of visitation."

1 PETER 2:12

CHAPTER PREVIEW

Sanctification is the continual process in a believer's life to die to sin and live in righteousness. The Holy Spirit plays an important role in both justification and sanctification. For one, a saved individual has been baptized in the Spirit through saving faith. Those who have the Holy Spirit are commanded to be "filled with the Spirit" and display the "fruit of the Spirit." The Holy Spirit also provides spiritual gifts so Christians can be equipped to serve. The two ordinances practiced by Christians are baptism in water and participating in communion with the local church body.

Faith without works is dead," Joan, a middle-aged woman, told me on a warm summer afternoon. "Why do Christians ignore the importance of doing good works?"

She approached me on the sidewalk outside the Ogden LDS temple during an open house event in August 2014. Whenever the LDS Church remodels an existing temple or builds a new structure, the public is invited (normally for a time period between two to five weeks) to see the interior of the building before it is closed to everyone except those Latter-day Saints who have valid "temple recommend" cards.

Joan had memorized the gist of James 2:20 and 26, which in the KJV states, "But wilt thou know, O vain man, that *faith without works is dead*?...For as the body without the spirit is dead, so *faith without works is dead* also." Her voice remained determined and sure.

"You're quoting from the second chapter of the book of James," I said. "And I must say that I am in complete agreement with James."

She seemed surprised that I not only knew the biblical reference but also agreed with what James wrote. But I needed to provide the complete context.

"James said that a true faith will be followed by good works," I said. "God has proclaimed that His followers must be holy because He is holy."[1] I then cited Ephesians 2:8-9, which we briefly discussed in the previous chapter of this book. It says that it is by grace that someone is saved through faith and not by works. Instead of stopping with verse 9, I continued with verse 10: "For we are his workmanship, created in Christ Jesus for good works, which God prepared beforehand, that we should walk in them."

SALVATION LIVED OUT
IN THE BELIEVER'S LIFE

As discussed in the previous chapter, justification takes place, once and for all, through faith. The righteousness of God is imputed to the believer through the work done by Jesus on the cross. Romans 5:15 says, "But the free gift is not like the trespass. For if many died through one man's trespass, much more have the grace of God and the free gift by the grace of that one man Jesus Christ abounded for many." Verse 18 adds that this "one act of righteousness leads to justification." The believer who is forgiven of all sins—past, present, and future—receives eternal life.

If forgiveness is a done deal, then someone like Joan may assume that good works are not important to the Christian. Good works are *not* optional in the life of the Christian in the process known as *sanctification*, as Christians have not been called to sin with impunity. As Colossians 3:2-3 commands, "Set your minds on things that are above, not on things that are on earth. For you have died, and your life is hidden with Christ in God." First Peter 2:24 states that Jesus sacrificed Himself on the cross so "that we might die to sin and live to righteousness."

The idea of good works as the Christian's response to God makes sense when the value of the atonement is understood. When it is, Timothy Keller writes that

> we now doubly owe it to Him to use it to please and imitate Him. We owe it to Him as our Creator, since He designed and owns us, and so He has both the wisdom to know how we are to live and the right to demand that we live that way. On the other hand, we now also owe it to Him as our Redeemer, since we gratefully want to please the one who saved us at such immeasurable cost.[2]

Such a mindset requires self-evaluation. R.C. Sproul explains:

> We need to regularly audit our value systems to see whether our values line up with the values of God. We're called to have the mind of Christ. That means we are to love what Jesus loves and to hate what Jesus hates. We pursue what Jesus pursues and flee from what Jesus flees from. That's what the life of the Christian is all about.[3]

While Christians have been set apart to be holy, this should not be misunderstood to mean that it is possible to become perfectly obedient in this life. While they still struggle with sin, Christians are called to become the "workmanship" of Christ. It is a false notion, J.I. Packer wrote, that "once we become Christians, God's power in us will immediately cancel our defects of character and make our whole lives plain sailing. This however is so unbiblical as to be positively dishonest."[4]

When considering the second chapter of Ephesians, it is important to note that Paul was addressing Christians who mistakenly thought that good works were necessary to gain God's favor. The apostle then had to emphasize that salvation was "not by works." James, on the other hand, was speaking to a group of believers who thought that good works were not required because of God's grace. This assumption is also wrong, James said, because good works in a believer's life ought to be evident to neutral observers. German pastor Dietrich Bonhoeffer compared Paul and James:

> St James is not concerned to deny justification by faith alone; rather he is urging the believer not to rest content on the laurels of faith, but to get on with the work of obedience. This is his way of leading him to genuine humility. Both apostles want Christians to have a genuine and complete dependence on grace, rather than on their own achievements.[5]

Philippians 2:12 says, "Therefore, my beloved, as you have always obeyed, so now, not only as in my presence but much more in my absence, *work out* your own salvation with fear and trembling." Notice how Paul said to "work *out* your own salvation," not "work *for*." Paul went on to say that "it is God who works in you, both to will and to work for his good pleasure." It is God who works in the believer's life to do good works. Through the power of the Holy Spirit, then, good works are accomplished in the life of the believer.

THE ROLE OF THE HOLY SPIRIT IN SALVATION

To understand the importance of the role of the Holy Spirit in salvation, several terms need to be understood. The first is *baptism of the spirit*. In the four Gospel accounts (Matthew 3:11; Mark 1:8; Luke 3:16; John 1:33), John the Baptist contrasted his baptism with the baptism of the Spirit that was originally predicted in Joel 2:28-32 and predicted again by Jesus in Acts 1:4-5. The Jews who comprised the early church received the full power of the Holy Spirit at Pentecost in Acts 2:1-13 while Gentile believers received this outpouring in Acts 10:44-45.

The Holy Spirit is not merely a force nor an impersonal being. Rather, He was sent by Jesus as promised in John 14:16-17: "And I will ask the Father, and he will give you another Helper, to be with you forever, even the Spirit of truth, whom the world cannot receive, because it neither sees him nor knows him. You know him, for he dwells with you and will be in you."

As Jesus promised in John 16:13, "When the Spirit of truth comes, he will guide you into all the truth, for he will not speak on his own authority, but whatever he hears he will speak, and he will declare to you the things that are to come." In fact, nobody can accept or reject Jesus as Lord "except in the Holy Spirit" (1 Corinthians 12:3). First Corinthians 2:9-10 says, "'What no eye has seen, nor ear heard, nor the heart of man imagined, what God has prepared for those who love him'—these things God has revealed to us through the Spirit." Verse 12 adds, "Now we have received not the spirit of the world, but the Spirit who is from God, that we might understand the things freely given us by God."

This indwelling happens when a person becomes a believer, as explained by Packer:

> God means all Christians as such to enjoy the full inward blessing of Pentecost (not the outward trimmings necessarily, but the communion of heart with Christ and all that flows from it) right from the moment of their conversion... for folk like you and me, who became Christians nearly two thousand years after Pentecost, the revealed program is that fullest enjoyment of the Spirit's new covenant ministry should be ours from the word "go." This is already clear in the New Testament, where Paul explains Spirit baptism as something that happened to the Corinthians—and, by parity of reasoning, happens to all other post-Pentecostal converts—at conversion.[6]

Paul told the Corinthian believers that the Holy Spirit came into their lives despite their dissension (1 Corinthians 1:10), carnality (3:1-3), disunity (6:1-8), and drunkenness at communion (11:21), among many other moral failures. In other words, they did not qualify for salvation based on their good works. Yet, at conversion, the Christian receives a full dose of the Holy Spirit who, as 2 Corinthians 5:5 says, is the "guarantee" for forgiveness of sins (Galatians 3:1-5; 4:6). Romans 5:5 states, "God's love has been poured into our hearts through the Holy Spirit who has been given to us." According to biblical teaching, anyone who does not possess the authentic Spirit of God is not a saved individual and should not be considered a Christian.

Citing Romans 8:3-4 and its reference to how "the righteous requirement of the law might be fulfilled in us...according to the Spirit," John Piper writes that more than just a future promise of heaven was accomplished in justification: "Christ accomplished *for* us the condemnation that the law demands *so that* he might accomplish *in* us the sanctification that the law commands...When God put Christ in our condemned place, he did this not only to secure heaven, but to secure holiness. Or even more precisely, not only to secure our life in paradise, but also to secure our love for people."[7] In other words, those good works performed by Christians are possible *only* through the work of the Spirit. These works are impossible without the power of the Holy Spirit.[8]

A second biblical term is the *filling of the Spirit*, which is referenced in Ephesians 5:18. The original Greek words literally mean "be being filled with the Spirit." In Acts 4, Peter was "filled with the Holy Spirit" when he spoke to the Jewish leaders after he and John were arrested (v. 8). When they were released, the two reported to the other believers what had happened (v. 23). Verse 31 says, "They were all filled with the Holy Spirit" as they worshiped God. Referring to the believers in whom Christ "dwell[s] in your hearts through faith," Paul asked God in Ephesians 3:18-19 to give them strength to comprehend "what is the breadth and length and height and depth, and to know the love of Christ that surpasses knowledge, that you may be filled with all the fullness of God."

Unlike the baptism of the Spirit, the filling of the Holy Spirit is a continuous pursuit. Not being filled with the Spirit does not mean that the believer has lost salvation. As Christians live their lives, they must be constantly refilled like a car that needs gasoline or a human who requires food. Just because a person ate dinner yesterday or filled the gas tank last week does not mean these don't have to be repeated. Like a cell phone that hasn't been charged for three days, so too is the Christian who is not connected to the spiritual source. When filled with God's Spirit, the Christian is empowered to do amazing things. Wayne Grudem writes:

> Someone might object that a person who is already "full" of the Holy Spirit cannot become more full—if a glass is full of water no more water can be put into it. But a water glass is a poor analogy for us as real people, for God is able to cause us to grow and to be able to contain much more of the Holy Spirit's fullness and power. A better analogy might be a balloon, which can be "full" of air even though it has very little air in it. When more air is blown in, the balloon expands and in a sense it is "more full." So it is with us: we can be filled with the Holy Spirit and at the same time be able to receive much more of the Holy Spirit as well. It was only Jesus himself to whom the Father gave the Spirit without measure (John 3:34).[9]

Third, the Christian is commissioned to display the *fruit of the Spirit*. An authentic conversion is experienced through the display of good rather than bad fruit. While speaking of false prophets in Matthew 7:16-20, Jesus explained the difference:

> "You will recognize them by their fruits. Are grapes gathered from thornbushes, or figs from thistles? So, every healthy tree bears good fruit, but the diseased tree bears bad fruit. A healthy tree cannot bear bad fruit, nor can a diseased tree bear good fruit. Every tree that does not bear good fruit is cut down and thrown into the fire. Thus you will recognize them by their fruits."

He also said in John 15:7-8, "If you abide in me, and my words abide in you, ask whatever you wish, and it will be done for you. By this my Father is glorified, that you bear much fruit and so prove to be my disciples."

Meanwhile, Romans 7:4-5 says, "Likewise, my brothers, you also have died to the law through the body of Christ, so that you may belong to another, to him who has been raised from the dead, in order that we may bear fruit for God. For while we were living in the flesh, our sinful passions, aroused by the law, were at work in our members to bear fruit for death."

According to Galatians 5:16-17, sinful passions are contrary to the desires of the Spirit. Paul admonished believers to "walk by the Spirit, and you will not gratify the desires of the flesh. For the desires of the flesh are against the Spirit, and the desires of the Spirit are against the flesh, for these are opposed to each other, to keep you from doing the things you want to do." He then provided a list of the "works of the flesh" in verses 19-21, including "sexual immorality, impurity, sensuality, idolatry, sorcery, enmity, strife, jealousy, fits of anger, rivalries, dissensions, divisions, envy, drunkenness, orgies, and things like these. I warn you, as I warned you before, that those who do such things will not inherit the kingdom of God." Verse 24 says, "And those who belong to Christ Jesus have crucified the flesh with its passions and desires." Another list of sins that needs to be eliminated can be found in Colossians 3:5-9.

As a replacement for these sinful desires, the fruit of the Spirit is given: "love, joy, peace, patience, kindness, goodness, faithfulness, gentleness, self-control" (Galatians 5:22-23). Other admonitions are given in the following verses:

- Ephesians 4:24: Christians are "to put on the new self."

- Colossians 3:12-16 commands "compassionate hearts, kindness, humility, meekness, and patience, bearing with one another...forgiving each other...put on love...let the peace of Christ rule in your hearts...And be thankful... Let the word of Christ dwell in you richly, teaching and admonishing one another in all wisdom, singing psalms and hymns and spiritual songs, with thankfulness in your hearts to God."

- Titus 3:14: "And let our people learn to devote themselves to good works, so as to help cases of urgent need, and not be unfruitful."

- Philippians 4:8: "Finally, brothers, whatever is true, whatever is honorable, whatever is just, whatever is pure, whatever is lovely, whatever is commendable, if there is any excellence, if there is anything worthy of praise, think about these things."

- 1 Timothy 6:11b: "Pursue righteousness, godliness, faith, love, steadfastness, gentleness."

In other words, action on the part of each individual believer is crucial. As J.I. Packer put it, "The Christian's motto should not be 'Let go and let God' but 'Trust God and get going!'"[10]

Finally, there are *gifts of the Spirit*, which are provided by God to edify others. These include service, teaching, giving, and wisdom, among others (Romans 12:6-8; 1 Corinthians 12:4-11; Ephesians 4:11; 1 Peter 4:10-11). Nobody possesses every available gift, but each Christian has at least one as provided by God (1 Corinthians 12:11). While there is an in-house church debate about the validity of the miraculous gifts (including tongues, healing, and prophecy) for today, there is no disputing that the Holy Spirit remains active in the church.

THE $10 MILLION GIFT: PART 2

Latter-day Saints usually have a difficult time understanding the evangelical Christian position on faith and the role of good works. As Joan and I stood on the public sidewalk outside the Ogden LDS temple, I decided to ask her if I could present the story of the loving grandfather's ten-million-dollar gift to his grandson as given in the previous chapter. After the incident the grandson had with the bank teller, I asked Joan if she could predict what his reaction would be once he learned he had ten million in his bank account.

"I'm sure he would be ecstatic," she said.

"Do you think the boy will go over to the grandfather's house, spray paint graffiti on the garage door, poison the grass in the front yard, and kick the man's dog?" I asked.

Joan looked at me as if I had lost my marbles.

"That's ridiculous," she said. "Why would he do that? Somebody who has received a gift that large would not purposely go out of his way to be so mean-spirited."

"I agree," I replied. "At the very least, I bet the boy went home and wrote a thank-you card."

She looked at me and shook her head. "No, this gift deserves much more of a response. I bet he might drive straight to the grandfather's house and give him a big hug."

"OK, then suppose after that big hug, the boy asked his grandfather if there was anything he needed. Looking around, the grandfather peeked through the kitchen window and pointed to the yard that needed to be mowed. He told the grandson that the lawn service had to be canceled because he had given the bulk of his estate to the boy and could no longer afford the extra expense.

"Any rational person would jump at this opportunity to help a benefactor as generous as this grandfather," I continued. "So that boy decided to dust off the lawnmower and get to work. His effort was satisfying, so much so that he decided to visit his grandfather's house every week for the next year, taking care of the yard work most of the year, raking leaves in the fall and shoveling the driveway snow in the winter." I paused, then asked, "What if, after the year was up, that same boy went to his grandfather and said, 'OK, I'm paid up'?"

"Even if the boy came over every week for a year, that would *not* be enough to pay back ten million dollars," Joan said.

She was right. There was no way this boy could have worked hard enough to pay back the gift. In the same way, a Christian can never repay the salvation provided by God. The story seemed to make sense to Joan, but she still was a little confused.

"By what you're saying, you make it appear that you don't think good works matter," she said.

I certainly did not want her to misunderstand. Nothing can be done to earn the forgiveness of sins, yet good works are commanded in the role of sanctification. As the prophet Samuel told Saul in 1 Samuel 15:22:

> "Has the LORD as great delight in burnt offerings
>   and sacrifices,
>   as in obeying the voice of the LORD?
> Behold, to obey is better than sacrifice,
>   and to listen than the fat of rams."[11]

Psalm 119 is the longest chapter in the Bible with a total of 176 verses. It contains eight verses for each of the twenty-two letters of the Hebrew alphabet. Each verse uses terms such as *laws*, *statutes*, *ways*, *precepts*, and *decrees* to emphasize the importance of keeping God's commandments.[12]

By misunderstanding the proper role of works in the life of the Christian, though, many Latter-day Saints like Joan assume that evangelical Christians believe they are free to be as bad as they want to be. After all, they wonder, what incentive would there be for a person guaranteed salvation to stop sinning? Dietrich Bonhoeffer coined the term "cheap grace" to refer to "the preaching of forgiveness without requiring repentance, baptism without church discipline, Communion without confession, absolution without personal confession. Cheap grace is grace without discipleship, grace without the cross, grace without Jesus Christ, living and incarnate."[13] He then went on to explain "costly grace":

> Such grace is *costly* because it calls us to follow, and it is
> *grace* because it calls us to follow *Jesus Christ*. It is costly
> because it costs a man his life, and it is grace because it gives
> a man the only true life. It is costly because it condemns sin,
> and grace because it justifies the sinner. Above all, it is *costly*
> because it cost God the life of his Son: "ye were bought at

a price," and what has cost God much cannot be cheap for us. Above all, it is *grace* because God did not reckon his Son too dear a price to pay for our life, but delivered him up for us. Costly grace is the Incarnation of God.[14]

Cheap grace does not grasp the significance of the cross, which Bonhoeffer said has "been the ruin of more Christians than any commandment of works."[15] He added, "Obedience remains separated from faith. From the point of view of justification it is necessary thus to separate them, but we must never lose sight of their essential unity. For faith is only real when there is obedience, never without it, and faith only becomes faith in the act of obedience."[16]

The idea that Christians believe they can be as bad as they want to be is not a biblical concept; rather, God's Word is replete with commands to flee sin. Romans 6:1-2 makes this clear: "What shall we say then? Are we to continue in sin that grace may abound? By no means! How can we who died to sin still live in it?" Verse 15 adds, "What then? Are we to sin because we are not under law but under grace? By no means!" For the true believer, sin is no longer considered the master. Other verses from this chapter in Romans confirm this idea:

- 6:6-7: "We know that our old self was crucified with him in order that the body of sin might be brought to nothing, so that we would no longer be enslaved to sin. For one who has died has been set free from sin."

- 6:11-14: "So you also must consider yourselves dead to sin and alive to God in Christ Jesus. Let not sin therefore reign in your mortal body, to make you obey its passions. Do not present your members to sin as instruments for unrighteousness, but present yourselves to God as those who have been brought from death to life, and your members to God as instruments for righteousness. For sin will have no dominion over you, since you are not under law but under grace."

- 6:19: "For just as you once presented your members as slaves to impurity and to lawlessness leading to more lawlessness, so now present your members as slaves to righteousness leading to sanctification."

Wayne Grudem provides a good summary for Romans 6 when he writes, "This initial break with sin, then, involves a reorientation of our desires so that we no longer have a dominant love for sin in our lives. Paul knows that his readers were formerly slaves to sin (as all unbelievers are), but he says that they are enslaved no longer."[17] While Christians *will* struggle with having the right attitude and doing the right things, this does not mean they are supposed to remain content giving in to their fleshly desires. John Piper plainly states, "No one should say, 'I am justified by faith; therefore, I do not need to obey God's commands.' That attitude is a sign that a person's heart has not been penetrated by the true nature of justifying faith."[18] As J.C. Ryle, a nineteenth-century bishop of Liverpool, England, put it, "If you and sin are friends, you and God are not yet reconciled."[19]

Paul teaches in Romans 7:15-20 that becoming a Christian is not a magical formula that will eliminate the sinful nature:

> For I do not understand my own actions. For I do not do what I want, but I do the very thing I hate. Now if I do what I do not want, I agree with the law, that it is good. So now it is no longer I who do it, but sin that dwells within me. For I know that nothing good dwells in me, that is, in my flesh. For I have the desire to do what is right, but not the ability to carry it out. For I do not do the good I want, but the evil I do not want is what I keep on doing. Now if I do what I do not want, it is no longer I who do it, but sin that dwells within me.

In verse 24, Paul added, "Who will deliver me from this body of death?" Many faithful Latter-day Saints strive to do the right things but are disappointed when their efforts continually fall short. Spencer

W. Kimball even said that "it is within his power to lift himself by his very bootstraps from the plane on which he finds himself to the plane on which he should be. It may be a long, hard lift with many obstacles, but it is a real possibility."[20] Tenth Mormon president Joseph Fielding Smith taught,

> All that we can do for ourselves we are required to do. We must do our own repenting; we are required to obey every commandment and live by every word that proceeds from the mouth of God. If we will do this, then we are freed from the consequences of our own sins. The plan of salvation is based on this foundation. No man can be saved without complying with these laws.[21]

The answer of these two general authorities is much different than what Paul said in Romans 7:25 to explain how the Christian is delivered from death "through Jesus Christ our Lord!" Then, in Romans 8:1-2, Paul promises, "There is therefore now no condemnation for those who are in Christ Jesus. For the law of the Spirit of life has set you free in Christ Jesus from the law of sin and death." Living the way God intends takes effort as the believer is empowered by God. As Hebrews 13:20-21 says, God will "equip you with everything good that you may do his will, working in us that which is pleasing in his sight." This comfort is provided so Christians can encourage others (2 Corinthians 1:3-4).

Still, there will be much opposition to the Christian's pursuit of holiness in both the physical and spiritual realms. According to Ephesians 6:11-12, Christians have been provided "the whole armor of God, that you may be able to stand against the schemes of the devil." This armor includes the belt of truth (v. 14a), the breastplate of righteousness (v. 14b), shoes with the gospel of peace (v. 15), the shield of faith to "extinguish all the flaming darts of the evil one" (v. 16), the helmet of salvation (v. 17), and "the sword of the Spirit, which is the word of God." Finally, there is the ability to pray "at all times in the Spirit" (v. 18).

Romans 12:1 directs Christians "to present [their] bodies as a living sacrifice, holy and acceptable to God." Animal sacrifices were intended to be killed, just as the Christian has been called to be "dead to sin," as cited above in Romans 6:11-14. Believers are told not to "be conformed to this world, but be transformed by the renewal of your mind, that by testing you may discern what is the will of God, what is good and acceptable and perfect" (Romans 12:2). This is because Christians should consider themselves as "sojourners and exiles" (1 Peter 2:11).

Romans 13:14 is a straightforward command for how the Christian is supposed to live: "But put on the Lord Jesus Christ, and make no provision for the flesh, to gratify its desires." Until a person decides to not conform to the ways of this world, contentment will never be found. The Bible makes it clear that following the will of God rather than going after fleshly desires is the key to victorious living.

REPENTANCE, BAPTISM, AND THE LORD'S SUPPER

At this point, Joan decided to bring up Acts 2:38, which says, "And Peter said to them, 'Repent and be baptized every one of you in the name of Jesus Christ *for* the forgiveness of your sins, and you will receive the gift of the Holy Spirit.'"

"Doesn't this show that baptism is a requirement for salvation?" she asked.

Acts 2:38 needs to be considered in context. First, *repentance* is feeling sorrow for sin and repudiating it, with a determination to obey. Second Corinthians 7:10 states, "For godly grief produces a repentance that leads to salvation without regret, whereas worldly grief produces death." When a person believes, repentance of sins is necessary, as described by J.I. Packer:

> The New Testament word for repentance means changing one's mind so that one's views, values, goals, and ways are changed and one's whole life is lived differently. The change is radical, both inwardly and outwardly; mind and judgment, will and affections, behavior and lifestyle, motives and purposes, are all involved. Repenting means starting a new life.[22]

Grudem writes that

> genuine repentance will result in a changed life. In fact, a
> truly repentant person will begin at once to live a changed
> life, and we can call that changed life the fruit of repen-
> tance. But we should never attempt to require that there be
> a period of time in which a person actually lives a changed
> life before we give assurance of forgiveness. Repentance is
> something that occurs in the heart and involves the whole
> person in a decision to turn from sin…When we turn to
> Christ *for* salvation from our sins, we are simultaneously
> turning *away* from the sins that we are asking Christ to save
> us from. If that were not true our turning to Christ for sal-
> vation from sin could hardly be a genuine turning to him
> or trusting in him.[23]

Those who believe that baptism is a requirement for salvation are
called "baptismal regenerationalists." Joan brought up Acts 2:38 in
support of this view. In response, some Greek scholars—including
Julius Mantey and A.T. Robertson—say the word *for* (Greek *eis*, pro-
nounced "ace") can mean "because of."[24] A similar usage is found in
Matthew 12:41. It says, "The men of Nineveh will rise up at the judgment with this generation and condemn it, *for* they repented at the
preaching of Jonah, and behold, something greater than Jonah is here."
Did the Ninevites repent *in order to get* the preaching of Jonah? Or did
they repent *because of* the preaching?

In discussing Acts 2:38, New Testament scholar Daniel Wallace
takes a slightly different approach by referencing Acts 10:44-46. This
passage states how "the gift of the Holy Spirit was poured out even
on the Gentiles," allowing them to speak using the gift of tongues.
When Peter observed this phenomenon, he commanded that the Gentiles get baptized (v. 48), even though they already had the gift of the
Holy Spirit. Water baptism came *after* this event, not *before*. H. Wayne
House writes, "The incident at Cornelius's house poses serious problems for baptismal regeneration."[25] Later, in defending his actions to
the church in Jerusalem, Peter adds, "If then God gave the same gift to

[Gentiles] as he gave to us when we believed in the Lord Jesus Christ, who was I that I could stand in God's way?" (Acts 11:17).

Thus, it was through the Christians' belief, not baptism, that the Holy Spirit entered the believers' lives. First Corinthians 12:13 says, "For in one Spirit we were all baptized into one body—Jews or Greeks, slaves or free—and all were made to drink of one Spirit." The baptism referred to here is the baptism of the Spirit, not water baptism, as described by Gordon Fee:

> Because of the verb "baptize," it is often assumed that Paul is referring to the sacrament of water baptism, and it is then often argued further that this text supports the close tie of the reception of the Spirit with baptism itself. But that assumes more than is actually said. While it is true that early on this verb became the technical term for the Christian initiatory rite, one may not thereby assume that *Paul* intended its technical sense here...one is hard pressed to find an equation between baptism and the reception of the Spirit in Paul's letters. Both are assumed to be at the beginning of Christian experience, to be sure, but the two are not specifically tied together in such a way that the Spirit is received at baptism.[26]

One other point concerning Acts 2:38 is that Peter gave a different sermon to a new audience in the following chapter and did not mention baptism at all. He commanded his listeners to repent so "that your sins may be blotted out" (Acts 3:19). If baptism is required for salvation, leaving the concept out in the next sermon to a new audience seems inconsistent.

Another passage often used to support baptismal regeneration is Romans 6:3-4. It says, "Do you not know that all of us who have been baptized into Christ Jesus were baptized into his death? We were buried therefore with him by baptism into death, in order that, just as Christ was raised from the dead by the glory of the Father, we too might walk in newness of life."

When the convert is immersed in the water, the symbolism is death (going into the grave). The baptized person who comes out of the water symbolizes being raised from the grave. A person is figuratively buried with Christ and raised to life to become a new spiritual creation. It can be likened to a caterpillar no longer forced to eat tasteless leaves. Through a metamorphosis, the transformed insect is free to fly and has a desire for nectar, a much tastier diet.[27]

There are other biblical reasons why Christians do not believe baptism is a requirement for a person to be justified from sins. As shown in the previous chapter, multiple verses declare that a person's works are incapable of cleansing sin. In addition, the apostle Paul said in 1 Corinthians 1:14-15 that he was grateful to God for the fact that he did not normally baptize converts, making it clear in verse 17 that "Christ did not send me to baptize but to preach the gospel." If baptism *is* a requirement for the forgiveness of sins, his admission makes no sense. As far as we know, even Jesus did not baptize anyone during His ministry.

Wayne Grudem writes, "To say that baptism or any other action is *necessary* for salvation is to say that we are not justified by faith alone, but by faith plus a certain 'work,' the work of baptism. The apostle Paul would have opposed the idea that baptism is necessary for salvation just as strongly as he opposed the similar idea that circumcision was necessary for salvation (see Gal. 5:1-2)."[28] Millard Erickson adds that "baptism *presupposes* faith and the salvation to which faith leads. It is, then, a testimony that one has already been regenerated. If there is a spiritual benefit, it is the fact that baptism brings us into membership or participation in the local church."[29]

At the same time, Christians *do* (or at least *should*) emphasize the importance of baptism in the role of sanctification. Jesus was baptized as an example for His followers. As G.R. Beasley-Murray puts it, this act was "his first step in bearing the sins of the world."[30] The purpose of baptism, then, "is an overt, public act that expresses inward decision and intent; since it is performed in the open, and not in secret, it becomes by its nature a confession of a faith and allegiance embraced... If baptism be an 'instrument of surrender' by one conquered by the love of Christ, it is equally the gracious welcome of the sinner by the Lord who has sought and found him."[31]

Every time a person displayed faith in the New Testament, baptism seemed to be the immediate response. For instance, Acts 2:41 says that "those who received [Peter's] word were baptized" (also see Acts 16:14-15,32-33; 1 Corinthians 1:16). Just as the grandson who received the enormous gift from his grandfather was pleased to mow his grandfather's grass, it is a privilege to do the right thing. It really is that simple. There is no qualification or payback through getting baptized. Bonhoeffer wrote,

> When he called men to follow him, Jesus was summoning them to a *visible act of obedience*. To follow Jesus was a public act. Baptism is similarly a public event, for it is the means whereby a member is grafted on to the visible body of Christ (Gal. 3:27f; 1 Cor. 12:13). The breach with the world which has been effected in Christ can no longer remain hidden; it must come out into the open through membership of the Church and participation in its life and worship. When he joins the Church the Christian steps out of the world, his work and family, taking his stand visibly in the fellowship of Jesus Christ.[32]

As far as the mode of baptism, there are three different methods practiced by Christians: immersion (a full submersion in water), affusion (pouring water over the head), and aspersion (sprinkling water). Some churches lightly sprinkle water over an infant's head, even when personal belief has not been displayed. Other churches prefer to reserve baptism for those who have professed faith in Christ, which is called believer's baptism. This mode eliminates infants as it involves immersion as a symbol of the new life that has taken place, as the Greek word for baptism means to immerse or dip. Colossians 2:12 says the Christian has "been buried with him in baptism, in which you were also raised with him through faith in the powerful working of God, who raised him from the dead."

Is baptism something done to gain justification and the forgiveness of sins? No. It is something done *because of* justification and the forgiveness of sins. If you are a Christian who has not been baptized, consider talking to your pastor about this, even if you had once been baptized in the LDS Church.

The second ordinance practiced in evangelical churches is *communion*, also known as the eucharist. This is also called the Lord's Supper since Jesus served bread and wine to His disciples the night before He died (Matthew 26:26-29). Observing communion commemorates the event and allows unity of Christian believers as they partake of the meal together. Unlike the weekly LDS *sacrament* where water and bread are the elements, Protestant Christian congregations generally use bread or wafers and grape juice or wine for the elements. This ordinance is celebrated in local Christian churches, whether weekly, monthly, or quarterly. It is done to symbolize the death of Jesus, with the bread or wafer representing His body and the grape juice or wine symbolizing His blood.[33] Paul says in 1 Corinthians 11:23-26,

> For I received from the Lord what I also delivered to you, that the Lord Jesus on the night when he was betrayed took bread, and when he had given thanks, he broke it, and said, "This is my body, which is for you. Do this in remembrance of me." In the same way also he took the cup, after supper, saying, "This cup is the new covenant in my blood. Do this, as often as you drink it, in remembrance of me." For as often as you eat this bread and drink the cup, you proclaim the Lord's death until he comes.

The elements provide powerful symbolism in this serious ceremony. Grudem shows how Jesus affirms His love through communion:

> The fact that I am able to participate in the Lord's Supper— indeed, that Jesus *invites me* to come—is a vivid reminder and visual reassurance that Jesus Christ loves *me*, individually and personally. When I come to take of the Lord's Supper I thereby find reassurance again and again of Christ's personal love for me…
>
> When I come at Christ's invitation to the Lord's Supper,

the fact that he has invited me into his presence assures me that he has abundant blessings for me. In this Supper I am actually eating and drinking at a foretaste of the great banquet table of the King. I come to his table as a member of his *eternal* family. When the Lord welcomes me to this table, he assures me that he will welcome me to all the other blessings of earth and heaven as well, and especially to the great marriage supper of the Lamb, at which a place has been reserved for me.[34]

Partaking of this ordinance should be done with great reverence, as Paul commanded in 1 Corinthians 11:27-28. In verses 29-30, he said that illness and death could be the result if communion is taken in the wrong manner. Many pastors may explain this before handing out the elements while stressing the ordinance is only for believers.

CONCLUSION

The conversation with Joan was coming to an end and I wanted to present a quick version of the gospel.

"It is possible to know you have eternal life. John wrote in 1 John 5:13, 'I write these things to you who believe in the name of the Son of God, that you may *know* that you have eternal life.' John did not say 'you may think' or 'you might hope' but rather 'you may *know* that you have eternal life.' There is no way to lay hold of the 'peace of God, which surpasses all understanding,' as described in Philippians 4:7, unless there is an assurance of salvation. And I want you to have that assurance. But you need to trust Jesus and not your works. You will never be able to do enough to cover your sin."

As far as the assurance of salvation, Keller makes a great point:

Assurance of salvation is not possible if we think we must earn or even maintain our salvation by our efforts. If we keep ourselves saved by good living, how could we ever be sure we were being good enough to retain God's favor? Yet the Bible often says that we Christians can know we are safe and saved (e.g.: 1 John 2:3). In other words, we didn't earn our salvation by our behavior, and we can't "un-earn" it by our behavior.[35]

Joan wasn't ready to commit. It is unlikely to get a person to change her mindset of "do better and be better" overnight. If nothing else, I wanted her to know that Christians do not minimize the spiritual fruit that Jesus said they are supposed to have. Perhaps the next Christian she would encounter could follow up and continue a gospel discussion with her. Maybe the next Christian in line is you?

DISCUSSION QUESTIONS

1. How can James 2:20 and 26 be reconciled with Ephesians 2:8-9? What role do works play in the Christian's life?

2. Suppose someone told you, "I don't need to do good works because I am saved by faith." If this believer felt there is freedom to willfully sin as a Christian, how would you answer using a biblical point of view?

3. In the ten-million-dollar illustration, the teenager may have thought that he had paid off his "gift" and had "earned" the ten million. Play the role of the grandfather when he learns this. What would be an appropriate response to help the boy learn from his understanding?

4. What role does water baptism play in the believer's life? When it comes to the mode of baptism, do you prefer sprinkling, pouring, or immersion in water? Why?

5. Why is celebrating the Lord's Supper important? What is the symbolism behind the elements?

RECOMMENDED RESOURCE

Dietrich Bonhoeffer, *The Cost of Discipleship* (New York: Collier Books, 1963).

CHAPTER 10

GROWING IN THE FAITH

A Passionate Pursuit

*"Now to him who is able to do far more abundantly than
all that we ask or think, according to the power at work
within us, to him be glory in the church and in Christ Jesus
throughout all generations, forever and ever. Amen."*

EPHESIANS 3:20-21

CHAPTER PREVIEW

*Being a Christian is not a passive experience. Instead, it is an active
passion. To grow as a Christian, dedication to spiritual disciplines is
required. For one, finding a healthy church is vital. This allows the
Christian individuals (collectively called the "body of Christ") to encourage and equip each other. In addition, believers need to take personal
responsibility for their faith by reading and studying the Bible while following its teachings. A consistent prayer life is also important because it
is the Christian's lifeline to God. All in all, living God's way will lead to
a life of fulfillment and joy.*

H al and his wife, Jenny, sat down in the chairs on the other side of
the desk where I was sitting at the Utah Lighthouse Bookstore on
a fall afternoon in 2015. As mentioned in chapter 3, I occasionally volunteer at this Christian bookstore located in Salt Lake City. Many folks
come to purchase research materials related to Mormonism. Others,
like this couple, are interested in discussing spiritual issues.

"What should we do now?" Hal asked in a forlorn manner after settling into his chair.

"I'm not sure what you mean," I said.

"We have belonged to the Church since we were born. What do we do now that we no longer believe Joseph Smith?"

The couple looked to be in their early seventies, so I was intrigued.

"Let me get this straight. You have been members of The Church of Jesus Christ of Latter-day Saints for your entire lives. And now the two of you have decided that Joseph Smith was *not* a true prophet of God?"

"That's right," he said with a firm resolve, adding that he and his wife were each 80 years old. "We have learned that Joseph Smith could not have been authorized by God. And we think the Church is in error."

The couple had become dismayed when they read the Gospel Topics essays, a series of articles quietly published from November 20, 2013, through October 23, 2015, on the official LDS Church website.[1] Although the number of essays has fluctuated, there were 13 original pieces authored by unnamed church historians providing information on a variety of controversial issues, including the multiple accounts of Joseph Smith's First Vision of God and an explanation on the restrictions placed on black members before 1978. These are sensitive issues for church members.[2]

The essays have not been mentioned in general conference addresses, nor were they ever advertised on the home page of the church's official website. Although authorized by church leaders, many Mormons may not know about them. One LDS teacher in Hawaii who used the information in the essays in his Sunday school class was released from his calling in mid-2015 by a local church leader who claimed erroneous information was being disseminated![3]

For many like Hal and Jenny, there was shock value when they did read them. One Brigham Young University–Idaho student said,

> Once I started searching, I came across this recently published essay on LDS.org. It talked openly about the translation process of the Book of Mormon. It shocked me. My issue with it was that the narrative it laid out was completely

different from the one I'd grown up learning about. I frantically searched the footnotes of the essay for some sort of an explanation. However, the more I searched the more confused I became.[4]

Most concerning for Hal and Jenny was the information about how Joseph Smith—who had married his wife, Emma, in 1827—had later polygamously married teenagers, some as young as 14. These girls made up a third of Smith's 30 to 40 wives![5] Smith also married women who were currently married to living husbands. This type of relationship is called polyandry, and these made up another third of his wives.

In addition, they were dismayed to learn how Smith claimed to use a seer stone to translate the Book of Mormon. Instead of looking at the plates to read the "Reformed Egyptian" characters, Smith took a stone he found while digging for buried treasure and placed it in his top hat. When he put his face in the hat, God supposedly allowed the magical stone to light up and provide the words for Smith to dictate to his scribe. This is how the Book of Mormon was composed.

I remained puzzled by Hal's question from earlier in the conversation. "When you asked me what you should do now, what did you mean?"

He responded, "If the LDS Church is not true, then what do we do? Should we stay in this church? Or do we leave it?"

Those who have discovered problems in Mormonism face a dilemma. Those who leave could risk losing relationships with family members, friends, neighbors, and coworkers. Fortunately, both Hal and Jenny were unified in their rejection of Mormonism, but many other couples are not as fortunate. Often divorces happen when only one person leaves the church and the other decides to stay.

"I believe that staying in a religion not based on the truth doesn't make sense," I said. "It's your decision, but I recommend you find a Christian church that teaches biblical truth."

R.C. Sproul agrees with this assessment:

> When the church is apostate, a Christian must leave. You may think you should stay within the church and try to

work for its change and recovery, but if the church is in fact apostate, you're not allowed to be there. Consider the showdown between the prophets of Baal and Elijah at Mount Carmel. After God displayed his power over Baal can you imagine somebody saying, "Well, I see now that Yahweh is God, but I'm going to stay here in the house of Baal as salt and light and try to work for its reform"? We're not allowed to do that. If the institution we are in commits apostasy, it is our duty to leave it.[6]

Hal said they had considered visiting services at a local Christian church, but they were unsure who could be trusted. His next question floored me because of his sincerity.

"We're not sure what to do at a Christian church service. What do we wear? When do we kneel? Could you help us?"

While many Mormons will not consider attending a Christian service, this did not seem to be the case with this couple. Of course, they were concerned because most Mormons wear their Sunday-best clothing to their church's services, with men normally donning white shirts with ties and dark slacks while women wear dresses. Going to an LDS service wearing casual clothing could result in judgmental stares.

I told the couple that many evangelical churches provide freedom in what the parishioners wear—one pastor I know even dons shorts in the summer when he preaches on Sundays! Still, some congregations do encourage suits or dresses. It just depends. I said they would not be wrong to dress conservatively for a first visit but recommended they skip the shirt/tie and dress and not be overly formal. Visiting could allow them to see what was typical and adjust their style if they decided to attend that church again.

As far as procedures in a typical Christian service, I explained that there were differences between congregations. While someone who attends a Roman Catholic service needs to know when to stand, kneel, and respond with a recitation of the right words at the right time, such a format is not typical at most evangelical Christian services. Generally, pastors or music leaders provide easy-to-follow oral instructions so nobody feels out of place.

THE GREAT APOSTASY

Those who do not understand Mormonism's teaching on the Great Apostasy may have missed why Hal and Jenny were struggling. Mormonism teaches that the authority of Christianity ended a few years after the death of Jesus's apostles, supposedly tainting all Christian churches and thus requiring a complete restoration to fix the corruption. Referencing Joseph Smith–History 1:19 in the Pearl of Great Price, LDS President Gordon B. Hinckley wrote, "The Prophet Joseph was told that the other sects were wrong. These are not my words. Those are the Lord's words. But they are hard words for those of other faiths."[7]

Mormon Apostle James E. Talmage taught, "From the facts already stated it is evident that the Church was literally driven from the earth; in the first ten centuries immediately following the ministry of Christ the authority of the Holy Priesthood was lost among men, and no human power could restore it."[8] Talmage also wrote, "Mankind had ceased to know God; and had invested the utterances of prophets and apostles of old, who had known Him, with a pall of mystery and fancy, so that the True and the Living God was no longer believed to exist."[9] As Henry B. Eyring, the second counselor in the LDS First Presidency, put it, "This is the true Church, the only true Church, because in it are the keys of the priesthood. Only in this Church has the Lord lodged the power to seal on earth and to seal in heaven as He did in the time of the Apostle Peter."[10]

The fear of leaving Mormonism for what LDS Apostle Bruce R. McConkie called "apostate Christendom"[11] has made an indelible impact on the psyche of many. To consider leaving Mormonism for biblical Christianity will not be taken seriously by many ex-Mormons who, in the back of their minds at least, continue to hold to the Great Apostasy.

During a discussion with former Latter-day Saints who express wariness of Christian churches because they don't have "authority," I like to ask, "Where did you learn that Christian churches are part of the Great Apostasy?" Of course, they admit, the idea came from LDS Church leaders. Then I will reply, "Let me get this straight. You reject Joseph Smith as a prophet of God and no longer believe the leaders of this church teach the truth. But you want to continue to hold on to a doctrine originating with an organization you no longer trust?" I have had former Mormons look at me quizzically and say, "I never thought of it that way." It is possible to reject Mormonism and the teachings of its leaders (such as the Great Apostasy) while keeping a belief in God and Jesus!

THE ROLE OF THE CHRISTIAN CHURCH

The Greek word *ekklesia* literally means "called out ones" and consistently refers to individual Christians who make up the (singular) "body of Christ." Finding a local body of believers (which I call the "local church") is important, as God did not intend for believers to survive on their own. Hebrews 10:24-25 says, "And let us consider how to stir up one another to love and good works, not neglecting to meet together, as is the habit of some, but encouraging one another, and all the more as you see the Day drawing near." First Thessalonians 5:11 adds, "Therefore encourage one another and build one another up, just as you are doing."

In the book of Acts, Luke described ways that the early believers worked together to further the kingdom of God. For example, Acts 4 lays out how Christians should take care of each other, as verse 34 says, "There was not a needy person among them." Believers sold everything they had to be able to share with others, while verses 32-37 describe how they had everything in common. This does not mean that there was no conflict. One dispute in Acts 6:1-7 took place between two sets of Jews; the solution decided upon by the leaders was to appoint local men to spread out the duties, thereby releasing the apostles for service. The result of working out the conflict is described in verse 7: "And the word of God continued to increase, and the number of the disciples multiplied greatly in Jerusalem, and a great many of the priests became obedient to the faith."

Local churches can worship through the spoken word (preaching), prayer, and singing. Wayne Grudem writes, "Because God is worthy of worship and seeks to be worshiped, everything in our worship services should be designed and carried out not to call attention to ourselves or bring glory to ourselves, but to call attention to God and to cause people to think about him." When it comes to the various parts of the worship service, church leaders ought to ask, "Are they really bringing glory to God in the way they are done?"[12] The benefits are many, including delighting God and drawing near to Him while allowing the Almighty to minister to our spirits.

Explaining how a Christian should be heaven-minded rather than focus on the things of this earth, John Piper says that "God *regards faithfulness to him as more important than life.*" Piper writes how "the instincts of many of today's preachers and churchgoers seem to go in the other direction: to treat life on earth as the great central value and the honor of God as subservient to that. If God does not serve our comforts here, then he is unworthy. This is a great sorrow and weakness in the church—and in her mission."[13]

There is a difference between a church that stresses a biblical view of doctrine versus one that relies on a secular worldview and gravitates toward the mindset dictated by an immoral culture. R.C. Sproul explains that liberal Christians who "pride themselves on being openminded quickly become closeminded. I believe the basic reason why liberal churches tolerate such a wide variety of doctrines is because doctrine doesn't matter to them much at all. They have no passion about the essential content of the Christian faith, whereas in the conservative milieu people are prepared to give their lives for the truth of the Scriptures because they see these things as having eternal significance."[14]

Just as Paul said to "test everything" (1 Thessalonians 5:21) and John said to "test the spirits to see whether they are from God, for many false prophets have gone out into the world" (1 John 4:1), proper investigation must be done when choosing a church. Grudem writes, "When there is an assembly of people who take the name 'Christian' but consistently teach that people cannot believe their Bibles—indeed a church whose pastor and congregation seldom read their Bibles or pray in any meaningful way, and do not believe or perhaps even understand the gospel of salvation by faith in Christ alone, then how can we say that this is a true church?"[15] The goal in leaving Mormonism, then, is to find a place where the truth is spoken. Going to another religion or church that espouses a false gospel is *not* the goal.

FINDING A LOCAL CHURCH

Depending on where a person lives, there can be a selection of Bible-believing churches to consider. Choosing one may involve personal taste or style. For instance, some congregations emphasize singing older hymns while others prefer contemporary songs. A number mix the genres. One church might excel with its children's or youth programs while another could be more attuned to empty nesters or senior citizens. Much depends on the giftings of the pastor(s), leaders (such as elders and deacons), and the congregation itself. I told Hal and Jenny they should visit several recommended churches before deciding.[16]

If a person lives in a place where there is a choice, here are some things that ought to be considered:

Correct doctrine. As mentioned above, this is a must. Among the essential issues are the authority of the Bible, the nature of Father/Son/Holy Spirit, and justification by faith alone.

Stimulating preaching. I recommend churches where expository preaching is utilized. This means that biblical books are covered systematically chapter by chapter while providing modern-day application. Some pastors regularly emphasize topical or self-help sermons with little emphasis on what the Bible teaches. If that is the case, consider another church. Doctrinal teaching is important. Utah pastor Bryan Hurlbutt explains, "Preaching should never be stale or a form of dead orthodoxy, but it had better include a healthy dose of orthodox theology. People need spiritual meat to survive in times where the devil is looking to eat their lunch. If Sundays continue to be solely about milk we will find our people malnourished and ready for the world, the flesh, and the devil to pick them off."[17]

Nearby location. If there are several possibilities, I recommend choosing a church that can be reached in a reasonable amount of time. Each person/family must decide what "reasonable" means. If a church is located too far away, it can be difficult to become actively involved or invite neighbors.

Emphasis on youth programs. For families with children, a church sponsoring programs that teach biblical truth to children and teens should be on the top of the priority list. A large-enough congregation might even have a youth or children's pastor on staff. AWANA programs[18] and youth group gatherings can help kids take ownership of their faith in a world filled with competing values.

Wise stewards of finances. Faithful Mormons are required to tithe if they want to participate in their church's temples. In Christianity, giving a set amount of money is not a requirement for salvation, but the Bible commands believers to be generous in kingdom building (2 Corinthians 8:1-15), as "God loves a cheerful giver" (2 Corinthians 9:7). One suggestion is to request a copy of a church's budget to consider its priorities. If the vast majority of the money received stays within the church walls (such as mortgage payments, utility bills, and staff salaries) and there is little to spend on local ministry and missionary endeavors, it is a likely indication that this congregation is too inward focused.

Clear discipline standards. What do the church leaders do when sin is detected? In 1 Corinthians 5, Paul told the Corinthian leaders to "purge" a sexually immoral believer from the church. He asked in verse 12, "Is it not those inside the church whom you are to judge?" Some pastors who shy away from conflict may say it is none of their business to criticize their members' behaviors, but unchecked sin in a church is problematic. Paul provides wise advice in verse 6 (as well as in Galatians 5:9) by saying "a little leaven leavens the whole lump."

Emotionally healthy. Unfortunately, some church leaders have harmed their congregations by placing unreasonable demands or restrictions upon the members that go beyond the teachings of the Bible.

Even in Utah where fewer than 2 percent of the residents are evangelical Christians, there are choices available in populated areas (though not so much in the rural communities). If you are the Christian who is doing the recommending, I would hope your home church would be a start! Encourage your friends to come to a service. Pick them up, sit with them, and make them feel welcome. I encourage you to take them out to lunch after the service, even if it is just fast food, and pay the tab. Based on the points listed above, give them freedom to visit other Bible-believing congregations.

One great place to get to know other believers is in a weekly Bible study, perhaps even held in a home. These allow a smaller group of believers to become more involved with each other's lives, including studying God's Word, praying specifically for needs, and making sure nobody falls through the cracks. When difficult times come and people struggle, fellow believers can help. James 5:19-20 says, "My brothers, if anyone among you wanders from the truth and someone brings him back, let him know that whoever brings back a sinner from his wandering will save his soul from death and will cover a multitude of sins." Since that conversation, Hal and Jenny have continued to attend a Bible study held in my home where they have learned more about God's Word.

PERSONAL SPIRITUAL DISCIPLINE

Besides becoming involved with a local body of believers, it is important for Christians to take responsibility for their spiritual health. Living fully and completely for Jesus is a choice. This does not come automatically, especially when living life with others who do not make God their priority. Piper explains that

> we are surrounded by unconverted people who think they *do* believe in Jesus. Drunks on the street say they believe. Unmarried couples sleeping together say they believe. Elderly people who haven't sought worship or fellowship for 40 years say they believe. All kinds of lukewarm, world-loving church attenders say they believe. The world abounds with millions of unconverted people who say they believe in Jesus.[19]

Just like getting in shape or eating healthier, spiritual discipline requires individual sacrifice, commitment, and effort. Merely attending church services is the perfect recipe for spiritual death through malnutrition and, ultimately, starvation. The apostle Paul had many "kick-in-the-tail" admonitions throughout his writing. For example, he said to "train yourself for godliness" in 1 Timothy 4:7. Second Corinthians 13:5 says, "Examine yourselves, to see whether you are in the faith. Test yourselves." And in 1 Corinthians 9:24-27, he likens the Christian to an Olympic athlete:

> Do you not know that in a race all the runners run, but only one receives the prize? So run that you may obtain it. Every athlete exercises self-control in all things. They do it to receive a perishable wreath, but we an imperishable. So I do not run aimlessly; I do not box as one beating the air. But I discipline my body and keep it under control, lest after preaching to others I myself should be disqualified.

For the Christian, "godliness is no optional spiritual luxury for a few quaint Christians of a bygone era or for some group of super-saints of today. It is both the privilege and duty of every Christian to pursue godliness, to train himself to be godly, to study diligently the practice of godliness."[20] Yet some Christians become fearful when they realize that Satan is, as described in 1 Peter 5:8, "a roaring lion, seeking someone to devour."

Should believers pull the blankets over their heads? Absolutely not! As Piper puts it, we can have

> a deep, unshakable confidence that Satan is not in control of this world. We are called in Scripture to have confidence that Satan will never have the final say. God wants his children to be confident that God's will is final and decisive, when his will and Satan's will clash, which they always do, since, even when they will the same act, they differ radically in how it should be done and to what end. Divine providence is never frustrated by Satan in its plan for this world—for the everlasting good of God's people in the all-satisfying praise of the glory of his grace.[21]

What does it mean to say God's will? There are two possible meanings. First, there are abundant references throughout the Bible concerning God's sovereign will, which include all events—past, present, and future—that are both good and evil. To know what God's sovereign will was for yesterday, watch the news. What will be His sovereign will for tomorrow? Wait until tomorrow. God sovereign will is a surety. In addition, the moral will of God is another possible meaning. This can be followed or broken through a person's own choices, as discussed in the previous chapter.

While we can know that God's sovereign will is never thwarted, individual responsibility in combatting the enemy's attacks is required to move forward in the battle. To be successful, there are two disciplines that are stressed more than any other in the Bible. For one, learning to utilize God's Word is crucial. Ephesians 6:10-18 talks about "the whole armor of God" to be "able to stand against the schemes of the devil." Borrowing the terminology of a Roman soldier (i.e., "belt" of truth, "breastplate" of righteousness, and "shield" of faith, among others), a proper handling of "the sword of the Spirit, which is the word of God" is commanded.

Without God's Word, the Christian will ultimately be defeated. When Jesus was personally confronted by Satan in Matthew 4:1-11, He cited the Old Testament three times.

It is not necessary to become a biblical expert overnight. First Peter 2:2 encourages "baby steps" when it says, "Like newborn infants, long for the pure spiritual milk, that by it you may grow up into salvation." In the previous verses (1:22-25), Peter talked about the Word of God, so *spiritual milk* is certainly a reference to the Bible. It will take effort and perseverance, as 2 Timothy 2:15 says, "Do your best to present yourself to God as one approved, a worker who has no need to be ashamed, rightly handling the word of truth."

Because finding the time to read and contemplate the Bible can be a challenge, a course of action is necessary. Some like to read from beginning to end. However, there are several drawbacks with such a plan. For one, missing a day or two of reading can cause legalistic guilt and result in abandonment of the once-promising goal. Genesis and Exodus are both interesting books, but the action bogs down in

Leviticus, Numbers, and Deuteronomy. For those who would like to read the entire Bible during the year, I recommend a "One Year Bible" that includes daily readings from the Old and New Testaments as well as part of the Psalms and Proverbs, providing variety while eliminating the likelihood of getting stuck in a tedious section.[22]

Another possibility is to study a particular book. A great place to start is the Gospel of John. Just reading one chapter a day in this Gospel will allow a person to complete the task in only three weeks. Another awesome book is Romans, which provides a systematic overview of salvation.[23] Of course, there are many good Christian websites offering material for a verse-by-verse study. A good discipline is keeping a reading journal and jotting down observations.

A wonderful gift to give someone from an LDS background is a modern version of the Bible. There is nothing wrong with the King James Version, but I have found that Latter-day Saints who have never really comprehended this hard-to-understand translation are in for a treat when they pick up a version that is easier to understand. It can be like putting on glasses for the first time when bad vision has made everything blurry. Another resource to consider is BibleGateway.com to compare several translations and experience the differences. Study Bibles can be extremely helpful because they provide commentary at the bottom of each page as well as feature articles.[24]

Talking about the importance of commitment, Jerry Bridges writes,

> Where can we find the time for quality Bible study? I once heard that question asked of a chief of surgery in a large hospital. Twenty-five years later, his answer continues to challenge me. He looked his questioner squarely in the eye and said, "You always find time for what is important to you." How important is the practice of godliness to you? Is it important enough to take priority over television, books, magazines, recreation, and a score of activities that we all find time to engage in?[25]

A second vital spiritual discipline is prayer. After bringing up the importance of the Bible, Paul wrote in Ephesians 6:18 that Christians should be "praying at all times in the Spirit, with all prayer and supplication. To that end, keep alert with all perseverance, making supplication for all the saints." As it has been said, "One might pray and not be a Christian, but one cannot be a Christian and not pray."[26]

Those who have lived as members of the LDS Church may assume that formal, stylized prayers are necessary to be heard by God. To show this is not the case, consider the parable of the Pharisee and the tax collector in Luke 18:9-14:

> He also told this parable to some who trusted in themselves that they were righteous, and treated others with contempt: "Two men went up into the temple to pray, one a Pharisee and the other a tax collector. The Pharisee, standing by himself, prayed thus: 'God, I thank you that I am not like other men, extortioners, unjust, adulterers, or even like this tax collector. I fast twice a week; I give tithes of all that I get.' But the tax collector, standing far off, would not even lift up his eyes to heaven, but beat his breast, saying, 'God, be merciful to me, a sinner!' I tell you, this man went down to his house justified, rather than the other. For everyone who exalts himself will be humbled, but the one who humbles himself will be exalted."

Compared to the religious leader, the prayer of the tax collector was straightforward and simple, demonstrating his humility before God. Jesus taught in Matthew 6:6, "But when you pray, go into your room and shut the door and pray to your Father who is in secret. And your Father who sees in secret will reward you." He also said in Luke 11:9-10, "And I tell you, ask, and it will be given to you; seek, and you will find; knock, and it will be opened to you. For everyone who asks receives, and the one who seeks finds, and to the one who knocks it will be opened."

Even when under stress, it is possible to know that God can be trusted. Jesus said in Matthew 10:28-31, "And do not fear those who kill the body but cannot kill the soul. Rather fear him who can destroy both soul and body in hell. Are not two sparrows sold for a penny? And not one of them will fall to the ground apart from your Father. But even the hairs of your head are all numbered. Fear not, therefore; you are of more value than many sparrows." Philippians 4:6 says that Christians can present their requests to God and "not be anxious about anything, but in everything by prayer and supplication with thanksgiving let your requests be made known to God."

Dietrich Bonhoeffer described what it means to have a reliance on God:

> Anxiety is characteristic of the Gentiles, for they rely on their own strength and work instead of relying on God. They do not know that the Father knows that we have need of all these things, and so they try to do for themselves what they do not expect from God. But the disciples know that the rule is "Seek ye first the kingdom of God and his righteousness, and all these things shall be added unto you."... After he has been following Christ for a long time, the disciple of Jesus will be asked "Lacked ye anything?" and he will answer "Nothing, Lord." How could he when he knows that despite hunger and nakedness, persecution and danger, the Lord is always at his side? [27]

It is necessary to look beyond ourselves, as seventeenth-century Puritan Thomas Brooks explained,

> God looks not at the elegancy of your prayers, to see how neat they are; nor yet at the geometry of your prayers, to see how long they are; nor yet at the arithmetic of your prayers, to see how many they are; nor yet at the music of your prayers, nor yet at the sweetness of your voice, nor yet at the logic of your prayers; but at the sincerity of your prayers, how hearty they are. There is no prayer acknowledged, approved, accepted, recorded, or rewarded by God, but that wherein the heart is sincerely and wholly. [28]

Even when a Christian is unsure what to pray for, God knows. And we're not alone. First Timothy 2:5 says, "For there is one God, and there is one mediator between God and men, the man Christ Jesus." Besides having Jesus as an advocate, the third member of the Trinity is also actively involved. Romans 8:26-27 says, "For we do not know what to pray for as we ought, but the Spirit himself intercedes for us with groanings too deep for words. And he who searches hearts knows what is the mind of the Spirit, because the Spirit intercedes for the saints according to the will of God."

We must not assume that God wants His children to gain material desires. "Name-it-and-claim-it" teachers who call themselves Christian often talk about a "seed of faith" necessary for God to automatically answer their every whim. It is true that Philippians 4:19 does say that "God will supply every need of yours according to his riches in glory in Christ Jesus." But notice, the promise is He will supply every *need*, not *greed*.

Meanwhile, some believe it is a lack of faith to pray for anything more than once. Yet Jesus emphasized the importance of persistence. Consider the parable of the persistent widow in Luke 18:1-8:

> And he told them a parable to the effect that they ought always to pray and not lose heart. He said, "In a certain city there was a judge who neither feared God nor respected man. And there was a widow in that city who kept coming to him and saying, 'Give me justice against my adversary.' For a while he refused, but afterward he said to himself, 'Though I neither fear God nor respect man, yet because this widow keeps bothering me, I will give her justice, so that she will not beat me down by her continual coming.'" And the Lord said, "Hear what the unrighteous judge says. And will not God give justice to his elect, who cry to him day and night? Will he delay long over them? I tell you, he will give justice to them speedily. Nevertheless, when the Son of Man comes, will he find faith on earth?"

R.A. Torrey wrote, "Be constant and persistent in your asking. Be importunate and untiring in your asking. God delights to have us 'shameless' beggars in this direction; for it shows our faith in Him, and He is mightily pleased with faith."[29] As Grudem appropriately explains, "If we were really convinced that prayer changes the way God acts, and that God does bring about remarkable changes in the world in response to prayer, as Scripture repeatedly teaches that he does, then we would pray much more than we do. If we pray little, it is probably because we do not really believe that prayer accomplishes much at all."[30]

As far as which person of the Trinity should be addressed, most prayers in the Bible are addressed to the Father. Since Jesus is God, prayers can be directed to Him as well. In Acts 1:24, the apostles prayed, "You, Lord [Jesus], who know the hearts of all…" In Acts 7:59, Stephen prayed to the "Lord Jesus" as he was being killed. Ananias also prayed to Jesus in Acts 9:10-16. Romans 10:10-12 says Jesus can be called upon in prayer. And Paul directly prayed to Jesus in 2 Corinthians 12:8 concerning having his spiritual "thorn" removed. While there are no examples of anyone praying to the Holy Spirit, this would be totally appropriate since the Spirit is also fully God.

At what time of the day should a person pray? The Bible talks about being in a constant state of prayer, as 1 Thessalonians 5:17 says to "pray without ceasing" while Ephesians 6:18 commands Christians to pray "at all times in the Spirit." Colossians 4:2 tells believers to "continue steadfastly in prayer." Throughout the day, prayers can be offered in an informal manner, especially when situations arise. A priority ought to be setting aside a certain time each day to focus on talking to God.

Personally, I like to dedicate time to do this in the morning since I am an early riser. David even prayed in Psalm 5:3, "O LORD, in the morning you hear my voice." For others, a time in the evening might be a better fit. There are no set rules. Bonhoeffer provided a good perspective on this topic:

> Prayer is the supreme instance of the hidden character of the Christian life. It is the antithesis of self-display. When men pray, they have ceased to know themselves, and know only God whom they call upon. Prayer does not aim at any direct effect on the world; it is addressed to God alone, and is therefore the perfect example of undemonstrative

action…The right way to approach God is to stretch out our hands and ask of One who we know has the heart of a Father.[31]

Some (like me) struggle with focus. Daydreaming, thinking about the many to-do lists, and interruptions (i.e., phone buzzing, someone walking into the room) can make intimate communication with God impossible. I suggest putting all electronic devices away while finding a place where family members will respect your "prayer closet."

To be successful in a personal devotional life, a plan is needed. One of my favorite techniques is ACTS, a model that I have used for more than five decades. This places prayer into four categories:

- A stands for *Adoration*, a time to praise God for who He is. I like to pick several attributes of God (talked about in chapter 4).

- C is for *Confession*, allowing a chance for sins to be uncovered and forgiven (1 John 1:9).

- T represents *Thanksgiving* and remembering God's many blessings and previous prayer requests that have been answered.

- S represents *Supplication* and bringing personal requests to God, both for other people as well as yourself. A whiteboard in our home is used to update the requests of friends, family members, missionaries, and organizations; when not sure who or what to pray for, this board is a helpful reminder.

It is important to allow time for the Spirit to speak. Instead of feeling like only audible or intentional prayers can be offered, there are times when stillness is needed. I sometimes find that God wants to introduce ideas into my mind as I wait on Him. Sometimes I am nudged to contact someone or request a prayer for someone or something I missed. Even the idea for this book came during a time such as this. All credit and glory to God!

What about those times when it feels like our prayers are not being answered? Millard Erickson responds,

> We do not always receive what we ask for. Jesus asked three times for the removal of the cup (death by crucifixion); Paul prayed thrice for the removal of his thorn in the flesh. In each case, the Father granted instead something that was more needful (e.g., 2 Cor. 12:9-10). The believer can pray confidently, knowing that our wise and good God will give us, not necessarily what we ask for, but what is best. For as the psalmist put it, "No good thing does [the LORD] withhold from those who walk uprightly" (Ps. 84:11).[32]

Waiting for answers can be difficult. Remember the time when Joseph was sold into slavery by his brothers in Genesis 37:23-36? Later, in Genesis 50:20, Joseph recounted this bad experience and understood that "God meant it for good." Admittedly, not every prayer request is answered the way we want. It may also be a case of God saying no. As Lloyd Ogilvie—a chaplain for many years in the United States Senate—wrote,

> Now we must consider unanswered prayers for things which *may not be best for us or are not in keeping with the Lord's timing for us.* When I think of some of my "unanswered" prayers, I am filled with thanksgiving and praise! Looking back on some ungranted petitions I am gratified that the Lord said no. If I had received them they would not have been maximum for me or the people around me.[33]

Other times, though, waiting on God results in answers far better and grander than could ever be imagined. One thing I have learned in my time as a Christian is this: God is faithful. He can be trusted to answer our prayers, but He can't answer unless we ask. It is freeing to cast "all [our] anxieties on him, because he cares for [us]" (1 Peter 5:7). The end result is complete satisfaction in God. Jesus explained in John 15:11: "These things I have spoken to you, that my joy may be in you, and that your joy may be full." He also said in John 10:10, "I came that they may have life and have it abundantly."

And you can bank on it!

CONCLUSION

As we conclude, let me share with you this quote from John Piper to explain the purpose of life:

> God is "seeing to it" that his people—his bride, the church (Eph. 5:25-27)—come to faith in Christ, repent of sin, experience forgiveness and justification and reconciliation with God as adopted children, walk by faith, be transformed into the image of Christ, live lives of love and good deeds, attain the resurrection of the dead, be perfected in glory, inhabit a renewed creation, and spend eternity glorifying God by treasuring him supremely with everlasting joy.[34]

Wow! There really is a God. Jesus really does love people. And it *is* possible to have a personal relationship with the One who not only created but also sustains this universe!

Those who are Bible-believing Christians are called "ambassadors for Christ" (2 Corinthians 5:20) and have been given a commission to faithfully represent the case for Christianity. Remember the farmer and his wife that I talked about in the introduction? Maybe you are the only person in the world of certain Mormons who has the ability to accurately introduce authentic Christianity into their lives. What a wonderful opportunity Christians have to tell others the good news!

If you are a Latter-day Saint or have left the LDS Church, *don't* give up a desire to discover the truth. In Proverbs 8:17, God explains, "I love those who love me, and those who seek me diligently find me." James 4:8 adds, "Draw near to God, and he will draw near to you."

May the Lord bless you as you pursue truth!

DISCUSSION QUESTIONS

1. What effect do you think the doctrine of the Great Apostasy has on those who have left the LDS Church when it comes to considering the case for Christianity?

2. How important is finding a good Christian church for a believer? What are the benefits that come from getting involved in a local congregation?

3. How difficult do you think it will be for the average Latter-day Saint to venture into a Christian church? What are some ways that church members can make visitors more comfortable at a church service? Explain your ideas as if a Christian pastor is listening.

4. Why is regularly reading the Bible important? What advice could you give in making this an interesting and beneficial time for those who are not used to reading it for themselves?

5. Why can a personal prayer life sometimes be difficult to manage? What advice would you give to someone who is struggling with this discipline in their Christian life?

RECOMMENDED RESOURCES

Entry-Level Resource

Stormie Omartian, *Prayer Warrior: The Power of Praying Your Way to Victory* (Eugene, OR: Harvest House Publishers, 2013).

Tony Evans, *Prayers for Knowing God* (Eugene, OR: Harvest House Publishers, 2021).

Middle-Level Resources

Gordon D. Fee and Douglas Stuart, *How to Read the Bible for All Its Worth* (Grand Rapids, MI: Zondervan, 2014).

R.A. Torrey, *How to Pray* (Westwood, NJ: Barbour and Company, 1989).

Advanced Resource

Dietrich Bonhoeffer, *The Cost of Discipleship* (New York: Collier Books, 1963).

Resources for Those Who Have Left Mormonism

If you know someone who has left Mormonism and wants to follow Jesus, here are three "post-Mormon" resources with community support and mentoring programs that can be recommended:

Ex-Mormon Christians:
www.facebook.com/groups/XMChristians

MIT: Mormons in Transition:
www.facebook.com/groups/mitmormontransition

Faith After Mormonism:
faithaftermormonism.org/

GLOSSARY

*A variety of theological and historical terms are used through-
out this book. This glossary offers concise definitions of unique
words. When the term is used differently by Christians and
Mormons, both definitions are given. Italicized words in the
definitions are defined elsewhere in this glossary.*

Adoption. Christian: Becoming a spiritual *child of God* by trusting in *Jesus*
for the *forgiveness* of *sins*.

Agnosticism. The belief that there is insufficient evidence to determine
if God exists.

Anti-Mormon. LDS: A designation, usually meant in a derogatory way,
for those who disagree with the LDS Church or its followers.

Anthropomorphism. Using human characteristics to describe God.

Apocrypha. Historical books written by Jews during the intertestamental period (300 BC to the time of Christ). These are not accepted as
authoritative scripture by Christians or Mormons.

Apostasy, Great. LDS: The belief that the true church ceased to exist soon
after the death of Jesus's apostles and was later restored when *Joseph
Smith* founded the LDS Church in 1830.

Apostle. Christian: Typically, a reference to one of the 12 New Testament
followers of *Jesus,* as well as Paul. LDS: Besides the followers of *Jesus,*

two counselors in the *First Presidency* and 12 men who currently serve under the authority of the *prophet*.

Articles of Faith. LDS: A set of 13 beliefs in *Mormonism* composed by *Joseph Smith* in 1842 and listed in the *Pearl of Great Price*.

Atheism. The belief that God does not exist.

Atonement. Christian: The death of *Jesus* on the cross provides the full payment for the *sins* of those who place their trust in Him. LDS: Jesus's suffering in the Garden of Gethsemane as well as on the cross allows every human to be resurrected to one of three *kingdoms of glory*.

Autograph. An original manuscript of *scripture*.

Baptism, water. Christian: An *ordinance* involving water to symbolize the washing away of *sins*. LDS: The first saving *ordinance* (Articles of Faith 1:4) administered by an LDS priesthood holder and involving full immersion. In addition, vicarious baptisms for the dead are performed in LDS *temples*.

Bible. Christian: The 66 books compiled into the Word of God provide access to true *doctrines* and God's moral commandments. LDS: One of four written scriptures. The King James Version of the Bible is the official translation, considered to be true "as far as it is translated correctly" (Articles of Faith 1:8).

Book of Abraham. LDS: A book found in the *Pearl of Great Price* that was translated by *Joseph Smith* from Egyptian papyri scrolls, which were purchased by the church in 1835 before they were lost a few years later. They resurfaced in the 1960s and are now owned by the LDS Church.

Book of Mormon. LDS: One of four written scriptures. It was officially published in 1830 by *Joseph Smith* who claimed he found the *autograph* (gold plates) and then translated them. It describes three different groups that migrated to the Americas before the time of Christ. The Israelites fleeing Jerusalem about 600 BC were divided into two main groups, the Nephites and Lamanites.

Born again. Christian: A description of a person who has been forgiven of all *sin* through faith in *Jesus*.

Canon. Christian: The combined 66 books of the Old and New Testaments. LDS: The four written works comprised of the *Bible* (KJV), the *Book of Mormon*, the *Doctrine and Covenants*, and the *Pearl of Great Price*.

Celestial kingdom. LDS: The highest of three *kingdoms of glory* and the ultimate destiny for faithful Latter-day Saints who have kept all the commandments as defined in *Mormonism*. Also called celestial glory. See *eternal life*.

Child(ren) of God. Christian: A person whose *sin*s are *forgive*n through trust in *Jesus* (John 1:12). LDS: All humans originally born as spirits in the *preexistence*.

Christian. Christian: A person who trusts *Jesus* alone for the *forgiveness* of *sin*. LDS: Anyone who believes in the divinity and teachings of *Jesus*.

Church. Christian: All true believers. LDS: Generally, a reference to The Church of Jesus Christ of Latter-day Saints.

Communion. Christian: Also called the Lord's Supper, the distribution of the bread and wine/grape juice in a local body of believers to symbolize the atoning work accomplished on the cross. LDS: See *sacrament*.

Dead Sea Scrolls. More than 900 manuscripts discovered in 11 mountainous caves between 1947 and 1955 near Qumran, Israel, located in the northwestern area of the Dead Sea. A quarter of the manuscripts (about 230) were Old Testament texts, most of which were fragmentary.

Deity. Christian: Referring to *Jesus* as being fully God.

Doctrine. A theological teaching.

Doctrine and Covenants (D&C). LDS: One of four written scriptures said to contain revelations God communicated mainly to church founder *Joseph Smith*.

Eternal life. Christian: Spending eternity with God in *heaven*. LDS: Exaltation to godhood in the highest level of the *celestial kingdom*.

Evangelical. Christian: A Protestant believer who holds the *Bible* to be the literal Word of God. This term is not typically used for those who belong to Roman Catholic, Eastern Orthodox, or liberal (mainline denominational) Protestant churches. See *Christian*.

Evangelism. The intentional act of sharing one's personal faith with others.

Fall. Christian: A reference to Adam and Eve's *sin* in the Garden of Eden and separation from the presence of God. LDS: Adam and Eve's "transgression" in the Garden of Eden, allowing spirits from the *pre-existence* to be born on the earth so they can progress to godhood.

First Presidency. The top three leaders in the LDS Church: the *prophet* and his two counselors.

Forgiveness. Christian: A complete washing away of a believer's past, present, and future *sins* through faith alone based on the death of *Jesus* on the cross. LDS: Obtained by an individual Mormon mainly by keeping all of God's commandments.

Fruit of the Spirit. Christian: In contrast to the "acts of the sinful nature," the *Christian* displays characteristics provided through the Holy Spirit.

General authority. LDS: A high-ranking leader in the LDS Church, including the *prophet*, his two counselors, 12 *apostles*, and the First Quorum of the *Seventy*.

General Conference. LDS: A biannual event held on the first weekend every April and October in Salt Lake City, UT. Talks given here are authoritative.

General (natural) revelation. God revealing Himself through nature and human conscience.

Gifts of the Spirit. Christian: Spiritual equipping provided to an individual through the *Holy Spirit*.

Glorification. Christian: The future state of *salvation* where believers will receive new bodies and reside with God in *heaven* for eternity.

God the Father. Christian: The first person of the *Trinity* who is uncreated and spirit in form (John 4:24). LDS: Also known as Elohim or Heavenly Father, He was once a righteous human in another realm who died and became the God of this world with a tangible body of flesh and bones (D&C 130:22).

Godhead. Christian: See *Trinity*. LDS: *God the Father, Jesus*, and the *Holy Ghost*, who remain separate deities but are one in purpose.

Gospel. Christian: 1) One of the four books at the beginning of the New Testament telling the story of *Jesus*. 2) The explanation of how *forgiveness* of *sin* is available through faith in *Jesus*. LDS: All doctrines, principles, laws, ordinances, and covenants necessary for a *Latter-day Saint* to receive *eternal life*.

Gospel Topics essays. LDS: A series of 13 articles written between 2013 to 2015 by LDS Church historians published on the church's website. These explain controversial issues such as plural marriage, the Book of Mormon translation, and Joseph Smith's behavior/practices.

Grace. Christian: Unmerited favor from God provided to those who place their trust in *Jesus*. LDS: Enabling power provided by God to help a person keep the commandments.

Heaven. Christian: Destiny for godly angels and forgiven believers to spend eternity in the presence of God. LDS: A general term referring to the three *degrees of glory*. See *celestial kingdom*.

Hell. Christian: A place where *Satan* and his angels as well as unforgiven people will spend eternity separated from the presence of God. LDS: Can refer to either *spirit prison* or *outer darkness*.

Heresy. False teaching.

Holy Spirit/Holy Ghost. Christian: The third person of the *Trinity* who spiritually baptizes believers and fills their lives with His presence. LDS: The third member of the *Godhead* who is a personage of spirit. Unlike *God the Father* and *Jesus*, the Holy Ghost does not have a body of flesh and bones.

Hypostatic union. Christian: *Jesus* as fully God and fully man (two natures) existing in one person.

Imputation. Christian: The righteousness of God credited to the believer's account and not earned through individual good works.

Incarnation. Christian: As the second person of the *Trinity*, the teaching that *Jesus* became fully human.

Inerrancy. Christian: The belief that the *Bible*, as originally written, was inspired by God and is without error.

Infallible. Christian: The belief that what the *Bible* teaches about matters of faith and practice are exactly the way God intended it to be communicated.

Inspiration. Christian: The belief that the authors of the *Bible* wrote according to the way God intended.

Jesus. Christian: The second person of the *Trinity*, who came to earth and lived a human life. His sacrifice on the cross allows believers to be forgiven of their *sins*. LDS: God the Father's firstborn son and humanity's oldest brother. Known as Jehovah, he became a god through obedience.

Joseph Smith. The founder and first prophet/president of The Church of Jesus Christ of Latter-day Saints.

Justification. Christian: Referring to *salvation*, the idea that believers are forgiven of their *sins* based solely on the *atonement* accomplished by *Jesus* on the cross.

Kingdom of glory. LDS: One of three places where most humans will spend eternity. The highest kingdom is called the *celestial kingdom*. The others are the *terrestrial* and *telestial kingdoms*.

Latter-day Saint. LDS: A person who belongs to The Church of Jesus Christ of Latter-day Saints.

Lord's Supper. See *communion*.

Mercy. Christian: The undeserved favor a believer receives from God by not getting what was justly due (punishment for *sin*). LDS: Favor provided through the *atonement* that allows obedient Latter-day Saints to return to the presence of *God the Father*.

Miracle. Christian: A divine act through the power of God, always with the intention of bringing glory to God.

Mormon. As a noun, a main character in the *Book of Mormon*. Also, an unofficial nickname for someone who belongs to The Church of Jesus Christ of Latter-day Saints. As an adjective, relates to the LDS Church.

Mormonism. The religion of The Church of Jesus Christ of Latter-day Saints.

Ordinance. Christian: A rite celebrated in churches. In Protestant Christianity, these are *baptism* and *communion*. LDS: A sacred ceremony involving promises to keep the commandments of God. These include water *baptism*, confirmation, ordination to the Melchizedek priesthood, the temple endowment, and marriage sealing.

Outer darkness. LDS: Punishment throughout eternity reserved for *Satan* and those considered to be the sons of perdition.

Pearl of Great Price. LDS: One of the four written scriptures that includes Joseph Smith's testimony, the Book of Moses, and the *Book of Abraham*.

Preexistence/Premortality. LDS: A previous existence where humans once existed as spirits. A war in heaven caused one-third of the spirits to be cast out for their disobedience, with the punishment of never receiving physical bodies. Obedient spirits who chose *Jesus* as their savior in this state are given the opportunity to be born on earth with physical bodies needed to progress.

President. LDS: See *prophet*.

Priesthood. Christian: An authority known as the royal priesthood given to every *Christian* regardless of race, nationality, or gender (1 Peter 2:9). LDS: The Aaronic priesthood is held by qualified males 11 years of age or older, while the Melchizedek priesthood is held by qualified males 18 years of age or older.

Prophet. Christian: A leader in the *Bible* who delivered God-ordained messages. LDS: The highest-ranking male leader in the LDS Church, also known as the church president.

Redemption. Christian: The deliverance from *sin* of its guilt, defilement, power, and liability through Christ's sacrifice.

Repentance. Christian: A willful change of mind and behavior as a person turns from *sin* to follow God. LDS: The acknowledgment and later successful abandonment of *sin*.

Resurrection (of Jesus). The raising of *Jesus* from the dead three days after He was crucified. A doctrine accepted by both Christians and Latter-day Saints.

Revelation. Christian: See *general* and *special revelation*. LDS: God's ongoing communication to humanity through prayer and the authoritative guidance of the LDS leaders.

Sacrament. Christian: For some denominations, a word that is synonymous with *ordinance*. LDS: The distribution of bread and water in the weekly church service to remember Christ's atoning sacrifice and a time for members to renew the covenants they made at their *baptism* when they promised to keep all of God's commandments.

Salvation. Christian: Depending on the context, a reference to one of the following: *justification*, *sanctification*, and *glorification*. LDS: 1) General salvation, or salvation by grace, provided to all humans through the *atonement*; 2) Individual salvation, or *eternal life*, earned by those who successfully *repent* and continually keep all of God's commandments as outlined by the LDS Church.

Sanctification. Christian: The Holy Spirit's transforming work in a *Christian* to continue to die to *sin* and live in righteousness.

Satan. Christian: A created being who tempts humans to *sin* and accuses *Christians*. He will one day be cast into the lake of fire. LDS: A spirit child of God known as Lucifer in the *preexistence* who rebelled against God and was cast down to the earth. His final destination is *outer darkness*.

Scripture. Christian: See *canon*. LDS: See *standard works*.

Seventy. LDS: A *general authority* position under the *president* and *apostles*.

Sin. Christian: All people are tainted with original sin through the disobedience of Adam (Romans 5:12). In addition, every person has individually broken God's commandments (Romans 3:10). LDS: Disobedience to the commandments of God who "cannot look upon sin with the least degree of allowance" (D&C 1:31).

Skeptic. In a general sense as used in this book, those who consider themselves *atheists* or *agnostics*.

Special revelation. Christian: God's *revelation* of Himself through *miracles* and the inspired words of the *Bible*.

Standard works. LDS: The four written scriptures: *Bible* (officially, KJV), the *Book of Mormon*, the *Doctrine and Covenants*, and the *Pearl of Great Price*.

Straw man fallacy. An argument presenting an opponent's view in an unfair manner to make it easy to argue against (e.g., "The *Trinity* teaches that there are three gods in one God").

Tell. An artificial hill in the Near East containing layers of multiple civilizations.

Temple. Christian: A building originally constructed by Solomon in Jerusalem as a house for the ark of the covenant and as a special place to worship God. It was destroyed by the Romans in AD 70. LDS: Special buildings around the world where sacred *ordinances* are performed, including marriages for "time and eternity" and work on behalf of the dead. As of 2022, there were more than 170 temples throughout the world, with many more being built.

Theology. The study of biblical *doctrines*.

Translation, Bible. Putting the words from the original languages (Greek, Hebrew, Aramaic) into another language. Modern scholars attempt to stick close to what was written in the ancient texts while making the wording understandable.

Transmission, Bible. The process by which the words of the original manuscripts were preserved and passed down throughout the centuries by a variety of scribes.

Trinity. Christian: The doctrine of one God as revealed in three persons: the Father, Son, and Holy Spirit.

Virgin birth. Christian: The conception of *Jesus* in Mary's womb through the power of the *Holy Spirit* (Matthew 1:18). LDS: The literal begetting of *Jesus* by God the Father and his spiritual daughter Mary.

Word (of God). Christian: Depending on the context, a reference to either the *Bible* or *Jesus*.

Worldview. The belief system each person has in interpreting reality. Each person has a particular spiritual worldview accumulated through family or the culture.

SCRIPTURE INDEX

1 Kings
8:60: 99
18:16-46: 135
20:20: 46

2 Kings
19:16: 104

1 Chronicles
16:35: 98
17:20: 99

Ezra
3:11: 98

Nehemiah
1:6: 105

Job
11:5: 104
33:4: 99
42:2: 100

Psalms
11:7: 98
16:10: 139
18:30: 98
19:1: 81
22:7-8: 139
22:16: 43, 139
22:18: 139
25:8: 97-98
33:5: 108
34:9: 101
34:15: 104
36:5: 98
36:7: 104
68:18: 139
75:1-7: 98

84:11: 239
86:15: 98
89:10: 104
90:2: 14, 82, 102, 136
91:1: 104
91:4: 104
92:15: 97
93:2: 82
96:15: 98
99:4: 98
103:12: 191
110:1: 139
111:10: 101
139:7-12: 99, 162
145:19: 101
146:7-9: 98

Proverbs
1:7: 101
3:7: 101
8:13: 101
8:17: 241
9:10: 101
15:3: 99
16:5: 101
19:23: 101
28:5: 108

Ecclesiastes
12:13: 101

Isaiah
1:17: 280
1:18: 23
6:3: 98, 108
6:8: 278
7:14: 119, 138
9:6-7: 117, 276

11:1-3: 117
28:29: 98
30:18: 98
30:27: 104
33:5: 108
35:5-6: 138
37:16: 99
40:3: 138
40:8: 31
40:28: 100
43:10-11: 14, 99, 105
44:6,8: 14, 99, 105, 136
45:18: 105
45:21-23: 99, 105, 123-124
46:9-10: 98
53: 138-139
53:5: 186
53:7: 126
54:10: 98
55:11: 129
61:8: 98, 108
64:6: 182
66:1: 99, 104

Jeremiah
1:5: 98
17:9: 71
23:23-24: 98-99
29:13: 92
32:17: 100

Lamentations
3:22-23: 183

Hosea
6:3-6: 280

Romans

1:3: 122
1:16-17: 279
1:18-20: 81
2:5-8: 110
2:14-15: 88-89
2:28-29: 279
3:2: 39
3:10: 107, 253
3:21: 98
3:22: 279
3:23: 181-182
3:24: 182
3:28: 183
4:1-5: 184-185, 279
4:5: 183
4:20-21: 136
4:24-25: 279
5:1-2: 279
5:5: 202
5:8: 98, 185
5:9: 182
5:10: 127
5:12: 107, 253
5:15: 198
5:18-19: 87, 127, 198
6:1-2: 208
6:6-7: 208
6:11-14: 208-209
6:14: 183
6:19: 209
6:23: 182
7:4,5: 204
7:15-20: 209
7:24-25: 210

8:1-2: 182, 210
8:3-4: 202
8:11: 163
8:14: 127
8:14-17: 192
8:26-27: 236
8:39: 98
9:5: 122
9:15-16: 98
10:9-13: 127, 237
11:6: 183
11:33: 98
12:1-2: 211
12:6-8: 206
13:14: 211

1 Corinthians

1:9: 98
1:10: 202
1:14-15: 214
1:16: 215
1:18: 146
1:22-25: 144
2:2: 146
2:9-10,12: 201
3:1-3: 202
6:1-8: 202
6:14: 100
8:4: 161
8:6: 99, 118
9:24-27: 231
10:13: 98
11:21: 202
11:23-26: 216
11:27-30: 217
12:3: 201

12:4-11: 205
12:11: 205
12:13: 213, 215
13:13: 24
15:1-3: 127
15:3-8: 133, 148, 151
15:29: 54
15:57: 182
15:58: 280

2 Corinthians

1:3-4: 210
3:17-18: 99, 162
4:4: 122
5:5: 202
5:6,12: 229
5:17: 191
5:20: 241
5:21: 120, 185
6:2: 266
7:10: 211-212
8:1-15: 229
8:9: 190
9:7: 229
9:8: 280
11:4: 115
11:16-33: 90
12:9-10: 90, 239
13:14: 157

Galatians

2:15-16: 183, 279
3:1-5: 202
3:11: 279
3:20: 161
3:26-28: 192
3:27: 215

1 Peter
1:3: 154, 183
1:15-16: 280
1:17-19: 275
1:22-25: 232
1:23: 191
2:2: 232
2:9: 192, 252
2:11: 211
2:12: 197
2:22: 122
2:24: 183, 185, 199
3:15: 22, 24
4:8: 202
4:10-11: 205
4:23: 202
4:31: 202
5:8: 232

2 Peter
1:19-21: 37
3:15-16: 38

1 John
1:5: 95, 136
1:9: 98, 183, 238
2:3: 218
2:4: 280
2:12: 183
3:1-2: 192
3:3-5: 136
3:5: 122
3:20: 98
4:1: 227
4:2-3: 122
4:7-8: 98
4:9-10: 189

5:6-8: 63
5:10-13: 127
5:13: 218
5:20: 122

2 John
6: 280
7: 122

3 John
4,11: 280

Jude
25: 117

Revelation
1:8: 118
1:17-18: 118
4:8: 98
20:15: 110
21:6: 118
21:22: 104
22:13: 118

BOOK OF MORMON

1 Nephi
15:34: 180

2 Nephi
10:24: 183
25:23: 183, 279

Alma
34:32-35: 179, 266

3 Nephi
11:29: 20

Moroni
8:18: 102

DOCTRINE AND COVENANTS

1:31-32: 181, 254
20:19: 278
20:21-28: 278
58:43: 179, 180
88:6,7,13: 99
88:34-40: 100
93:13,17: 121
93:29,33,35: 100
130:22: 14, 99, 103, 249

PEARL OF GREAT PRICE JOSEPH SMITH-HISTORY

1:19: 225

BOOK OF ABRAHAM

3:22: 100
4:1: 99-100

SUBJECT INDEX

NOTES

INTRODUCTION

1. The official Bible translation for The Church of Jesus Christ of Latter-day Saints is the King James Version (KJV), but many English speakers have a hard time understanding the archaic language of a work originally published in 1611 and later modified in 1769 (the edition most used today). I will regularly cite the reputable English Standard Version (ESV) throughout this book, unless otherwise noted. If it makes the LDS reader more comfortable, feel free to compare the ESV with the KJV.

2. The dialogues used throughout this book are based on actual encounters I have had since 1987. While the example from any single chapter could incorporate two or three different discussions, all are authentic. All names have been changed.

3. For our purposes, an "evangelical/born again/biblical" Christian is someone who holds that the Bible is the Word of God and, generally, considers its words to be taken literally, differentiated from Roman Catholic, Eastern Orthodox, or liberal mainstream Protestant churches. My purpose in this book is not to quibble with the members of these other churches but to present a conservative Protestant (biblical) worldview with the LDS religion.

4. For more information on the use of "Mormon," "Mormonism," and "LDS" as shortened terms to refer to the religion and the people, see "A Revelation from God?" at mrm.org/no-more-mormon.

5. For more on this topic, see chapter 1 in the book *Answering Mormons' Questions: Ready Responses for Inquiring Latter-day Saints* (Grand Rapids, MI: Kregel Publications, 2013).

6. Dallin Oaks, "Apostasy and Restoration," *Ensign*, May 1995, 84. For additional citations, see mrm .org/we-never-criticize. It should be noted that semiannual general conference sessions are held in Salt Lake City on the first weekends of April and October. The English church magazine *Ensign* (1970–2020)/*Liahona* (2021–) provides in the May and November editions the transcripts for the talks given by church leaders. What is taught in these sessions is supposed to be obeyed by the church membership.

7. Bruce R. McConkie, *Mormon Doctrine* (Salt Lake City, UT: Deseret Book Company, 1966), 525. Ellipsis mine. A creed is a written statement of belief. There are ancient creeds that several churches recite regularly, especially the Apostles' Creed and the Nicene Creed.

8. The first chapter in Joseph Smith–History found in the Pearl of Great Price portrays nineteenth century Christians as spiritual buffoons who, at best, were ignorant or, worse yet, concerted opposers of spiritual truth. For LDS leader citations, see mrm.org/index-great-apostasy.

9. Primary 3, "Lesson 6: Jesus Christ's Church Has Been Restored," churchofjesuschrist.org/study/manual/primary-3/lesson-6-jesus-christs-church-has-been-restored?lang=eng. Ellipsis mine.

10. Generally, Mormonism teaches that efficacious work of an individual is possible after this life. Thus, a good person might get a second chance at celestial glory, although church leaders have not provided specific details as to how this works (i.e., how much ignorance about Mormonism's teachings is necessary to have a chance to reach the celestial kingdom after death). The Bible never teaches second-chance salvation (2 Corinthians 6:2; Hebrews 9:27) and neither, for that matter, does the Book of Mormon (Alma 34:32-35).

11. Joseph Fielding Smith, *Doctrines of Salvation* (Salt Lake City, UT: Bookcraft, 1954), 1:135.

12. J.P. Moreland, *Love Your God with All Your Mind: The Role of Reason in the Life of the Soul* (Colorado Springs, CO: NavPress, 1997), 74.

13. Ibid., 101.

14. Norman L. Geisler, *Baker Encyclopedia of Christian Apologetics* (Grand Rapids, MI: Baker Books, 1999), 745. The statement used here illustrates the law of noncontradiction, which states that both propositions can be false but both cannot be true. In other words, a proposition cannot be A and non-A at the same time.

15. Millard J. Erickson, *Introducing Christian Doctrine* (Grand Rapids, MI: Baker Academic, 2001), 16. Italics in original. Ellipsis mine.

16. R.C. Sproul, *Does God Control Everything?* (Orlando, FL: Reformation Trust, 2012), 6.

17. Harold O.J. Brown, *Heresies: The Image of Christ in the Mirror of Heresy and Orthodoxy from the Apostles to the Present* (Grand Rapids, MI: Baker, 1984), 19, 21. Ellipsis mine. Among the important early creeds were the Apostles' Creed (AD 120–250); Creed of Nicaea (AD 325 at the Council of Nicaea); Nicene Creed (AD 381 at Constantinople); the Chalcedonian Creed (AD 451 at the Council of Chalcedon); and the Athanasian Creed (AD 500).

18. Roger E. Olson, *The Story of Christian Theology* (Downers Grove, IL: InterVarsity Press, 1999), 16.

19. Harold O.J. Brown, *Heresies: The Image of Christ in the Mirror of Heresy and Orthodoxy from the Apostles to the Present* (Grand Rapids, MI: Baker, 1984), 22.

20. A good verse to use when someone uses this argument is Mormon 7:7 in the Book of Mormon. It says those found guiltless will "dwell in the presence of God in his kingdom, to sing ceaseless praises with the choirs above, unto the Father, and unto the Son, and unto the Holy Ghost, which are one God, in a state of happiness which hath no end"!

21. Corey Miller, *Engaging with Mormons: Understanding Their World Sharing Good News* (Epsom, UK: Good Book Company, 2020), 103.

22. J. Gresham Machen, *What Is Christianity? (And Other Addresses)* (Grand Rapids, MI: Eerdmans, 1951), 132-33. *Polemic* means a strong argument or refutation of other views.

23. If my intention is to harm rather than help the LDS people, I am no better than Saul of Tarsus who persecuted Christians before he encountered Jesus on the road to Damascus. For more, see "Why should I care about sharing my faith with Latter-day Saints?" found at mrm.org/sharing-faith-with-mormons.

24. D. Michael Quinn, ed., *J. Reuben Clark: The Church Years* (Provo, UT: Brigham Young University Press, 1983), 24. The law school at the LDS Church-owned Brigham Young University is named after Clark who was a member of the First Presidency.

25. Timothy Keller, *Galatians for You* (Epsom, UK: Good Book Company, 2013), 114-15.

26. This book's purpose is not to necessarily provide a full description of Mormonism. To read more about LDS teaching as contrasted with Christianity, I recommend *Mormonism 101: Examining the Religion of the Latter-day Saints* (Grand Rapids, MI: Baker Books, 2015) that I wrote with Bill McKeever. For a simple layout of LDS teaching, see the articles found at CrashCourseMormonism.com.

27. For a variety of different evangelistic tactics, *Sharing the Good News with Mormons* (Eugene, OR: Harvest House Publishers, 2018), a book I co-edited with Sean McDowell, may be helpful. Each of the 24 chapters is authored by a different Christian apologist or pastor.

28. For more about my personal history, visit IntroducingChristianity.com/introducing-introduction.

CHAPTER 1—THE BIBLE: GOD'S SPECIAL REVELATION

1. Today the Wycliffe Bible Translators (wycliffe.com), a Christian missionary group, attempts to translate the Bible into as many languages as possible. According to this organization, there are at least 7000 languages in the world, yet the full Bible has been translated into fewer than a tenth of them. About a third of the world's languages do not have a portion of God's Word. This means that about two billion people have no access to any part of the Bible in their mother tongue.

2. A helpful article on this issue can be found at namb.net/apologetics/resource/the-new-world -translation-of-the-holy-scriptures-the-jehovah-s-witnesses-bible/.

3. For an overview of how Jehovah's Witnesses interpret John 1:1, see carm.org/jehovahs-witnesses/ john-11-the-word-was-a-god. For a scholarly 2014 article titled "Jehovah's Witnesses and John 1:1: New Evidence Advances the Discussion" by Brian J. Wright and Tim Ricchuiti, see equip.org/ article/jehovahs-witnesses-john-11-new-evidence-advances-discussion.

4. Neil A. Maxwell, "The Wondrous Restoration," *Ensign*, April 2003, 35. For other LDS teachings on the Bible, visit mrm.org/bible-quotes.

5. Ezra Taft Benson, Gordon B. Hinckley, and Thomas Monson, "Letter Reaffirms Use of King James Version of Bible," *Church News*, June 20, 1992, 3.

6. Robert J. Matthews, *A Bible! A Bible!* (Salt Lake City, UT: Bookcraft, 1990), 72. Italics in original.

7. Joseph Fielding Smith, ed., *Teachings of the Prophet Joseph Smith* (Salt Lake City, UT: Deseret Book, 1977), 327.

8. Wayne Grudem, *Systematic Theology: An Introduction to Biblical Doctrine* (Grand Rapids, MI: Zondervan Academic, 1994), 132. Most errors in Mormonism stem from the LDS leaders' 1) low view of the Bible's authority/reliability; 2) misreading of biblical texts; and 3) emphasized appeal to additional scripture.

9. Roger E. Olson, *The Story of Christian Theology* (Downers Grove, IL: InterVarsity Press, 1999), 131-32. Ellipsis mine.

10. Grudem, *Systematic Theology*, 57.

11. William Lane Craig, *The Son Rises: Historical Evidence for the Resurrection of Jesus* (Eugene, OR: Wipf & Stock Publishers, 2001), 34.

12. Craig L. Blomberg, *Can We Still Believe the Bible? An Evangelical Engagement with Contemporary Questions* (Grand Rapids, MI: Brazos Press, 2013), 68. Ellipsis mine. The Coptic Gospel of Thomas providing 114 sayings attributed to Jesus is often accepted by liberal scholars even though it was composed in the second century AD. On pages 71-74, Blomberg provides reasons why this

book was rejected by early Christians, concluding on page 81 that the Gospel of Thomas "merits close scrutiny, but after such scrutiny it becomes clear it does not belong in the canon."

13. Ibid., 67. Italics in original.

14. Lee Strobel, *The Case for Christ: A Journalist's Personal Investigation of the Evidence for Jesus* (Grand Rapids, MI: Zondervan Publishing, 1998), 90. Ellipsis mine.

15. Generally, I recommend not using the word *scripture* to reference the Bible in conversations with Mormons. Rather, say *Bible* to be clear.

16. R.C. Sproul, *Can I Trust the Bible?* (Sanford, FL: Reformation Trust Publishing, 2017), 19.

17. Norman Geisler and Ron Brooks, *When Skeptics Ask: A Handbook on Christian Evidences* (Wheaton, IL: Victor Books, 1990), 146.

18. Grudem, *Systematic Theology*, 60-61. Ellipsis mine.

19. Gleason L. Archer, *Encyclopedia of Bible Difficulties* (Grand Rapids, MI: Zondervan, 1982), 19. Italics mine. For more on the topic of inerrancy, see "Why Inerrancy of the Bible Is So Important to Evangelical Christians" at mrm.org/bible-inerrancy.

20. Many scholars believe that 1 Timothy was composed in the middle AD 60s, just a few years before Luke wrote his Gospel.

21. Norman L. Geisler, *Baker Encyclopedia of Christian Apologetics* (Grand Rapids, MI: Baker Books, 1999), 79.

22. Archaeologists identify the 11 caves by using the chronological number in which each was discovered. Thus, Cave 1 is the first cave found and Cave 11 is the last. Several other caves have been uncovered, though any manuscripts once hidden in them are gone.

23. No copies of the book of Esther were discovered, although a section of a commentary on this book was located.

24. Randall Price, *Secrets of the Dead Sea Scrolls* (Eugene, OR: Harvest House Publishers, 1996), 127.

25. Ibid., 145-46. Italics in original. Ellipsis mine.

26. Gleason Archer, *A Survey of the Old Testament* (Chicago, IL: Moody Press, 1994), 25. Ellipsis and italics mine.

27. John D. Currid, *The Case for Biblical Archaeology: Uncovering the Historical Record of God's Old Testament People* (Phillipsburg, NJ: P&R Publishing, 2020), 3. Ellipsis mine.

28. One secular archaeological publication declared in 2021 that there is "evidence from archaeology and ancient texts for the historical existence of 53 *real* people in the Hebrew Bible and, in the New Testament, Jesus plus 23 political figures." The article lists six additional New Testament figures, and "when added to the documented real people in the Hebrew Bible, we arrive at a grand total of 83 real Bible people—for now." Meanwhile, the number of positively identified biblical sites from the Holy Lands are many hundreds, with new sites being found on a regular basis (Lawrence Mykytiuk, "New Testament Religious Figures Confirmed," *Biblical Archaeological Review*, Summer 2021, vol. 47, no. 2, 38, 47). In contrast, not even one Book of Mormon character or historical site can be positively verified as support for Mormonism's most emphasized scripture.

29. Joel P. Kramer, *Where God Came Down: The Archaeological Evidence* (Brigham City, UT: Expedition Bible, 2020), 8.

30. An example is Shimon Gibson, a respected Israeli biblical archaeologist whom I met on an Israel trip in 2013. He has been involved in many important New Testament excavations at a variety

of Israeli sites, including Jerusalem and Bethlehem. Gibson wrote a book titled *The Final Days of Jesus: The Archaeological Evidence* (New York: Harper One, 2010), yet he remains an agnostic who denies the deity of Jesus.

31. On pages 256-259 in their book *I Don't Have Enough Faith to Be an Atheist* (Wheaton, IL: Crossway, 2004), Norman Geisler and Frank Turek provide 84 different facts about how Luke accurately depicted the first century Roman world in the book of Acts despite having no access to modern maps or nautical charts. For instance, he knew "the correct title grammateus for the chief executive magistrate in Ephesus (19:35)" and "Felix being governor at this time (23:24)."

32. Titus Kennedy, *Unearthing the Bible: 101 Archaeological Discoveries that Bring the Bible to Life* (Eugene, OR: Harvest House Publishers, 2020), 48-61. Kennedy lists several other discoveries from Egypt that further support the historicity of Hebrew people who left Egypt.

CHAPTER 2—THE NEW TESTAMENT: TRUSTWORTHY AND RELIABLE

1. For instance, Ehrman has produced popular multi-episode programs for the Great Courses, including *History of the Bible*, *History of the New Testament*, and the best-selling *How Jesus Became God*, none of which are recommended.

2. We don't have room to fully cover the teachings of Bart Ehrman, but the appendix ("Responding to the Challenges of Bart Ehrman") in Josh and Sean McDowell, *Evidence that Demands a Verdict* (Nashville, TN: Thomas Nelson, 2017), 705-22, is recommended. The McDowells say Ehrman's "arguments that attempt to undermine the deity of Christ and the value of the New Testament texts can and should be challenged because of their significant weaknesses. Taken as a whole, his arguments do not in any way undermine the accuracy of the New Testament and the traditional claims of Christianity."

3. John MacArthur and Richard Mayhue, *Biblical Doctrine* (Wheaton, IL: Crossway, 2017), 111-12. Italics in original.

4. Darrell L. Bock and Daniel B. Wallace, *Dethroning Jesus: Exposing Popular Culture's Quest to Unseat the Biblical Christ* (Nashville, TN: Thomas Nelson, 2007), 46. Copyists who may have used any of the autographs as their source might not have taken special care (i.e., wearing gloves, sanitizing the area where the manuscript laid, avoiding direct sunlight) to have prolonged the life of these scrolls. We will never know.

5. Lee Strobel, *The Case for the Real Jesus: A Journalist Investigates Current Attacks on the Identity of Christ* (Grand Rapids, MI: Zondervan, 2011), 73. Ellipsis mine.

6. F.F. Bruce, *The New Testament Documents: Are They Reliable?* (Grand Rapids, MI: Wm. B. Eerdmans Publishing Co., 1981), 10. Ellipsis mine.

7. Daniel Wallace in Nabeel Qureshi, *Seeking Allah, Finding Jesus: A Devout Muslim Encounters Christianity* (Grand Rapids, MI: Zondervan, 2016), 305.

8. Bock and Wallace, *Dethroning Jesus*, 49.

9. Ibid., 50.

10. Daniel Wallace in Appendix 1 ("Testing the New Testament"), in Qureshi's *Seeking Allah, Finding Jesus*, 305.

11. Ibid.

12. Craig L. Blomberg, *Can We Still Believe the Bible? An Evangelical Engagement with Contemporary Questions* (Grand Rapids, MI: Brazos Press, 2013), 18.

13. Norman L. Geisler, *Baker Encyclopedia of Christian Apologetics* (Grand Rapids, MI: Baker Books, 1999), 537.

14. The LDS Church website maintains that many biblical books may have "perhaps even [been] willfully destroyed" (churchofjesuschrist.org/study/scriptures/bd/canon?lang=eng). There is no evidence for this claim.

15. Blomberg, *Can We Still Believe the Bible?*, 27. Italics in original.

16. Wallace in Qureshi, *Seeking Allah, Finding Jesus*, 306.

17. F.F. Bruce, *The New Testament Documents: Are They Reliable?* (Grand Rapids, MI: Wm. B. Eerdmans Publishing Co., 1981), 14-15.

18. Blomberg, *Can We Still Believe the Bible?*, 15.

19. Ibid., 17.

20. Bruce M. Metzger, *A Textual Commentary on the Greek New Testament* (Germany: United Bible Societies, 1971), 43.

21. Wallace in Lee Strobel, *The Case for the Real Jesus: A Journalist Investigates Current Attacks on the Identity of Christ* (Grand Rapids, MI: Zondervan, 2011), 89.

22. Ibid., 97.

23. F.F. Bruce, *The New Testament Documents: Are They Reliable?* (Grand Rapids, MI: Wm. B. Eerdmans Publishing Co., 1981), 14-15.

24. "Manuscript Discoveries of the New Testament in Perspective," Papers of the Fourteenth Annual Symposium on the Archaeology of the Scriptures, Presented April 13, 1963, 57-58.

25. It should be noted that the Book of Mormon cites Mark 16:16-18 word-for-word in Mormon 9:23-24. These verses are not included in any other Gospel.

26. Wallace in Qureshi, *Seeking Allah, Finding Jesus*, 307.

27. For an overview on this topic by Daniel Wallace, see bible.org/article/textual-problem-1-john-57-8.

28. Greg Koukl, "'Misquoting' Jesus? Answering Bart Ehrman," str.org/w/-misquoting-jesus-answering-bart-ehrman. Timothy Paul Jones responds to Ehrman's claims in his rebuttal book titled *Misquoting Truth: A Guide to the Fallacies of Bart Ehrman's 'Misquoting Jesus'* (Downers Grove, IL: InterVarsity Press, 2007).

29. B.H. Roberts, ed., *History of the Church of Jesus Christ of Latter-day Saints* (Salt Lake City, UT: Deseret Book Company, 1976), 1:368.

30. For more on the Joseph Smith translation, visit mrm.org/jst-passion-week.

31. Millard J. Erickson, *Christian Theology* (Grand Rapids, MI: Baker Book House, 1986) 1:237. Italics in original.

32. Ibid., 1:236.

33. Thaddeus J. Williams, *Confronting Justice Without Compromising Truth: 12 Questions Christians Should Ask About Social Justice* (Grand Rapids, MI: Zondervan Academic, 2020), 203-4. Italics in original.

34. For a study guide on Romans, see mrm.org/romans-road.

35. For more on this issue, see "Why a Modern Translation of the Bible Can be Beneficial," mrm.org/modern-translation.

36. Consider the story of Micah Wilder, who, as a Mormon missionary in Florida, was told by a pastor to read the Bible as a little child. Micah read the New Testament more than a dozen times during his mission over the next two years and ended up becoming a Christian. This incredible story is found at *Passport to Heaven: The True Story of a Zealous Mormon Missionary Who Discovers the Jesus He Never Knew* (Eugene, OR: Harvest House Publishers, 2021) and is highly recommended.

37. Wayne Grudem, *Systematic Theology: An Introduction to Biblical Doctrine* (Grand Rapids, MI: Zondervan Academic, 1994), 717. Italics in original.

CHAPTER 3—THE EXISTENCE OF GOD:
REASONABLE REASONS FOR BELIEF

1. To see more on this issue, visit mrm.org/book-of-mormon-translation-essay.

2. To see more on this issue, visit mrm.org/book-of-abraham-essay.

3. Referring to the "Neo-atheists," Paul Copan points out how their "arguments against God's existence are surprisingly flimsy, often resembling the simplistic village atheist far more than the credentialed academician." Paul Copan, *Is God a Moral Monster?: Making Sense of the Old Testament God* (Grand Rapids, MI: Baker Books, 2011), 17.

4. On page 220 of her book *The Next Mormons: How Millennials Are Changing the LDS Church* (New York: Oxford University Press), Mormon blogger Jana Riess reports that 44 percent of former Mormons classify themselves as atheist, agnostic, or nothing at all. This is a very troubling statistic, especially since she recorded only 10 percent who ended up as evangelical Christians.

5. Josh and Sean McDowell, *Evidence that Demands a Verdict* (Nashville, TN: Thomas Nelson, 2017), xxxix.

6. Norman L. Geisler and Frank Turek, *I Don't Have Enough Faith to Be an Atheist* (Wheaton, IL: Crossway, 2004), 26. Italics in original.

7. Alex McFarland, *The 10 Most Common Objections to Christianity* (Ventura, CA: Regal, 2007), 37-38.

8. Frank Turek, *Stealing from God: Why Atheists Need God to Make Their Case* (Colorado Springs, CO: NavPress, 2014), xxiii-xxv. Ellipses mine.

9. Paul Copan, *That's Just Your Interpretation: Responding to Skeptics Who Challenge Your Faith* (Grand Rapids, MI: Baker Publishing, 2001), 22.

10. Antony Flew, *There Is a God: How the World's Most Notorious Atheist Changed His Mind* (New York: HarperCollins, 2007), 132.

11. Ibid., 158. Flew said on page 185, "I think that the Christian religion is the one religion that most clearly deserves to be honored and respected whether or not its claims to be a divine revelation is true."

12. Norman L. Geisler, *Baker Encyclopedia of Christian Apologetics* (Grand Rapids, MI: Baker Books, 1999), 277.

13. Stephen C. Meyer, *Return of the God Hypothesis: Three Scientific Discoveries that Reveal the Mind Behind the Universe* (New York: Harper One, 2021), 382. For those who want to overdose on scientific evidence, I recommend this resource as well as other works by Meyer.

14. Ibid., 238.

15. Geisler, *Baker Encyclopedia of Christian Apologetics*, 26-27.

16. Michael J. Behe, *Darwin's Black Box: The Biochemical Challenge to Evolution* (New York: Free Press, 2006), 42. Behe responded to critics in *A Mousetrap for Darwin: Michael J. Behe Answers His Critics* (Seattle, WA: Discovery Institute Press, 2020).

17. C.S. Lewis, *Mere Christianity* (New York: MacMillan Publishing, 1943), 45. Italics in original.

18. Geisler, *Baker Encyclopedia of Christian Apologetics*, 279. Italics in original. Ellipsis mine.

19. Turek, *Stealing from God*, 97.

20. Ibid., 98.

21. Geisler and Turek, *I Don't Have Enough Faith to Be an Atheist*, 172. Italics in original.

22. For evidence of religious persecution that continues today, visit the Voice of the Martyrs website at persecution.com.

23. C.S. Lewis, *The Problem of Pain* (New York: Macmillan Publishing, 1962), 110.

24. For a comparison of five different views, see Chad Meister and James K. Dew Jr., eds., *God and the Problem of Evil: Five Views* (Downers Grove, IL: IVP Academic, 2017).

25. John Piper, desiringgod.org/interviews/what-is-so-important-about-christian-hope. Italics in original.

26. J.P. Moreland, *Love Your God with All Your Mind: The Role of Reason in the Life of the Soul* (Colorado Springs, CO: NavPress, 1997), 39.

CHAPTER 4–THE NATURE OF GOD:
ATTRIBUTES WORTHY OF WORSHIP

1. For example, see "Does Lorenzo Snow's famous couplet no longer have a functioning place in LDS theology?" (mrm.org/snow-couplet). This couplet has been taught in recent church manuals assigned for members to read, including chapter 14 in *Teachings of Presidents of the Church: George Albert Smith* (Salt Lake City, UT: The Church of Jesus Christ of Latter-day Saints, 2011) and chapter 5 in *Teachings of Presidents of the Church: Lorenzo Snow* (Salt Lake City, UT: The Church of Jesus Christ of Latter-day Saints, 2012). As far as becoming gods, an official Gospel Topics essay published by the LDS Church explains that "the divine nature that humans inherit can be developed to become like their Heavenly Father's." See mrm.org/becoming-like-god.

2. Found at GodNeverSinned.com, a site created by MRM associate Aaron Shafovaloff. youtube .com/watch?v=WyH61ybnPBE. Ellipses mine.

3. The God of Heavenly Father—whomever He might be and whatever His name—is not considered by Mormons to be the "grandfather" God of humanity. In reality, though, that is who this god would be if the concept is true.

4. A.W. Tozer, *The Knowledge of the Holy* (New York: Harper & Row, 1961), 1-2. Ellipses mine.

5. Ibid., 12.

6. Millard J. Erickson, *Christian Theology* (Grand Rapids, MI: Baker Book House, 1986), 1:28. "Theology" literally means the "study of God" (*theos* = God, *logy* = study of). More than once I have told my students that every Christian should love theology because what could be more important than studying God!

7. See news-ca.churchofjesuschrist.org/article/mormonism-101-faq.

8. The choir's name was changed to the Tabernacle Choir at Temple Square in 2018.

9. Jerry Bridges, *The Practice of Godliness* (Colorado Springs, CO: NavPress, 1983), 26-27. Ellipsis mine.

10. On page 8 of the July 1973 *Ensign* magazine, Marion G. Romney—a member of the First Presidency—said, "The truth is, my beloved brethren and sisters, man is a child of God—a God in embryo." This idea was also taught by Spencer W. Kimball in *The Miracle of Forgiveness* (Salt Lake City, UT: Bookcraft, 1969), 3.

11. Wayne Grudem, *Systematic Theology: An Introduction to Biblical Doctrine* (Grand Rapids, MI: Zondervan Academic, 1994), 442-43. Italics in original. For an article titled "Responding to the Claim that God was Once a Man," visit mrm.org/god-once-a-man.

12. See John 1:18 as well as 1 Timothy 1:17; 6:15-16.

13. Grudem, *Systematic Theology,* 188. Italics in original.

14. Even Adolf Hitler is qualified for one of Mormonism's kingdoms of glory since vicarious work on his behalf was accomplished in the London, England, LDS temple in 1993–1994. To see Hitler's scanned baptismal and endowment listing, visit mrm.org/adolph-hitler-record.

15. See Matthew 5:22,28 and James 2:10.

16. R.C. Sproul, *Does God Control Everything?* (Orlando, FL: Reformation Trust, 2012), 21.

17. Greg Koukl, *The Story of Reality* (Grand Rapids, MI: Zondervan, 2017), 117.

18. The Book of Mormon teaches the existence of hell. For more, see beggarsbread.org/2017/03/05/the-book-of-mormon-and-the-eternality-of-hell.

19. Koukl, *The Story of Reality*, 160. Ellipsis mine.

CHAPTER 5—JESUS: SAVIOR OF HIS PEOPLE

1. Michael J. Wilkins and J.P. Moreland, eds., *Jesus Under Fire: Modern Scholarship Reinvents the Historical Jesus* (Grand Rapids, MI: Zondervan, 1995), 221-22. Italics in original.

2. J.I. Packer, *Keep in Step with the Spirit* (Old Tappan, NJ: Fleming H. Revell, 1984), 42.

3. Gordon B. Hinckley, "Crown of Gospel Is Upon Our Heads," *Church News*, June 20, 1998, 7.

4. Gordon B. Hinckley, "We Look to Christ," *Ensign*, May 2002, 90. For other LDS citations on the topic of Jesus, see mrm.org/jesus-quotes.

5. Milton R. Hunter, *The Gospel Through the Ages* (Salt Lake City, UT: Deseret Book, 1957), 51.

6. Bruce R. McConkie, *Mormon Doctrine* (Salt Lake City, UT: Deseret Book Company, 1966), 323.

7. Robert D. Hales, "Your Sorrow Shall Be Turned to Joy," *Ensign*, November 1983, 67.

8. *Gospel Fundamentals* (Salt Lake City, UT: The Church of Jesus Christ of Latter-day Saints, 2002), 5.

9. Ron Rhodes, *Christ Before the Manger: The Life and Times of the Preincarnate Christ* (Grand Rapids, MI: Baker Book House, 1992), 41.

10. Robert M. Bowman Jr. and J. Ed Komoszewski, *Putting Jesus in His Place* (Grand Rapids, MI: Kregel, 2007), 103. Italics in original.

11. Harold O.J. Brown, *Heresies: The Image of Christ in the Mirror of Heresy and Orthodoxy from the Apostles to the Present* (Grand Rapids, MI: Baker, 1984), 148.

12. James Talmage, *Jesus the Christ* (Salt Lake City, UT: The Church of Jesus Christ of Latter-day Saints, 1981), 9.

13. McConkie, *Mormon Doctrine*, 547.

14. Ezra Taft Benson, *The Teachings of Ezra Taft Benson* (Salt Lake City, UT: Bookcraft, 1988), 7.

15. Rhodes, *Christ Before the Manger,* 16.

16. Ibid., 191.

17. Millard J. Erickson, *Christian Theology* (Grand Rapids, MI: Baker Book House, 1986), 2:756.

18. Millard J. Erickson, *Introducing Christian Doctrine* (Grand Rapids, MI: Baker Academic, 2001), 228.

19. John MacArthur and Richard Mayhue, *Biblical Doctrine* (Wheaton, IL: Crossway, 2017), 262.

20. Ibid., 262-63.

21. The teaching that Heavenly Father—who has a physical body with "parts and passion"—created Jesus through a physical relationship with Mary is highly offensive to Bible-believing Christians. If God had literally impregnated Mary—His spirit daughter in the preexistence according to Mormonism—it would be an incestuous act. For more on this topic, see mrm.org/virgin-birth-doctrine.

22. Ezra Taft Benson, *Sermons and Writings of President Ezra Taft Benson* (Salt Lake City, UT: The Church of Jesus Christ of Latter-day Saints, 2003), 3. Italics in original.

23. "The Atonement Can Secure Your Peace and Happiness," *Ensign*, May 1997, 53.

24. Wayne Grudem, *Systematic Theology: An Introduction to Biblical Doctrine* (Grand Rapids, MI: Zondervan Academic, 1994), 535.

25. Norman Geisler and Peter Bocchino, *Unshakable Foundations: Contemporary Answers to Crucial Questions about the Christian Faith* (Minneapolis, MN: Bethany House, 2001), 287.

26. William F. Arndt and F. Wilbur Gingrich, *A Greek-English Lexicon of the New Testament and Other Early Christian Literature* (Chicago, IL: University of Chicago Press, 1979), 716.

27. Ibid., 717.

28. Bowman Jr. and Komoszewski, *Putting Jesus in His Place,* 20.

29. Geisler and Bocchino, *Unshakable Foundations*, 296. Ellipsis mine.

30. Grudem, *Systematic Theology*, 553. Ellipsis mine.

31. Ibid., 558. Italics in original. Ellipsis mine.

32. MacArthur and Mayhue, *Biblical Doctrine*, 265.

33. Richard G. Scott, "The Atonement Can Secure Your Peace and Happiness," *Ensign*, May 1997, 53.

34. "Divine Love," *Ensign*, February 2003, 24. Italics in original.

35. For more, see "Why Don't Latter-day Saints Pray to Jesus?" at mrm.org/pray-to-jesus.

36. For example, see "Mormonism's Confusion over Christ's Atonement for Sin" (mrm.org/mormonisms-confusion-over-Christs-atonement-for-sin).

37. Joseph Fielding Smith, *Doctrines of Salvation* (Salt Lake City, UT: Bookcraft, 1954), 1:106.

38. C.S. Lewis, *Mere Christianity* (New York: MacMillan Publishing, 1943), 55-56. Ellipses mine.

CHAPTER 6–THE RESURRECTION:
THE CORNERSTONE OF CHRISTIANITY

1. The phrase "Peace Be Upon Him" (abbreviated PBUH) is used by many Muslims whenever the name of one of their prophets is written or spoken out loud. Jesus is considered one of the seven greatest prophets of Allah (God).

2. This translation of Islam's book of scripture is taken from Abdullah Yusuf Ali, *The Meaning of the Holy Qur'an* (Brentwood, MD: Amana Corporation, 1992). A footnote says, "The end of the life of Jesus on earth is as much involved in mystery as his birth…It is not profitable to discuss the many doubts and conjectures among the early Christian sects and among Muslim theologians." Ali added that, for Christians, the death and resurrection "is necessary for the theological doctrine of blood sacrifice and vicarious atonement for sins, which is rejected by Islam."

3. The imam was referencing the apocryphal Gospel of Barnabas to support his assertion. However, this book was written no earlier than the fifteenth century and may have been authored by a Muslim. See "Gospel of Barnabas," Norman L. Geisler, *Baker Encyclopedia of Christian Apologetics* (Grand Rapids, MI: Baker Books, 1999), 67-68.

4. Violence took place during the time of the Crusades, as both Christians and Muslims were in the wrong. Still, a religion should never be judged based on the bad behavior by some of its adherents. Ironically, this man (an immigrant from Syria) once told me in a private conversation how unfair he thought it was that Americans unfairly judged Islam based on the events of 9/11.

5. William Lane Craig, *The Son Rises: Historical Evidence for the Resurrection of Jesus* (Eugene, OR: Wipf & Stock Publishers, 2001), 40. Italics in original.

6. See archive.spurgeon.org/sermons/2197.php.

7. Gary R. Habermas and Michael R. Licona, *The Case for the Resurrection of Jesus* (Grand Rapids, MI: Kregel, 2004), 26-27. Italics in original.

8. Wayne Grudem, *Systematic Theology: An Introduction to Biblical Doctrine* (Grand Rapids, MI: Zondervan Academic, 1994), 355. Italics in original.

9. Geisler, *Baker Encyclopedia of Christian Apologetics*, 488.

10. Millard J. Erickson, *Christian Theology* (Grand Rapids, MI: Baker Book House, 1986), 1:277.

11. Thomas Jefferson, *The Jefferson Bible: The Life and Morals of Jesus of Nazareth* (Boston, MA: Beacon Press, 1904), 146. Spelling intact. The commonly used word in those days was *sepulchre*.

12. Norman Geisler and Ron Brooks, *When Skeptics Ask: A Handbook on Christian Evidences* (Wheaton, IL: Victor Books, 1990), 41.

13. Josh McDowell and Dave Sterrett, *Is the Bible True…Really?* (Chicago, IL: Moody Publishers, 2011), 55. Italics in original.

14. Fulfilled in Matthew 27:12-14. See Acts 8:32 and 1 Peter 1:17-19.

15. Fulfilled in Matthew 27:57-60.

16. Fulfilled in Matthew 20:28.

17. Fulfilled in Matthew 27:38.

18. Fulfilled in Luke 23:43.

19. Greg Koukl describes this strategy in Part 1 of his book *Tactics: A Game Plan for Discussing Your Christian Convictions* (Grand Rapids, MI: Zondervan, 2019).

20. William D. Edwards, Wesley J. Gabel, and Floyd E. Hosmer, "On the Physical Death of Jesus Christ," *Journal of American Medical Association*, March 21, 1986, 1463. The article can be found at jamanetwork.com/journals/jama/article-abstract/403315.

21. Gordon B. Hinckley, "The Symbol of Our Faith," *Ensign*, April 2005, 3.

22. Bruce R. McConkie, *Doctrinal New Testament Commentary* (Salt Lake City, UT: Bookcraft, 1965), 1:774. For more, see mrm.org/gethsemane-atonement.

23. Joseph Fielding Smith, *Answers to Gospel Questions* (Salt Lake City, UT: Deseret Book, 1963), 4:17.

24. J.C. Ryle, *Matthew: Expository Thoughts on the Gospels* (Abbotsford, WI: Aneko Press, 2019), 296.

25. Robert M. Bowman Jr., *Jesus' Resurrection and Joseph's Visions: Examining the Foundations of Christianity and Mormonism* (Tampa, Fl: DeWard Publishing, 2020), 16.

26. Erickson, *Christian Theology*, 2:816. Ellipsis mine.

27. John MacArthur and Richard Mayhue, *Biblical Doctrine* (Wheaton, IL: Crossway, 2017), 492. Italics in original.

28. J.C. Ryle, *The Cross: Crucified with Christ and Christ Alive in Me* (Abbotsford, WI: Aneko Press, 2019), 14-15. Italics in original.

29. Paul Copan, *Is God a Moral Monster?: Making Sense of the Old Testament God* (Grand Rapids, MI: Baker Books, 2011), 33.

30. These points come from a September 18, 1997, debate between William Lane Craig and atheist Gerd Lüdemann at Boston College. Lüdemann considered himself a Christian at that debate but later decided he was an atheist. Paul Copan and Ronald K. Tacelli, eds., *Jesus' Resurrection Fact or Figment? A Debate Between William Lane Craig and Gerd Lüdemann* (Downers Grove, IL: InterVarsity Press, 2000), 32-35.

31. Several dozen prominent scholars are used as support by William Lane Craig in *The Son Rises: Historical Evidence for the Resurrection of Jesus* (Eugene, OR: Wipf & Stock Publishers, 2001), 84-85.

32. These are the three main reasons why people lie and commit crimes, but none of these fit the situation of the disciples, according to J. Warner Wallace, *Cold-Case Christianity: A Homicide Detective Investigates the Claims of the Gospels* (Colorado Springs, CO: David C. Cook, 2013), 239-40.

33. Craig, *The Son Rises*, 23.

34. Ibid., 127. Craig reports, "Even though Jesus had predicted His resurrection, the gospels are clear that the disciples did not understand Him. They had no conception of a dying, much less a rising, Messiah, for the Scriptures said that the Messiah would reign forever (Isaiah 9:7; compare John 12:34). Thus Jesus' crucifixion shattered any hopes they might have entertained that He was the Messiah."

35. Ibid., 77, 118.

36. For an overview of the problems with the "Jesus Tomb," see Gary Habermas, *The Secret of the Talpiot Tomb: Unraveling the Mystery of the Jesus Family Tomb* (Nashville, TN: Holman, 2008). A video titled *Expedition Bible: Jesus Tomb Unmasked* by Joel Kramer is available on Amazon Prime Video.

37. Craig, *The Son Rises*, 85.

38. Ibid., 120-21.

39. *Hymns for the Family of God* (Nashville, TN: Paragon Associates Inc., 1972), 95.

CHAPTER 7–THE TRINITY: ONE GOD, THREE PERSONS

1. The LDS Church's official website states how "Latter-day Saints believe God the Father, Jesus Christ and the Holy Ghost are separate personages, but one in will and purpose—not literally the same being or substance, as conceptions of the Holy Trinity commonly imply." This is a straw man logical fallacy. See newsroom.churchofjesuschrist.org/article/latter-day-saints-101.

2. Joseph Fielding Smith, ed., *Teachings of the Prophet Joseph Smith* (Salt Lake City, UT: Deseret Book Company, 1977), 372. Ellipsis mine.

3. Dallin H. Oaks, "Apostasy and Restoration," *Ensign*, May 1995, 84.

4. Jeffrey R. Holland, "The One True God and Jesus Christ Whom He Hath Sent," *Ensign*, November 2007, 40. Italics in original.

5. James R. White, *The Forgotten Trinity: Recovering the Heart of Christian Belief* (Minneapolis, MN: Bethany House, 1998), 194-95. Italics in original.

6. Wayne Grudem, *Systematic Theology: An Introduction to Biblical Doctrine* (Grand Rapids, MI: Zondervan Academic, 1994), 226.

7. White, *The Forgotten Trinity*, 247.

8. R.C. Sproul, *What Is the Trinity?* (Sanford, FL: Reformation Trust, 2019), 59.

9. "Mother in Heaven," churchofjesuschrist.org/study/manual/gospel-topics-essays/mother-in-heaven?lang=eng.

10. When I wrote this paragraph, this appeal had been used on my youngest daughter and me that morning by two older Mormons we met on a mountain trail hike.

11. White, *The Forgotten Trinity*, 26.

12. This point is readily accepted by Latter-day Saints.

13. As talked about in chapter 5, it is important to show how Jesus is not just "a" god or a "lesser" god, but that He is God in the same sense as the Father.

14. The Holy Spirit is not just a "personage of Spirit who acts on behalf" of God, as Mormonism teaches, but is the third person of the Trinity with His own unique personality.

15. This is not the only time there is such a construction; other supporting verses include Genesis 3:22, 11:7, and Isaiah 6:8. For an article titled "Does Genesis 1:26,27 Prove God Has a Physical Body?" visit mrm.org/genesis-1-26-27.

16. Consider how easy it would be to memorize these three references to show how each person in the Trinity created the universe: Genesis 1:1, 1:2, and John 1:3!

17. White, *The Forgotten Trinity*, 66.

18. Harold O.J. Brown, *Heresies: The Image of Christ in the Mirror of Heresy and Orthodoxy from the Apostles to the Present* (Grand Rapids, MI: Baker, 1984), 20.

19. Roger E. Olson, *The Story of Christian Theology* (Downers Grove, IL: InterVarsity Press, 1999), 153-54. Ellipsis mine.

20. Ibid., 147, 150. Ellipses mine.

21. White, *The Forgotten Trinity*, 27-28. Italics in original.

22. Michael W. Barrett, *Simply Trinity: The Unmanipulated Father, Son, and Spirit* (Grand Rapids, MI: Baker, 2021), 141. Ellipsis mine.

23. For example, the D&C uses "one God" (v. 28), "Almighty God" (v. 21), "Only Begotten Son" (v. 21), "crucified, died, and rose again the third day" (v. 23), "ascended into heaven, to sit down on the right hand of the Father" (v. 24), and "who believed in the words of the holy prophets" (v. 26). Unlike verse 19 ("the only living and true God…should be the only being whom they should worship"), the Nicene Creed declares that "the Son is worshiped and glorified."

24. Norman L. Geisler, *Baker Encyclopedia of Christian Apologetics* (Grand Rapids, MI: Baker Books, 1999), 608.

25. Grudem, *Systematic Theology*, 256. Ellipsis mine.

26. Louis Berkhof, *Systematic Theology* (Grand Rapids, MI: Wm. B. Eerdmans, 1976), 89. Italics in original.

27. Brown, *Heresies*, 128. Italics in original.

28. "Godhead," churchofjesuschrist.org/study/manual/gospel-topics/godhead?lang=eng.

29. John MacArthur and Richard Mayhue, *Biblical Doctrine* (Wheaton, IL: Crossway, 2017), 192-93. Italics in original. Ellipsis mine.

30. Grudem, *Systematic Theology*, 240.

31. John Piper, *Providence* (Wheaton, IL: Crossway, 2020), 167. Italics in original.

32. For more on this topic, see mrm.org/council-of-nicea.

33. Some Christians mistakenly believe they have failed if the Mormon does not decide to become a Christian on the spot. Providing someone a better understanding of Christian doctrine should be considered an evangelistic success. Christians are commissioned to faithfully present God's Word as accurately as they can and leave the final results to God's sovereignty.

CHAPTER 8–JUSTIFICATION: FORGIVENESS OF SINS BY FAITH ALONE

1. "Anti-Mormon" is a designation used by some Latter-day Saints to describe a person who dislikes or even hates Mormons. By giving away a book authored by an LDS leader, the argument seems to lose its teeth. Randy Sweet and I discuss this tactic in chapter 19 of *Sharing the Good News with Mormons: Practical Strategies for Getting the Conversation Started* (Eugene, OR: Harvest House Publishers, 2018), edited by Sean McDowell and me. For additional information, go to TheMiracleofForgiveness.com.

2. *Conference Reports*, April 1970, 16; "Finding Forgiveness," *Ensign*, May 1995, 76; and "The Path to Peace and Joy," *Ensign*, November 2000, 26.

3. Different books—from the LDS scriptures to James E. Talmage's *Jesus the Christ* and *The Articles of Faith*—were given away each year at Christmastime from 1981–2017. For more, see mrm.org/books-employee-gift.

4. Spencer W. Kimball, *The Miracle of Forgiveness* (Salt Lake City, UT: Bookcraft, 1969), 286.

5. Christian apologist Keith Walker describes this as an "impossible gospel"—one that requires a complete abandonment of sin—in the final chapter of *Sharing the Good News with Mormons*.

6. For a more detailed explanation of 2 Nephi 25:23, see mrm.org/2nephi2523.

7. This idea was detailed in Robinson's famous "bicycle parable" given in a May 29, 1990, BYU devotional titled "Believing Christ: A Practical Approach to the Atonement." See speeches.byu.edu/talks/stephen-e-robinson/believing-christ-practical-approach-atonement/.

8. Stephen E. Robinson, "Believing Christ," *Ensign*, April 1992, 7. Ellipses his.

9. In Roman 4:5 of the Joseph Smith Translation, Smith added the word "not" between the words "justifies" and "the ungodly," contradicting what Paul meant. No manuscript supports his interpretation.

10. Wayne Grudem, *Systematic Theology: An Introduction to Biblical Doctrine* (Grand Rapids, MI: Zondervan Academic, 1994), 678. Italics in original.

11. Millard J. Erickson, *Christian Theology* (Grand Rapids, MI: Baker Book House, 1986), 3:958-59. Ellipsis mine.

12. Timothy Keller, *Galatians for You* (Epsom, UK: Good Book Company, 2013), 99.

13. R.C. Sproul, *How Can I Be Right with God?* (Sanford, FL: Reformation Trust, 2017), 18, 21. Italics in original. Ellipsis mine.

14. In the Gospel of John, Jesus taught that faith, not works, justifies a person before God. See John 5:24; 6:40; 11:25-26; 12:46. Paul also taught this truth in Acts 16:31; Romans 1:16-17; 2:28-29; 3:22; 4:4-5,24-25; 5:1-2; 10:9-13; Galatians 2:16; 3:11; and Titus 3:5-7.

15. Kimball, *The Miracle of Forgiveness*, 206. For other citations from LDS sources on the topic of grace, go to mrm.org/grace-quotes.

16. Grudem, *Systematic Theology*, 711.

17. Keller, *Galatians for You*, 127.

18. Martin Luther, *The Bondage of the Will* (Grand Rapids, MI: Baker Academic, 2012), 264.

19. John MacArthur and Richard Mayhue, *Biblical Doctrine* (Wheaton, IL: Crossway, 2017), 611. Ellipsis mine.

20. Roger E. Olson, *The Story of Christian Theology* (Downers Grove, IL: InterVarsity Press, 1999), 382.

21. MacArthur and Mayhue, *Biblical Doctrine*, 617-18.

22. Charles Spurgeon, *Christian Classics Ethereal Library Volume 3*, 2009, 130.

23. John Stott, *The Cross of Christ* (Downers Grove, IL: InterVarsity Press, 1986), 162.

24. R.C. Sproul, *What Does It Mean to Be Born Again?* (Orlando, FL: Reformation Trust, 2010), 23.

25. Charles Hodge, *Systematic Theology* (Peabody, MA: Hendrickson Publishers, 1999), 3:238.

26. William Lane Craig, *Reasonable Faith: Christian Truth and Apologetics* (Chicago, IL: Moody Press, 1994), 35-36.

CHAPTER 9–SANCTIFICATION:
A LIFE MARKED BY GOOD WORKS

1. See Leviticus 11:44-45; 19:2; 20:7; 1 Peter 1:15-16.

2. Timothy Keller, *Galatians for You* (Epsom, UK: Good Book Company, 2013), 143.

3. R.C. Sproul, *What Do Jesus' Parables Mean?* (Orlando, FL: Reformation Trust, 2017), 31.

4. J.I. Packer, *Keep in Step with the Spirit* (Old Tappan, NJ: Fleming H. Revell, 1984), 26-27.

5. Dietrich Bonhoeffer, *The Cost of Discipleship* (New York: Collier Books, 1963), 333.

6. Packer, *Keep in Step with the Spirit*, 91. Ellipsis mine.

7. John Piper, *Providence* (Wheaton, IL: Crossway, 2020), 626. Italics in original. Ellipsis mine.

8. Regardless of one's view on the sign gifts—including tongues, interpretation of tongues, healing, miracles, and prophesying—the Bible *never* teaches that a person must speak in tongues (or exercise any of these other gifts) to be considered a Spirit-baptized believer. Paul wrote in 1 Corinthians 13 that love trumps the gifts of tongues and prophecies. In the next chapter, he taught how it would be better for someone to "speak five words" intelligently "than ten thousand words in a tongue" (v. 19).

9. Wayne Grudem, *Systematic Theology: An Introduction to Biblical Doctrine* (Grand Rapids, MI: Zondervan Academic, 1994), 782.

10. Packer, *Keep in Step with the Spirit*, 157.

11. Also see Hosea 6:3-6 and Micah 6:6-8.

12. So many other verses support the idea that good works will follow belief, including Isaiah 1:17; John 14:15,21; 1 Corinthians 15:58; 2 Corinthians 9:8; Colossians 3:23-24; Titus 2:7; 3:14; Hebrews 10:24-25; 1 John 2:4; 2 John 6; 3 John 4,11.

13. Bonhoeffer, *The Cost of Discipleship*, 47.

14. Ibid., 47-48. Italics in original.

15. Ibid., 59.

16. Ibid., 69.

17. Grudem, *Systematic Theology*, 748.

18. Piper, *Providence*, 593.

19. J.C. Ryle, *Old Paths* (Carlisle, PA: Banner of Truth, 1999), 199-200.

20. *Doctrines of the Gospel Student Manual (Religion 430 and 431)* (Salt Lake City, UT: The Church of Jesus Christ of Latter-day Saints, 1986), 52.

21. Joseph Fielding Smith, *The Way to Perfection* (Salt Lake City, UT: Deseret Publishing, 1984), 172.

22. J.I. Packer, *Concise Theology: A Guide to Historic Christian Beliefs* (Carol Stream, IL: Tyndale House Publishers, 1993), 162.

23. Grudem, *Systematic Theology*, 713-14. Italics in original. Ellipsis mine.

24. The construction is called an "accusative of cause" whereby "the substantive indicates the ground for the action. It answers the question, Why?" James A. Brooks and Carlton L. Winbery, *Syntax of New Testament Greek* (Lanham, MD: University Press of American, 1988), 60.

25. H. Wayne House, "Baptism for the Forgiveness of Sins (Part 2)," *Christian Research Journal*, vol. 22, no. 3, 2000.

26. Gordon D. Fee, *The First Epistle to the Corinthians* (Grand Rapids, MI: William B. Eerdmans, 1987), 604. Italics in original. Ellipsis mine.

27. For several other common passages used by baptismal regenerationists, see chapter 13 in Bill McKeever and Eric Johnson, *Mormonism 101: Examining the Religion of the Latter-day Saints* (Grand Rapids, MI: Baker Books, 2015).

28. Grudem, *Systematic Theology*, 981.

29. Millard J. Erickson, *Christian Theology* (Grand Rapids, MI: Baker Book House, 1986) 3:1096. Italics in original.

30. G.R. Beasley-Murray, *Baptism in the New Testament* (Grand Rapids, MI: William B. Eerdmans, 1990), 49.

31. Ibid., 101-2.

32. Bonhoeffer, *The Cost of Discipleship*, 259-60. The role of the church will be covered in chapter 10.

33. It is hard to understand how water used in the LDS sacrament is supposed to symbolize the blood of Jesus.

34. Grudem, *Systematic Theology*, 991. Italics in original. Ellipsis mine.

35. Timothy Keller, *Galatians for You* (Epsom, UK: Good Book Company, 2013), 134. To answer the question about whether salvation can be lost, see "Is It Possible for Christians to Lose Their Salvation?" at mrm.org/lose-salvation.

CHAPTER 10 – GROWING IN THE FAITH: A PASSIONATE PURSUIT

1. See churchofjesuschrist.org/study/manual/gospel-topics-essays/essays?lang=eng.

2. For more information on the essays, including a series of Viewpoint on Mormonism podcasts, see mrm.org/gospel-topics.

3. See sltrib.com/news/mormon/2015/05/27/this-mormon-sunday-school-teacher-was-dismissed-for-using-churchs-own-race-essay-in-lesson.

4. Matthew L. Harris and Newell G. Bringhurst, eds., *The LDS Gospel Topics Series: A Scholarly Engagement* (Salt Lake City, UT: Signature Books, 2020), 23.

5. Endnote 24 in the essay states "careful estimates put the number between 30 and 40." See churchofjesuschrist.org/study/manual/gospel-topics-essays/plural-marriage-in-kirtland-and-nauvoo?lang=eng.

6. R.C. Sproul, *What Is the Church?* (Orlando, FL: Reformation Trust, 2013), 68.

7. Gordon B. Hinckley, "Inspirational Thoughts," *Ensign,* June 2004, 3.

8. James E. Talmage, *The Articles of Faith* (Salt Lake City, UT: The Church of Jesus Christ of Latter-day Saints, 1987), 203.

9. James Talmage, *Jesus the Christ* (Salt Lake City, UT: The Church of Jesus Christ of Latter-day Saints, 1981), 754.

10. Henry B. Eyring, "The True and Living Church," *Ensign,* May 2008, 20.

11. Bruce R. McConkie, *Mormon Doctrine* (Salt Lake City, UT: Deseret Book Company, 1966), 131.

12. Ibid., 1005.

13. John Piper, *Providence* (Wheaton, IL: Crossway, 2020), 371-72. Italics in original.

14. Sproul, *What Is the Church?,* 16. Some mainline denominations even promote unbiblical practices such as homosexuality, euthanasia, and abortion.

15. Wayne Grudem, *Systematic Theology: An Introduction to Biblical Doctrine* (Grand Rapids, MI: Zondervan Academic, 1994), 867.

16. Mormonism Research Ministry hosts a website (utahchurches.org) that helps people find godly Bible-based churches in the state of Utah.

17. Bryan Hurlbutt, *Tasty Jesus: Liberating Christ from the Power of Our Predilections* (Eugene, OR: Resource Publications, 2013), 58.

18. AWANA is a program held in many Christian churches in 120 countries that provides children

"an opportunity to know, love and serve Jesus for a lifetime." Memorization of verses and gaining general Bible knowledge is emphasized. To learn more about this organization, visit awana.org.

19. John Piper, *Desiring God* (Colorado Springs, CO: Multnomah Books, 2003), 54-55. Italics in original.

20. Jerry Bridges, *The Practice of Godliness* (Colorado Springs, CO: NavPress, 1983), 16.

21. Piper, *Providence*, 259.

22. One example is *The One Year Bible ESV* (Wheaton, IL: Good News Publishers, 2020). Different versions are available as well.

23. See mrm.org/romans-road.

24. I contributed articles and notes as an associate editor for the *CSB Apologetics Study Bible for Students* published in 2017. There are dozens of other possibilities available online.

25. Jerry Bridges, *The Practice of Godliness* (Colorado Springs, CO: NavPress, 1983), 52.

26. R.C. Sproul, *Does Prayer Change Things?* (Sanford, FL: Reformation Trust, 2009), 1.

27. Dietrich Bonhoeffer, *The Cost of Discipleship* (New York: Collier Books, 1963), 200-201.

28. Compiled by I.D.E. Thomas, *A Golden Treasury of Puritan Quotations* (Carlisle, PA: Banner of Truth, 1977), 212.

29. R.A. Torrey, *How to Pray* (Westwood, NJ: Barbour and Company, Inc., 1989), 5.

30. Grudem, *Systematic Theology*, 378.

31. Bonhoeffer, *The Cost of Discipleship*, 181, 183. Ellipsis mine.

32. Millard J. Erickson, *Christian Theology* (Grand Rapids, MI: Baker Book House, 1986), 1:406.

33. Lloyd John Ogilvie, *You Can Pray with Power* (Ventura, CA: Regal Books, 1988), 95. Italics in original.

34. Piper, *Providence*, 515.

OTHER RELATED
READING
FROM HARVEST
HOUSE PUBLISHERS

FOREWORD BY
JOSH McDOWELL

SHARING THE GOOD NEWS
WITH MORMONS

ERIC JOHNSON
SEAN McDOWELL
GENERAL EDITORS

PRACTICAL STRATEGIES
FOR GETTING
THE CONVERSATION STARTED

Sharing the Good News with Mormons

Eric Johnson and Sean McDowell, General Editors

How do you share the gospel with those who don't think they need it?

Someone you know is a Mormon—a family member, a coworker, a friend, or a neighbor—and you long to present the truth about Jesus and what God's Word teaches. But where do you start? How can you convey what's on your heart in a way that will be well received?

Every relationship and situation is unique, and that's why these essays from respected scholars, apologists, and pastors—including Sandra Tanner, Robert Bowman, David Geisler, Bill McKeever, Mark Mittelberg, J. Warner Wallace, Lynn Wilder, and others—lay out a variety of creative methods for sharing the gospel effectively so you can...

- initiate authentic conversations

- respond with compassion and clarity to Mormon teachings

- understand your Mormon friends and find ways to keep the dialogue going

Speaking the truth to Mormons can feel daunting when you're unprepared. Let the suggestions in this book give you solid ideas for reaching those who are lost but don't realize it.

Passport to Heaven
Micah Wilder

"You have a call, Elder Wilder."

When missionary Micah Wilder set his sights on bringing a Baptist congregation into The Church of Jesus Christ of Latter-day Saints, he had no idea that *he* was the one about to be changed. Yet when he finally came to know the God of the Bible, Micah had no choice but to surrender himself—no matter the consequences.

For a passionate young Mormon who had grown up in the Church, finding authentic faith meant giving up all he knew: his community, his ambitions, and his place in the world. Yet as Micah struggled to reconcile the teachings of his Church with the truths revealed in the Bible, he awakened to his need for God's grace. This led him to be summoned to the door of the mission president, terrified but confident in the testimony he knew could cost him everything.

Passport to Heaven is a gripping account of Micah's surprising journey from living as a devoted member of a religion based on human works to embracing the divine mercy and freedom that can only be found in Jesus Christ.

ADDITIONAL RESOURCES FROM ERIC JOHNSON

For more materials relating to this book, visit
IntroducingChristianity.com

For other resources, consider…

Mormonism Research Ministry
P.O. Box 1746
Draper, UT 84020
(801) 572-2153
www.mrm.org

The website contains hundreds of articles, videos, and other informa-tion to help you better understand Mormonism from a Christian point of view while learning how to better share the Christian faith.

Request a free two-year subscription to the ministry newsletter *Mormonism Researched* by emailing contact@mrm.org and mention-ing this book in the subject line.

PODCAST

Since 2011, MRM has aired a daily show, which plays on radio stations in five different states. More than 2500 broadcasts are indexed by categories at mrm.org/viewpoint-on-mormonism-catalog.

BOOKS

Mormonism 101: Examining the Religion of the Latter-day Saints (Grand Rapids, MI: Baker Books, 2015). Bill McKeever and Eric Johnson provide a general overview of the differences between the doctrines of Mormonism and biblical Christianity.

Answering Mormons' Questions: Ready Responses for Inquiring Latter-day Saints (Grand Rapids, MI: Kregel Publications, 2013). Bill McKeever and Eric Johnson answer 38 common questions Latter-day Saints ask Christians.

Mormonism 101 for Teens (Sandy, UT: Mormonism Research Ministry, 2016). Written especially for Christian young people who want to better understand the teachings of Mormonism.

Sharing the Good News with Mormons: Practical Strategies for Getting the Conversation Started (Eugene, OR: Harvest House Publishers, 2018). Written for Christians who want to learn specific techniques on how to share their Christian faith with Latter-day Saints.